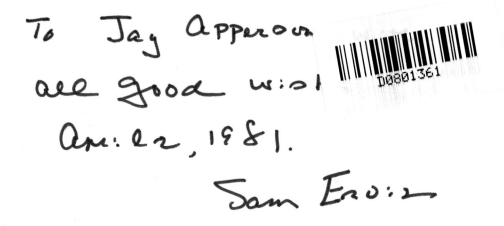

To Jay Apperson

all good wish

April 22, 1981.

Sam Ervin

THE
WHOLE
TRUTH

Sam J. Ervin, Jr.

THE WHOLE TRUTH

THE WATERGATE CONSPIRACY

RANDOM HOUSE
NEW YORK

Grateful acknowledgment is made to the following for permission to reprint previously published material:

The Charlotte Observer: Excerpt from the May 17, 1973, issue. Reprinted by permission of The Charlotte Observer.

The New York Times: Excerpt by Anthony Lewis, September 1974. Copyright © 1974 by The New York Times Company. Reprinted by permission.

Omaha World-Herald: Excerpt from the May 8, 1974, issue. Reprinted by permission of the Omaha World-Herald, Omaha, Nebraska.

Library of Congress Cataloging in Publication Data

Ervin, Samuel James, 1896–
The whole truth: The Watergate Conspiracy.

Includes index.
1. Watergate Affair, 1972–   2. Ervin, Samuel
James, 1896–   I. Title.
E860.E78   364.1'32'0973   78-21821
ISBN 0-394-48029-5

Manufactured in the United States of America
24689753

To my beloved wife,
Margaret Bell Ervin,
whose steadfast love has been
my inspiration and joy
for more than fifty-six years

PROLOGUE

If President Nixon had entrusted his campaign for reelection to the Republican National Committee, there would have been no Watergate. Its members would have known that the activities of Watergate were outside the political pale.

He gave control of his campaign, however, to close associates who were virtually without experience in politics or government apart from their association with him.

The series of untoward events known collectively as Watergate were parts of two successive conspiracies. The ultimate objective of the parties to the first conspiracy was a lawful one, which was shared by multitudes of law-abiding Americans. They sought President Nixon's reelection. But they resorted to improper, illegal, and unethical means to further their objective. They surreptitiously hired spies to obtain secret information concerning the plans of those seeking the Democratic nomination for President and the Democratic nominee for that office by fraud, infiltration, and burglary; and they surreptitiously hired saboteurs to frustrate those plans by deception, "dirty tricks," forgery, libel, and other devices.

The first conspiracy had its origin at a time when Senators Hubert H. Humphrey, Henry M. Jackson, and Edmund S. Muskie were the strongest contenders for the Democratic nomination for the presidency, and one of them, Senator Muskie, was outrunning President Nixon in the polls.

The views of Humphrey, Jackson, and Muskie in respect to economics and national defense were shared by millions of Americans, and the nomination of one of them by the Democratic party would have put President Nixon's reelection bid in jeopardy.

As a consequence, one of the prime purposes of the parties to the first conspiracy was to eliminate Humphrey, Jackson, and Muskie from the running for the Democratic nomination. This they did by various foul tactics, including the "Canuck letter" and the forged document purporting to be on Senator Muskie's campaign letterhead falsely charging Senators Humphrey and Jackson with sexual offenses, which their hired saboteur, Donald Segretti, disseminated in the Florida Democratic presidential primary.

The second conspiracy arose when the burglars were caught in the headquarters of the National Democratic Committee in the Watergate Office Building. The objective of the parties to it was to conceal from law enforcement officers, the press, and the public the activities and identities of those responsible for the burglary and the other improper, illegal, and unethical acts incident to the first conspiracy.

The efforts of the conspirators to cover up the truth about Watergate were materially assisted by some persons who cannot be justly suspected of any knowledge of the conspiracies, or of the truth concerning Watergate. The activities and identities of the parties to the first conspiracy were hidden until after President Nixon had been over-whelmingly reelected in the general election of November 1972. Meanwhile, Gordon Liddy, Howard Hunt, and James McCord, and the four Miami residents had been indicted for complicity in the burglary, and the Department of Justice had solemnly assured the American people there was no evidence that anybody else was involved in the Watergate affair.

Nevertheless, Bob Woodward and Carl Bernstein, investigative reporters for the *Washington Post*, began to unearth circumstances which engendered grave suspicion that the Watergate break-in might have been more than a "third-rate burglary."

Senator Mike Mansfield, who was then the Majority Leader of the Senate, is as fair and forthright a man as I have ever known. After the election, he expressed to me his concern about some of the publicly known "dirty tricks" which had been practiced on Senators Humphrey,

Jackson, Muskie, and McGovern during the primary and election campaigns, and about the suspicion which the Woodward and Bernstein investigation had aroused concerning the Watergate break-in. He was convinced it was the duty of the Senate to investigate these matters impartially.

He and I agreed that either of two of the standing committees of the Senate—the Judiciary Committee, of which Senator James O. Eastland was chairman, and the Government Operations Committee, of which I was chairman—would be an appropriate committee under Senate Rules to conduct an investigation of these matters.

Senator Mansfield was reluctant, however, for either of these committees to conduct such an investigation. He knew that neither of them could conduct the investigation with dispatch because of its large size. Besides, he knew that the investigation was likely to be surcharged with political overtones, and apprehended it would add to those overtones if Senators Jackson and Muskie, who were victims of publicly known "dirty tricks" and members of the Government Operations Committee, or Senator Edward M. Kennedy, a supposed aspirant for a future Democratic nomination for the presidency and a member of the Judiciary Committee, participated in the investigation.

For these reasons, Senator Mansfield decided to urge the Senate to establish by resolution a small select or special committee to conduct the investigation after the trial of the seven original Watergate defendants had been concluded.

While I was icebound in North Carolina during the early days of January 1973, the Democratic Policy Committee and the Democratic Caucus of the Senate, acting on Senator Mansfield's recommendation, unanimously adopted resolutions urging that the Senate establish a select or special committee to investigate the Watergate affair and that I be named its chairman.

Upon my return to Washington, Senator Mansfield gave me three reasons why he wanted me to serve as chairman of the proposed select committee. They were that I had had more judicial experience than any other senator; that I was "the most nonpartisan Democrat" in the Senate; and that nobody could justly accuse me of ever having harbored any presidential or vice-presidential aspirations. While I did not covet the assignment, I accepted it as a duty I owed to the Senate and my country.

Walter Malone, the Tennessee judge and poet, put these verses in his poem "To a Judge":

O thou who wieldest for one fleeting day
The Power that belongs alone to God:
O idol moulded out of common clay,
To sway one little hour an iron rod,

Dost thou not tremble to assume thy seat,
And judge thy fellow-travelers to the tomb?
Dost thou not falter as thy lips repeat
Thy Comrade's downfall, thy Companion's doom?

A word from you, and Fortune flies away,
While silks and satins tatter into rags;
The banquet revellers scatter in dismay,
And Pride and Pomp haul down their flaunting flags.

During the thirty-two years before I entered the Senate, I participated in the administration of justice as a trial lawyer and trial and appellate judge. In so doing, I acquired the abiding conviction that the most sacred obligation which can devolve upon any human being is that of judging his "fellow-travelers to the tomb," and that this sacred obligation requires him to judge them with fairness and without fear or favor.

I strove to perform this obligation with fidelity in my capacity as chairman of the Senate Select Committee. I was under no temptation to do otherwise because I was then seventy-six years of age and neither desired nor expected any further political preferment.

Like other conspiracies, the Watergate conspiracies were formed and carried out in secrecy. The trial of the seven original Watergate defendants did nothing to dispel the mystery in which they were shrouded. The defendants refused to talk or testify, and the prosecution assured the trial jurors that they were engaged in "a lark of their own" when they burglarized the headquarters of the National Democratic Committee.

As a consequence, the Senate Select Committee had no evidence available to it when it began its labors, and was confronted by a herculean task in its search for the truth respecting Watergate.

With the aid of its dedicated and diligent staff, the Senate Select Committee discovered the truth respecting Watergate in fragments, day by day and bit by bit. To the maximum extent possible, I recount its discoveries as they were made. For the sake of continuity of narration and clarity of understanding, however, I have anticipated the discovery of the clandestine meetings President Nixon had with John Dean, H. R.

Haldeman, John Ehrlichman, and John Mitchell during the late winter and early spring of 1973.

At that time they frantically feared the Senate Select Committee was about to reveal the truth about the Watergate affair and desperately sought ways to thwart its doing so. In describing these meetings, I refrain from making inferences and permit Nixon, Dean, Haldeman, Ehrlichman, and Mitchell to portray themselves in their own words as they were subsequently revealed by Nixon's secretly recorded tapes.

The only security America has against anarchy on the one hand and tyranny on the other is to be found in reverential obedience to the Constitution by those entrusted with governmental power. When Senator Mansfield said I was the "most nonpartisan Democrat in the Senate," he meant that I was an independently minded senator who supported Presidents when I thought them right and opposed them when I deemed them wrong, regardless of their political labels.

I did that in respect to President Nixon. I stoutly opposed his attempts to usurp and exercise powers denied him by the Constitution. At the same time I supported his recommendations when I believed them to be sound. Besides, my research had satisfied me that the Gulf of Tonkin Resolution was tantamount to a congressional declaration of war, and I stoutly resisted the attempts of Congress to strip him of some of his constitutional powers as Commander in Chief of our forces in Southeast Asia after the invasion of the North Vietnamese sanctuary in Cambodia.

The committee never received any hard evidence indicating that President Nixon had any prior knowledge of the plans of the parties to the first conspiracy to burglarize and bug the headquarters of the Democratic National Committee in the Watergate Office Building.

When it began its labors, I suspected the committee might discover by its investigation that some overzealous aides of President Nixon had overstepped the bounds of political decency in the Watergate affair. It was inconceivable to me at that time, however, that President Nixon was personally involved in the cover-up operations incident to the second conspiracy.

As time passed, however, President Nixon took certain actions that tended to shatter my faith in his fidelity to truth and his constitutional obligation "to take care that the laws be faithfully executed." For the sake of brevity, I enumerate only three of them.

1. Before the committee was even organized, he declared publicly

that he would withhold the testimony of his aides and former aides from it, and invited the committee to contest the constitutionality of such action by time-consuming litigation, which could not possibly be concluded before the time appointed for the duration of the committee to expire.

2. When the committee discovered the existence of his secretly recorded tapes and the committee and Special Prosecutor Cox sought access to them, he refused to produce them, notwithstanding he claimed they would exonerate him from any complicity in Watergate.

3. When he sought to justify the firing of Special Prosecutor Cox, he falsely assured the American people that Senator Baker and I had approved his offer to furnish transcripts of the contents of the tapes to the Special Prosecutor in lieu of the tapes themselves, notwithstanding Senator Baker and I had no knowledge he had ever made any such offer to the Special Prosecutor.

In and of themselves, however, these outrageous acts did not conclusively establish President Nixon's complicity in the conspiracy to hide the truth about Watergate. They were reconcilable with a misguided loyalty to guilty aides, or with a perverted notion that the constitutional separation of the powers of government separated the President from any obligation to heed the Constitution and the laws. Hence, I continued to cling to the fading hope that the committee would be able to exonerate President Nixon from complicity in the cover-up conspiracy when it concluded its investigation and filed its final report.

I retired from the Senate with the intention of never writing anything about Watergate additional to the observations appearing in the committee's final report. I changed my mind, however, when I read President Nixon's *Memoirs*. They convinced me that I owed my country and history the obligation to set down on paper the truth respecting Watergate.

Nixon's *Memoirs* hurl foul epithets at those whose only offense was that they sought to ascertain the truth about Watergate by constitutional and legal processes in obedience to legal duty. The *Memoirs* complain bitterly of the refusal of the committee to investigate William C. Sullivan's allegations that J. Edgar Hoover, the FBI director, did improper things for the White House during the administration of President Lyndon B. Johnson. As chairman, I rightly ruled that the committee had no authority to investigate these allegations. Under the resolution establishing it, the committee's investigative power was limited to events connected with the presidential election of 1972. According to decisions of the Supreme Court, the committee would have violated the Constitution if it had undertaken to investigate Sullivan's allegations.

The correctness of my ruling was not impaired by the virtual certainty that those who asked the committee to make an unconstitutional investigation were trying to drag a red herring across the committee's investigative path.

Nixon's *Memoirs* insinuate that he was driven from the presidency by a hostile press and vindictive partisans, and not by his own misdeeds. This insinuation is totally incompatible with these circumstances:

1. Senator Hugh Scott, Republican Leader of the Senate, Representative John Rhodes, Republican Leader of the House, and Republican Senator Barry Goldwater, a staunch Republican conservative, visited the White House in a body on August 7, 1974, and advised Nixon, in essence, that he would be impeached by the House and convicted by the Senate if he did not resign.

2. The ten Republican representatives who voted against all impeachment proposals in the House Judiciary Committee made a report to the House of Representatives in August 1974 in which they stated that the subsequent release of the devastating tapes of June 23, 1972, convinced them that Nixon had obstructed justice in the Watergate affair; and that he had not been "hounded from office" by political opponents and media critics, but that on the contrary the tragedy which finally engulfed him was self-inflicted. They made this specific observation: "Our gratitude for his having by his resignation spared the nation further agony should not obscure for history our judgment that Richard Nixon, as President, committed certain acts for which he should have been impeached and removed from office."

3. The words imprinted by President Nixon's own voice on his own tapes reveal that he became personally involved in the efforts to cover up the truth respecting Watergate as early as June 23, 1972, six days after the burglary.

The controversies occasioned by Nixon's refusal to comply with the demands of the committee and the Special Prosecutor for crucial evidence controlled by him arose in various ways, and at various times, and endured for many months. For these reasons, the narration of these controversies, which is essential to the complete story of Watergate, may seem somewhat repetitious.

I wrote this book without the help of a ghost writer. Except for its quotations, all its words are my own. Originally I put them down on yellow tablets with a pencil.

I want to acknowledge my gratitude to the three persons who aided me in the making of this book: Grant Ujifusa, my editor, who encouraged me to write it; Mary Black McBryde, my secretary, who deciphered and typed my obscure words, and copied and recopied the resulting pages; and Margaret Bell Ervin, my wife, whose gentle patience and quiet inspiration harmonized during the writing of the book with the same happy qualities exhibited by her ever since we plighted our troth.

CONTENTS

THE
WHOLE
TRUTH

1

THE WATERGATE CONSPIRACIES

To explain Watergate, I must rely largely on facts unknown to me and the nation until the Senate Select Committee on Presidential Campaign Activities revealed them.

Richard M. Nixon was narrowly defeated for the presidency by John F. Kennedy in 1960, and narrowly won the Presidency over Hubert H. Humphrey in 1968. The motivation for Watergate had its origin in these events.

President Nixon and his aides who participated in the planning of his reelection campaign were determined that the presidential election of 1972 should not be a cliff-hanger.

At the outset this determination did not seem easy of accomplishment. Registered Democrats vastly outnumbered registered Republicans; Democrats controlled Congress; and nationally known Democrats, such as Senators Edmund S. Muskie, Edward M. Kennedy, Hubert H. Humphrey, and Henry M. Jackson, who had high vote-getting potentials, were prospective candidates for the Democratic presidential nomination. At least one of them, Muskie, was substantially outrunning Nixon in the polls.

Nevertheless, Nixon and his closest aides devised a campaign strategy to effect their purpose to demolish his Democratic opponent in the election of 1972.

Instead of entrusting his campaign for reelection to the Republican National Committee, President Nixon set up two special committees to manage it. One of them, the Committee for the Reelection of the President, which had jurisdiction over political activities, was chaired by John N. Mitchell, who resigned as Attorney General to accept the assignment, and the other, the Finance Committee to Reelect the President, which had jurisdiction over raising campaign funds, was headed by Maurice Stans, who relinquished the office of Secretary of Commerce for that purpose.

By so doing, President Nixon divorced his campaign from those of Republican candidates for other offices, and monopolized for his own reelection the $60 million in campaign funds the Stans' Committee collected.

The Mitchell and Stans committees occupied quarters in the same office building in Washington and worked in close cooperation. They had a joint budget committee composed of Mitchell and two officers of his committee and Stans and two officers of his committee. This budget committee was empowered to decide how much money was to be allocated to finance political projects.

The Mitchell and Stans committees were known collectively as CRP or CREEP.

It is obvious in retrospect that Watergate comprised two conspiracies. The active conspirators were those officers and employees of CREEP and those White House aides of President Nixon who knowingly shared and furthered the objectives of the conspiracies. They were aided in some instances by acts or omissions of innocent persons who were wholly unconscious of the existence of the conspiracies.

The first conspiracy was deliberately conceived, planned, and executed. It was designed to destroy insofar as the presidential election of 1972 was concerned the integrity of the process by which the President of the United States is nominated and elected.

The objective of the first conspiracy was consummated by numerous activities, largely secret in nature, which frustrated the campaigns of the most potent candidates for the Democratic nomination, implanted bitter controversies within the Democratic Party, and induced the

4

Democratic Party to deny its nomination to any candidate having the capacity to defeat President Nixon's bid for reelection.

The second conspiracy was instinctive and spontaneous. Its objective was to hide from law enforcement officers, the press, and the public the identities and secret activities of those who were chiefly responsible for formulating and executing the first conspiracy.

The second conspiracy postponed beyond the election and for several succeeding months the discovery and revelation of the truth about Watergate.

To effect the first conspiracy, the participating officers and employees of CREEP and the participating White House aides engaged in varying ways in one or more of these secret activities:

1. They exacted enormous contributions—frequently in cash—from corporate executives by impliedly implanting in their minds the impression that the making of the contributions was necessary to ensure that the corporations would receive governmental favors, or avoid governmental disfavors, while President Nixon remained in the White House. A substantial portion of the contributions was made out of corporate funds in violation of a statute enacted by Congress a generation ago.

2. They hid substantial parts of these contributions and other campaign funds in safes and secret deposits to conceal their sources and the identities of those who made them.

3. They disbursed substantial portions of these hidden contributions and other campaign funds in a surreptitious manner to finance the burglary and bugging of the offices of the Democratic National Committee in the Watergate complex in Washington for the purpose of obtaining political intelligence; and to sabotage by dirty tricks, espionage, and scurrilous and false libels and slanders the campaigns and the reputations of honorable men, whose only offenses were that they sought the nomination of the Democratic Party for President and the opportunity to run against President Nixon for that office in the presidential election of 1972.

4. They deemed the departments and agencies of the federal government to be the political playthings of the Nixon administration rather than impartial instruments for serving the people, and undertook to induce them to channel federal contracts, grants, and loans to areas, groups, or individuals so as to promote the reelection of President Nixon rather than the welfare of the people.

5. They branded as enemies of the White House individuals and

members of the news media who dissented from President Nixon's policies and opposed his reelection, and conspired to urge the Department of Justice, the Federal Bureau of Investigation, the Internal Revenue Service, and the Federal Communications Commission to pervert the use of their legal powers to harass them for so doing.

6. They borrowed from the Central Intelligence Agency disguises that E. Howard Hunt used in political espionage operations and photographic equipment that White House employees known as the Plumbers and their hired confederates used in connection with burglarizing a psychiatrist's office, which they believed contained information concerning Daniel Ellsberg that the White House was anxious to secure.

7. They assigned to E. Howard Hunt, who was at the time a White House consultant occupying an office in the Executive Office Building, the gruesome task of falsifying State Department documents to defame the memory of former President John F. Kennedy, who, as the hapless victim of an assassin's bullet, had been sleeping in the silence of the dreamless dust for nine years. The documents were to be altered to make it appear that President Kennedy was guilty of complicity in the murder of Ngo Dinh Diem, president of South Vietnam, who was assassinated in the coup of 1963, and were to be used in their altered state to discredit the Democratic Party in general and Senator Edward M. Kennedy in particular in case he sought or received the Democratic nomination for President.

8. They used campaign funds to hire saboteurs to forge and disseminate false and scurrilous libels of honorable men running for the Democratic Presidential nomination in Democratic Party primaries.

In retrospect, the most reprehensible act of sabotage perpetrated by a hired saboteur during the 1972 presidential campaign was that committed by Donald Segretti upon three front-running candidates for the Democratic nomination—Muskie, Humphrey, and Jackson—in the Democratic primary of Florida.

Segretti was a collegemate at the University of Southern California of Dwight L. Chapin, President Nixon's appointments secretary, and Gordon C. Strachan, assistant to H. R. ("Bob") Haldeman, President Nixon's longtime crony and the White House chief of staff.

In June 1971 Chapin and Strachan hired Segretti to frustrate by dirty tricks the campaigns of candidates for the Democratic nomination. Their action in so doing was approved by Haldeman, who authorized Herbert W. Kalmbach, Nixon's personal attorney and one of his

6

principal fund-raisers, to pay Segretti's salary and expenses out of campaign funds.

In March 1972 Segretti counterfeited a letter on stationery of Muskie's campaign organization, Citizens for Muskie, which falsely purported to be the composition of the "Senator Ed Muskie Staff," and to be a solicitation for support of his candidacy in the forthcoming Florida Democratic primary. In addition to so doing, the counterfeited letter charged that Senator Jackson, one of Muskie's primary opponents, had fathered an illegitimate child during his high school days in Everett, Washington, and had been arrested on homosexual charges in Washington, D. C., in 1955 and 1957. The counterfeited letter further charged that another of Muskie's primary opponents, Senator Humphrey, had been arrested in Washington in 1967 for drunken driving after colliding with two other automobiles and that at the time he was accompanied by a well-known call girl who had been employed by a lobbyist to entertain him.

Segretti and his confederates surreptitiously mailed copies of the counterfeited letter to Florida voters three days before the primary.

When he subsequently testified before the Senate Select Committee, Segretti stated he reported to Chapin this incident as well as other dirty tricks he perpetrated on candidates for the Democratic nomination, and that Chapin was hilariously pleased.

Since Chapin had the task of scheduling appointments for President Nixon, one wonders whether he had sufficient restraint to avoid recounting this incident at the time to Nixon.

Be this as it may, this incident and the multitude of other dirty tricks perpetrated upon candidates for the Democratic nomination in connection with the 1972 presidential campaign by persons acting in President Nixon's behalf illustrate the depths of degradation to which that campaign descended.

In the dark of the early morning of Saturday, June 17, 1972, the Washington police caught five burglars in the headquarters of the Democratic National Committee on the sixth floor of the office building in the Watergate complex in the nation's capital. The burglars were wearing blue surgical gloves, and carrying walkie-talkies and photographic equipment.

The burglars were James W. McCord, of the Washington area, and Bernard L. Barker, Virgilio R. Gonzalez, Eugenio R. Martinez, and Frank Sturgis, all of whom resided in Miami, Florida. Barker, Gonzalez, and Martinez were of Cuban ancestry. Sturgis, a native-born American,

7

had long since adopted Cuba as his country. They were united in hatred of Fidel Castro's regime. For convenience of narration, I will hereafter adopt the practice of the contemporary press and call them collectively the Cubans or the four Cubans.

At the time of their arrest, the four Cubans had thirteen new $100 bills on their persons. Armed with search warrants, Washington police searched their rooms in the nearby Watergate Hotel a few hours later, and found in them more electronic equipment, more blue surgical gloves, a small check issued to some third person by E. Howard Hunt, a small notebook containing the entry "E. Hunt, W.H.," and four packs containing eight new $100 bills each, making $3,200 in new $100 bills additional to those that had been found on the persons of the Cubans. The new $100 bills bore serial numbers in sequence, and the Washington police gave their serial numbers to the FBI to enable it to trace them to their source.

Although the relevant facts remained concealed for months, some CREEP officials and White House aides were struck with consternation when they learned the burglars had been apprehended in the headquarters of the Democratic National Committee. They were fearful the revelation of the truth might be injurious to the reelection of President Nixon.

As a consequence, they instinctively and spontaneously formed the second Watergate conspiracy, which was designed to cover up the identities and activities of those officers of CREEP and those White House aides who were parties to the first conspiracy and really responsible for the burglary.

The cover-up was initiated by John N. Mitchell by a statement he issued on Sunday, June 18, in response to newspaper reports identifying McCord as security chief for CREEP. Mitchell said, "McCord and the other four men arrested in Democratic headquarters Saturday were not operating either in our behalf or with our consent in the alleged bugging." He added, "There is no place in our campaign or in the electoral process for this type of activity, and we will not permit or condone it."

The *Washington Post* did not find Mitchell's statement convincing. Besides, it gave no credence to the attempt of Ronald L. Ziegler, Nixon's press secretary, to dismiss the Watergate episode as a "third-rate burglary."

On the contrary, the *Post* forthwith assigned two of its most gifted reporters, Carl Bernstein and Bob Woodward, to the task of investigating the Watergate affair. They did a remarkable job in digging up hidden information, and undoubtedly prompted other media of communications to give their investigative reporters similar tasks.

Within a few weeks the *Washington Post* and other media of communications published astounding articles relating to the burglary. They disclosed that E. Howard Hunt was a consultant on the White House payroll with an office in the Executive Office Building, and that he and G. Gordon Liddy, the legal adviser to the Stans committee, had masterminded the burglary. They likewise revealed that at the direction of Jeb Stuart Magruder, deputy chairman of the Mitchell committee, Hugh W. Sloan, Jr., treasurer of the Stans committee, had taken from safes in the quarters of the Stans committee substantial Nixon campaign funds in cash and delivered them to Liddy; and that the $4,500 in new $100 bills discovered by the Washington police on the persons and in the hotel rooms of the four Cubans on the day of their arrest represented a portion of the Nixon campaign funds which Sloan had delivered to Liddy.

During this period the Federal Bureau of Investigation, which was headed by President Nixon's appointee, L. Patrick Gray, and a federal grand jury, which had been impaneled by Judge John J. Sirica in the United States District Court for the District of Columbia, officially investigated the criminal aspects of the Watergate affair.

Assistant Attorney General Henry E. Petersen, a registered Democrat and a career man, had supervision of the Justice Department's Watergate investigation; Earl J. Silbert, chief assistant United States Attorney for the District of Columbia, and his aides, Seymour Glanzer and Donald E. Campbell, had responsibility for presenting the government's evidence to the grand jury.

The CREEP officials and White House aides who sanctioned and participated in the secret cover-up were desirous above all things that the grand jury should limit any indictments it might return to Liddy, Hunt, McCord, and the four Cubans.

The cover-up made this desire a reality. Although they were able to show that Hugh W. Sloan, Jr., treasurer of the Stans committee, had delivered $199,000 in cash out of Nixon campaign funds to Liddy and that Liddy had used a part of these funds to finance the burglary of the Watergate, Petersen and Silbert could not obtain any evidence they deemed sufficient to disprove Jeb Stuart Magruder's false assurance to them and the grand jurors that the money was given to Liddy to finance legitimate intelligence operations and that Liddy and his confederates engaged in an unauthorized prank of their own when they burglarized the Watergate.

As a consequence, the grand jury returned indictments on September 15, 1972, charging Liddy, Hunt, McCord, Barker, Gonzales, Martinez, and Sturgis with a number of crimes arising out of the Watergate episode, and adjourned.

Attorney General Richard Kleindienst and the Justice Department's director of public information, John W. Hushen, forthwith issued public statements assuring the nation that the Department of Justice had completed its investigation and that it had no evidence whatever to indicate that any persons other than the seven defendants named in the indictments of September 15 were involved in the Watergate affair. Petersen also made a statement citing the vast number of man-hours FBI agents had used in their investigation to prove his assurance that there had been no "whitewash."

The secret cover-up had succeeded, and the ultimate truth about Watergate remained hidden until the general election of November 7, 1972, was over. President Nixon was returned to the White House over his Democratic opponent, Senator George S. McGovern, by a landslide victory in which he received 520 of the nation's 538 electoral votes and 60.8 percent of its popular votes.

The Constitution says that the President "shall take care that the laws be faithfully executed." The Department of Justice is the instrument by which the President performs this responsibility. He appoints the Attorney General and other high officials of the department. They hold their offices at his pleasure. It is not surprising, therefore, that they hold the President in high esteem, and are susceptible to requests which they believe come from him.

Spokesmen for CREEP and the White House repeatedly assured law enforcement officers, the press, and the public that Liddy, Hunt, McCord, and the four Cubans were not operating by the authority or with the knowledge of CREEP when they burglarized and bugged the Watergate, and that no persons connected in any way with CREEP or the White House other than Liddy, Hunt, and McCord were implicated in any way in the Watergate affair.

Assistant Attorney General Petersen accepted these assurances at face value until April 1973, when the cover-up operation began to become unraveled. In the meantime he did certain things in good faith which tended to aid the cover-up.

Established procedures contemplate that able-bodied witnesses must appear in person before grand juries, and subject themselves to their inquiries. Instead of requiring Maurice Stans, chairman of the Finance Committee to Reelect the President, the White House aides Charles Colson, Egil Krogh, and David Young, and Charles Colson's secretary to appear in person and testify before the grand jury investigating Watergate, Petersen allowed them to make out-of-court statements in writing for presentation to that body.

It was later expressly revealed by evidence in the Senate Select Committee's hearing that Petersen took this action in respect to Stans at the request of John D. Ehrlichman, President Nixon's chief adviser on domestic affairs, who informed him that President Nixon did not want Stans to suffer the embarrassment of appearing before the grand jury.

Petersen's action in excusing these persons from making personal appearances before the grand jury was not compatible with the principle that all persons are entitled to equal treatment under the law. It also made it impossible for any inquisitive grand jurors to ask them any questions calculated to shed light on the matters they were investigating.

In August 1972 Donald Segretti was subpoenaed to testify before the grand jury. He contacted John W. Dean, III, President Nixon's counsel, for advice concerning what testimony he should give. Dean instructed him not to say anything about his relationships with Chapin, Strachan, and Kalmbach unless he was specifically asked about them.

Dean afterwards testified before the Senate Select Committee that he forthwith contacted Petersen and informed him that Segretti had no involvement in the Watergate incident, but that he had been hired by Chapin and Strachan and paid by Kalmbach to carry out some campaign activities for the White House. Dean further testified he told Petersen that these facts, if revealed, would be quite embarrassing and cause political problems during the remaining weeks of the campaign.

When he appeared before the Senate committee, Petersen testified he did not recall any conversation with Dean on this subject. He stated, however, that he had discussed the "dirty tricks" of Segretti with Earl Silbert, and that they had concluded that the dirty tricks had no connection with Watergate activities and were not violations of law. Petersen also stated: "In any event, I told Silbert I didn't want him getting into the relationships between the President and his lawyer or the fact that the President's lawyer might be involved in somewhat, I thought, illegitimate campaign activities on behalf of the President."

When Segretti appeared before the grand jury, Silbert asked him no questions about his dirty tricks or his relationships with Chapin, Strachan, and Kalmbach. But a grand juror did, and Segretti stated he was hired by Chapin and Strachan and paid by Kalmbach for his services.

Hindsight is easier than foresight. Nevertheless, it is reasonable to infer that, by their failure to follow up Segretti's testimony to the grand jury, Petersen and Silbert muffed an opportunity to discover as early as August 1972 that two White House aides, Chapin and Strachan, and Nixon's personal attorney and fund dispenser, Kalmbach, were seriously implicated in an important phase of the first conspiracy.

In August 1972 Representative Wright Patman, chairman of the House Committee on Banking and Currency, announced his plans to have that committee conduct a hearing to determine whether banking or election laws had been violated by members of CREEP in connection with collecting and disbursing Nixon campaign funds, and to call Stans and approximately forty other CREEP officers and employees and several White House aides to testify as witnesses.

The White House was deeply distressed by this development, and was determined to forestall any public disclosure of matters relating to Watergate before the election.

When Nixon was afterwards compelled to release it, his tape of September 15, 1972, disclosed that on that day Nixon, Haldeman, and Dean discussed in the Oval Office ways to prevent Wright Patman's hearing.

Dean expressed their consensus by saying, "We don't just want Stans up there in front of the cameras with Patman asking all these questions."

He reported to Nixon and Haldeman what had been done to prevent the hearing. A movement was on foot to persuade some of the attorneys for the seven defendants who had been indicted on that day to protest to the members of Patman's committee that the proposed hearing would jeopardize the right of their clients to a fair trial. Someone was approaching the American Civil Liberties Union to induce it to make like overtures to committee members. Garry Brown, a Republican representative from Michigan and a member of the committee, had written Attorney General Kleindienst asking him if the proposed hearing "isn't going to jeopardize your criminal case." Dean also informed Nixon and Haldeman that Stans was "going to see Jerry Ford [the Republican Leader of the House] and try to brief him and explain to him the problems he has."

After suggesting that Jerry Ford talk to Representative William B. Widnall, of New Jersey, the ranking Republican on Patman's committee, about the matter and "that they ought to raise hell about these hearings," Nixon gave this instruction to Haldeman and Dean: "Tell Ehrlichman to get Ford and [Garry] Brown in together, and they can work out something." Using a vulgarity, Nixon added, ". . . they ought to push it. No use to let Patman have a free ride here."

All relevant activities following the Oval Office discussion of Patman's proposal have not been revealed. Nevertheless, evidence afterwards presented to the Senate Select Committee indicate some of them.

White House congressional liaison aides William E. Timmons and Richard K. Cook urged ranking Republican members of the House and Republican members of the House Committee on Banking and Currency to block the proposed hearing. Mitchell, Stans, and counsel for CREEP pressured Dean to obtain a response from the Department of Justice to Representative Brown's inquiry of Kleindienst in the hope that it could be used to persuade members of Patman's committee to vote to block the hearing. After Dean talked to him about the potential implications of the breadth of the proposed Patman hearings, Petersen wrote Patman a letter setting forth the Department of Justice's view that the hearing he proposed to hold could jeopardize the prosecution of the seven Watergate defendants, and asking the committee to give serious consideration to this view before proceeding further.

Dean submitted to Patman's committee copies of Brown's inquiry and Petersen's letter on October 2, 1972. On the next day the Committee on Banking and Currency voted 20 to 15 to deny their chairman, Wright Patman, authority to hold the proposed hearing. Those so voting included all Republicans and several Southern Democrats. As Dean subsequently testified before the Senate Select Committee, the committee's action provoked "another sigh of relief . . . at the White House that we had leaped one more hurdle in the continuing cover-up."

Conspiracies are made in secret, and are ordinarily executed in ways designed to conceal the activities and identities of the conspirators. Consequently, their exposure is oftentimes dependent on revelations by parties to them.

The only person connected with the Watergate affair who made an honest revelation between the time of the arrest of the five burglars and the trial of the seven original Watergate defendants was Alfred C. Baldwin, III, who went with his attorney, Robert C. Minto, to Silbert and his associates on July 5, 1972, and received from them an assurance that he would not be prosecuted if he cooperated in their investigation.

As a consequence, he revealed to them the essential facts relating to the burglary itself. Acting on the directions of Liddy and Hunt, McCord, Barker, Gonzalez, Martinez, and Sturgis surreptitiously entered Democratic National Committee Headquarters in the Watergate a first time on May 28, 1972. Martinez photographed documents, and McCord planted bugging devices on the phones of Lawrence F. O'Brien, the chairman of the Democratic National Committee, and R. Spencer Oliver, another Democratic Party official.

Pursuant to his employment by McCord, Baldwin, using electronic receiving sets in a room of the Howard Johnson Motel across the street from the Watergate, monitored the intelligible conversations on the tapped phones, and gave daily logs of two hundred of them to McCord. It was discovered, however, that the bugging device on O'Brien's phone was malfunctioning, and Liddy and Hunt directed McCord to replace it. McCord and the four Cubans had burglarized the headquarters of the Democratic National Committee a second time for the primary purpose of replacing the bugging device on O'Brien's phone when the Washington police arrested them in the early morning of June 17.

Liddy, Hunt, McCord, and the four Cubans were placed on trial upon the indictments of September 15, 1972, before Judge Sirica and a petit jury in the United States District Court of the District of Columbia on January 8, 1973.

The trial lasted sixteen days and sixty-two witnesses testified. After several days Hunt, Barker, Gonzalez, Martinez, and Sturgis pleaded guilty on all counts, and the trial continued as to Liddy and McCord. Although they denied being pressured into entering their pleas, or being paid by anybody for anything, Hunt, Barker, Gonzalez, Martinez, and Sturgis did not take the witness stand or make any revelations during the trial. This was likewise true in respect to Liddy and McCord.

As evidence taken by the Senate Select Committee months later disclosed, everything relating to the trial did not occur in Judge Sirica's courtroom.

Hunt and McCord had retired from the Central Intelligence Agency after many years of service. Two of their codefendants, Barker and Martinez, had performed temporary chores for the agency. McCord entertained an intense loyalty to his former employer. He was fearful that some effort might be made during the trial to make it appear that the CIA had burglarized and bugged the Watergate as a national security measure to ascertain whether there was any link between the Democratic presidential campaign and the Cuban revolutionary dictator, Fidel Castro.

As a consequence, he wrote several letters to CIA officials warning them of his fear. Apparently knowing that John J. Caulfield, an erstwhile White House employee, had performed secret missions for Haldeman at Ehrlichman's request in times past, McCord wrote him a letter containing a thinly veiled threat to tell what he knew about Watergate if any effort should be made to portray it as a CIA operation.

Shortly thereafter Caulfield, acting on an assignment by Dean, made three clandestine contacts with McCord during the trial. On these occasions Caulfield complained that McCord was "fouling up the game plan," urged him to plead guilty and keep silent, and assured him he would receive presidential clemency and rehabilitation after a brief interval in case he was sentenced to prison on his plea of guilty. Caulfield told McCord that the assurances he was conveying came from "the very highest levels of the White House."

According to McCord's subsequent testimony before the Senate Select Committee, the crucial importance of his pleading guilty and keeping silent was emphasized by Caulfield with these words: "The President's ability to govern is at stake. Another Teapot Dome is possible, and the government may fall. Everybody else is on track but you, you are not following the game plan, get closer to your attorney."

McCord later told the Senate Select Committee that Caulfield added a threat to his importunities and promises by warning him that the administration would undoubtedly take action against him if he made public allegations against high administration officials.

McCord refused to plead guilty, but he did keep silent throughout the trial.

Earl Silbert, who was the chief government prosecutor in the trial, declared to the petit jury in his opening statement and again in his summation of the case against Liddy and McCord that the seven original Watergate defendants were engaged in a caper of their own when they burglarized and bugged the headquarters of the Democratic National Committee.

On January 30, 1973, the petit jury adjudged Liddy and McCord guilty of all charges against them, and Judge Sirica postponed sentencing them and their codefendants until March 23rd.

Judge Sirica, a courageous, experienced, and wise jurist, was not pleased with the way in which the lawyers were trying the case. On several occasions he excused the petit jurors from the courtroom, and observed in their absence that the lawyers were not asking the witnesses these critical questions: Who hired the burglars, and what was their object?

Shortly after the verdict Judge Sirica stated he was not satisfied that the full Watergate story had been revealed at the trial, and that he hoped the Senate would empower the investigative committee it was planning to establish "to get to the bottom of what had happened."

2

THE SENATE COMMITTEE

I have never known a more forthright and honorable man than Mike Mansfield, who served so well for many years as Democratic leader of the Senate. While he entertained great compassion for those who erred through human frailty, he abominated chicanery.

As a result of personal conversations with him in the waning weeks of 1972, I knew that the Watergate incident and certain other events of the presidential campaign of 1972 had engendered in his mind grave misgivings and the conviction that the Senate was obligated to the country to investigate that incident and campaign fully and fairly.

Mansfield realized that such an investigation would be fraught with more political overtones than any other congressional investigation in the nation's history. As one who revered the Senate as an institution, he was determined to do everything in his power to ensure that not only should any Senate investigation of this presidential campaign be fair, but that it should appear to the nation to be fair.

To this end, he decided he would not assign any Democratic senator to serve on any Senate committee empowered to conduct the investigation if there was reason to believe he harbored presidential or vice-presidential aspirations, or was likely to be influenced by partisanship rather than patriotism.

Mansfield also thought the investigation ought to be made by a small special committee rather than a large standing committee, such as the Government Operations Committee or Judiciary Committee, and that the committee ought not to begin its work until the trial of the seven original Watergate defendants by Judge Sirica and the petit jury had been completed.

While I was detained at my home in North Carolina by ice-covered highways in early January 1973, the Democratic Policy Committee and the Democratic Caucus of the Senate unanimously approved Senator Mansfield's proposals that the Senate establish a special committee to investigate the Watergate incident and the presidential campaign of 1972, and that I be asked to serve as its chairman.

When I returned to Washington, Mike Mansfield gave me these reasons why he wanted me to serve as chairman of the Senate special committee: first, I had had more judicial experience than any other member of the Senate; second, nobody could accuse me of harboring presidential or vice-presidential aspirations; and, third, I was the most nonpartisan Democrat in the Senate. In explaining his choice of me for the chairmanship, Mansfield afterwards paid me this high compliment publicly: "Senator Ervin was the only man we could have picked on either side of the aisle who'd have had the respect of the Senate as a whole." *The Congressional Quarterly*, which reports congressional activities to the nation, stated I was chosen to head the committee because of my "reputation for fairness and nonpartisanship."

I advised Senator Mansfield I accepted his selection of me as a call to patriotic service, and undertook to draft a resolution creating a special committee with purposes and powers conforming to our joint views.

As John Dean later testified, the White House was displeased by the action of the Senate Democrats in selecting me to head the inquiry into the Watergate incident and related matters.

The New York Times book *The Watergate Hearings* states:

> In the running tug-of-war between Congress and the White House in 1973, Senator Ervin seems to be holding the rope at the east end of Pennsylvania Avenue on virtually every issue. It is his bill that seeks to limit the President's power to impound funds and his committees that are looking into the questions of newsmen's right to withhold

their sources of information and the President's right to withhold information and staff members from Congressional scrutiny.

This statement inferentially suggests the White House's displeasure over my selection may have been occasioned by my opposition on constitutional grounds to some of its actions. A statement made by President Nixon himself to Dean indicates, however, that the White House may have feared I would be too diligent from its point of view in discharging the duties devolving upon me as chairman. When the White House released its transcripts of certain presidential tapes on April 30, 1974, the transcript of the tape of February 28, 1973, revealed that on that day Nixon made this comment to Dean: "Ervin works harder than most of our Southern gentlemen. They are great politicians. They are just more clever than the minority. Just more clever!"

As a result of my long involvement in the administration of justice as a trial lawyer and judge, I was wedded to the abiding conviction that the most sacred obligation devolving upon any human being is the task of judging those whom Walter Malone, the Tennessee judge and poet, called "our fellow travelers to the tomb."

I accepted the chairmanship of the Senate Select Committee with the determination to seek the truth and be just to all. For example, I refused to let the committee staff present on television the evidence it had collected purporting to link John B. Connally, of Texas, with illegal actions in respect to the so-called milk funds. In explaining my reason for so doing, I said, "I don't believe a word of the testimony against him, and I'm unwilling to expose any human being to public disgrace on the basis of evidence I believe incredible." My view of the evidence against Connally was confirmed by the verdict of the jury which subsequently acquitted him when he was tried on the identical charges in the United States District Court for the District of Columbia.

When I accepted the chairmanship, I suspected the Select Committee might find that some overzealous officers or employees of CREEP and possibly some overzealous White House aides had committed some unethical or even illegal acts. It was simply inconceivable to me, however, that President Nixon could have been involved in the tragic events the Select Committee was ordered by the Senate to investigate.

I stated publicly with complete sincerity on numerous occasions that I hoped the Select Committee would be able to make a final report exonerating the President.

To make it invulnerable to legal attacks and red herrings, I drafted with meticulous care a resolution to establish "a select committee of the Senate . . . to conduct an investigation and study of the extent, if any, to which illegal, improper, or unethical activities were engaged in by any persons, acting either individually or in combination with others, in the presidential election of 1972, or in any related campaign or canvass conducted by or in behalf of any person seeking nomination or election as the candidate of any political party for the office of President of the United States in such election, and to determine whether in its judgment any occurrences which may be revealed by the investigation and study indicate the necessity or desirability of the enactment of new congressional legislation to safeguard the electoral process by which the President of the United States is chosen."

Although it was officially named The Select Committee on Presidential Campaign Activities, the committee was popularly known as the Ervin committee or the Senate Watergate committee. For convenience, I call it the Senate Select Committee.

In its original form, the resolution stipulated that three of the members of the committee should be Democratic senators appointed by the president of the Senate on the recommendation of Senator Mike Mansfield, the Democratic leader in the Senate, and two members of the committee should be Republican senators appointed by the president of the Senate on the recommendation of Senator Hugh Scott, the Republican leader in the Senate.

In addition to stating in general terms its overall objective, the resolution conferred upon the committee specific powers to investigate and study the breaking, entering, and bugging of the Watergate and every other incident related to the presidential campaign and election of 1972.

The resolution gave the committee ample authority to require by subpoena or otherwise any person who it believed had knowledge or information concerning any of the matters it was authorized to investigate and study to appear before it and testify as a witness. The resolution also expressly conferred on the committee this power to compel the production of evidential material:

> To require by subpoena or order any department, agency, officer, or employee of the executive branch of the United States Govern-

ment, or any private person, firm or corporation, or any officer or former officer or employee of any political committee or organization to produce for its consideration or for use as evidence in its investigation and study any books, checks, cancelled checks, correspondence, communications, documents, papers, physical evidence, records, recordings, tapes, or materials relating to any of the matters or questions it is authorized to investigate and study which they or any of them may have in their custody or under their control.

The resolution empowered the committee to employ a professional and clerical staff to assist in its investigation and study, allocated $500,000 to it for expenses, and ordered it to report its findings and recommendations for legislation to the Senate "at the earliest practicable date, but no later than February 28, 1974."

By subsequent resolutions of the Senate, additional sums of $1.5 million were allotted to the committee for expenses, and the time for making its report to the Senate was extended to June 30, 1974.

The resolution creating the Senate Select Committee, which was designated as Senate Res. 60, was considered by the Senate on February 7, 1973. The Senate rejected Republican-sponsored amendments to make the committee consist of three Democrats and three Republicans, and to require the committee to investigate the presidential elections of 1964 and 1968 as well as that of 1972. I opposed the first of these amendments because it created the possibility that the committee might suffer from paralysis. I objected to the second on the ground that there were no charges of improprieties in the presidential elections of 1964 and 1968, and that if the Senate directed the committee to investigate them, it "would be about as foolish as the man who went bear hunting and stopped to chase rabbits."

The Senate then amended the resolution with my approval by increasing the number of committee members to four Democrats and three Republicans, and by providing that "the minority members of the Select Committee shall have one third of the professional staff of the Select Committee (including a minority counsel) and such part of the clerical staff as may be adequate."

After so doing, the Senate passed S. Res. 60 by the unanimous vote of 77 to 0.

Upon the recommendation of the Democratic Leader of the Senate, the president of the Senate appointed Herman E. Talmadge, Daniel K. Inouye, Joseph M. Montoya, and me the Democratic members of the committee, and upon the recommendation of the Republican Leader of the Senate, the president of the Senate appointed Howard H. Baker, Jr., Edward J. Gurney, and Lowell P. Weicker, Jr., its Republican members.

Shortly after the appointment of its members, the Senate Select Committee held an organizational meeting, and formally elected me its chairman and Senator Baker its vice-chairman.

As a result of the cover-up, the identities and activities of those really responsible for debasing the presidential election of 1972 were hidden. There was a public outcry for the investigation to proceed with dispatch. Consequently, the committee assembled with promptness a staff composed of approximately seventy-five lawyers, investigators, administrative aides, and secretaries to assist it in its monumental task.

While the members of the staff varied from time to time, the names of all who served the committee at any time during its life are set forth in the committee's final report.

In conformity to Senate custom, I named Samuel Dash, professor of law in Georgetown University Law Center, to be chief counsel and staff director, and Rufus L. Edmisten, a long-time aide of mine, to be deputy chief counsel. I also appointed Arthur S. Miller, professor of constitutional law at George Washington University, chief consultant. I borrowed from the Senate Subcommittee on Separation of Powers, of which I was chairman, Walker F. Nolan, Jr., and J. F. Pecore, who served the Senate Select Committee as counsel and assistant counsel, respectively.

Since he was responsible for supervising the staff in general and its Democratic members in particular, I delegated to Dash the power to select all other Democratic appointees to the staff. These actions of mine were sanctioned by my three Democratic colleagues, who extended to me complete cooperation in all phases of the committee's work.

Dash exercised his delegated authority with great wisdom. He named David M. Dorsen, James Hamilton, and Terry F. Lenzner, as assistant chief counsel; Mark J. Biros, Eugene Boyce, Donald Burris, M. Philip Haire, Marc Lackritz, Robert McNamara, William Mayton, James Moore, Robert Muse, Ronald D. Rotunda, Barry Schochet, W. Dennis Summers, and Alan S. Weitz, as assistant counsel; Carolyn M. Andrade and Laura Matz, as administrative assistants; Carolyn E. Cohen, as office manager; Carmine S. Bellino, as chief investigator; and Wayne Bishop, as chief field investigator.

Pursuant to the letter and spirit of S. Res. 60, one-third of the professional and clerical members of the staff at all times were the appointees of the three Republican members of the committee. They named Fred D. Thompson, a former U.S. District Attorney of Tennessee, as minority counsel; Donald G. Sanders, as deputy minority counsel; and Howard S. Liebengood, Michael Madigan, Richard Schutz, H. William Shure, and Robert Silverstein, as assistant minority counsel.

I assured the Republican members of the committee that they were free to use their appointees to the staff to any extent they wished to investigate the campaigns of candidates seeking the Democratic Party's nomination for President in 1972.

The committee was singularly blessed in having Samuel Dash as its chief counsel. He did not seek this post, and was greatly surprised when I offered it to him. I chose him because I was convinced he was ideally fitted for it. He had received a fine legal education at Harvard Law School, had had vast trial experience as district attorney of the city of Philadelphia, and was a highly respected professor of law in Georgetown University Law Center at the time he was given a leave of absence to serve the committee. Besides, he had made a profound study of surreptitious activities and written *The Eavesdroppers*, an excellent treatise on the subject.

He and I shared a common devotion to constitutional government and the rule of law. Instead of humiliating witnesses who invoked their constitutional right to plead the Fifth Amendment by exposing them to public view while so doing, as was customary in congressional investigations, we permitted them to make their pleas in executive sessions. The committee allowed Liddy and Colson to plead the Fifth Amendment in this fashion, and did not even call Chapin as a witness because of advance information that he would plead the Fifth Amendment if called. Dash and I discussed all of the committee's problems as they arose in private meetings, and were always able to agree on a position we could both support. It would have been impossible for anyone to have been of greater help to me in my work as chairman.

For chronology's sake, it is necessary to recount an event which was unknown until June 25, 1973, when Dean testified before the Senate Select Committee.

Before the committee held its organizational meeting, on February

10 and 11, 1973, Haldeman, Ehrlichman, Dean, and a fourth White House aide, Richard A. Moore, met at the La Costa Resort Hotel near San Clemente to devise strategy for the White House to pursue in respect to the Select Committee. After twelve to fourteen hours of discussion, the White House aides reached these conclusions:

1. The Senate Committee was unlike the courts, grand jury, and the Federal Bureau of Investigation which "had been dealt with earlier," and "it was going to take an all-out effort by the White House to deal with the Senate inquiry, because of the scope of the resolution, the composition of the Committee, the investigative powers of the Committee, and the general feelings that the Senate was a hostile world for the White House."

2. The White House could not look for any help from the Democratic members of the committee; "Senator Gurney would help the White House"; "Senator Weicker was an independent who could give the White House problems"; and "Senator Baker was an unknown," and an effort should be made without delay to determine how he "planned to operate."

After reaching these conclusions, the White House aides agreed on this strategy for dealing with the Senate inquiry:

> The White House will take a public posture of full cooperation, but privately will attempt to restrain the investigation and make it as difficult as possible to get information and witnesses. A behind-the-scenes media effort would be made to make the Senate inquiry appear very partisan. The ultimate goal would be to discredit the hearings and reduce their impact by attempting to show that the Democrats have engaged in the same type of activities.

For the sake of clarity, I will narrate events occurring after the La Costa conference in their relation to kindred events rather than in chronological order.

The La Costa strategy was compatible with the cover-up conspiracy. It is intriguing, however, when laid alongside something that President Nixon had said in a news conference on August 29, 1972. At that time he stated, in essence, that on the basis of a complete investigation of the Watergate incident by his counsel, John W. Dean, III, he could declare "categorically . . . that no one in the White House staff, no one in this administration, presently employed, was involved in this very bizarre incident." He then added, "What really hurts in matters of this sort is not the fact that they occur, because overzealous people in campaigns do things that are wrong. What really hurts is if you try to cover it up."

After that statement, Lawrence O'Brien requested the release of the report of Dean's Watergate investigation, and President Nixon's press agent, Ronald L. Ziegler, replied that such report would not be released.

I digress to observe that subsequently Dean testified before the Senate Select Committee that he had never made any report justifying Nixon's statement of August 29, 1972, and Ziegler publicly admitted that Dean had never made any "formal" report to that effect.

Pursuant to the La Costa strategy, the White House initiated efforts to discredit the Senate Select Committee by having it portrayed by White House advocates in the news media as an exceedingly partisan group. This effort fell far short of its objective because of the actions of two of its Republican members.

Senator Baker, who is a stalwart East Tennessee Republican, entertains a strong sense of loyalty to the Republican Party as an institution. I suspect that the White House undertook to bring much pressure on him to influence his conduct as a member of the committee. If it did, it failed in its purpose. As vice-chairman, Senator Baker rendered faithful service to the committee in its quest for the truth relating to Watergate, and earned my enduring gratitude for so doing.

Senator Weicker, who is a most courageous and forthright individual, stated publicly that the people had lost faith in politicians and the only way to change their attitude was "to bring dirty business like the Watergate out in the open." He practiced what he preached by being most zealous in seeking the truth concerning this tragedy.

White House aides also sought to smear individual members of the committee. According to a charge made by Senator Weicker on June 28, 1973, Colson was trying to intimidate him by planting with newsmen false stories concerning campaign contributions he had received.

On May 17, 1973, the Charlotte, North Carolina, *Observer* carried this article:

> The White House made an attempt two months ago to enlist North Carolina Republicans in a campaign to discredit Senator Sam J. Ervin, Jr., reliable sources have told the Observer. High officials in

the North Carolina Republican Party confirmed Wednesday that H. R. "Bob" Haldeman, at that time President Nixon's Chief of Staff, made two attempts to get local party officials to "dig up something to discredit Ervin and blast him with it."

When a reporter queried me about this incident, I told him it did not disturb me because all the indiscretions I had committed in the past were barred by the statute of limitations and I had lost my capacity to commit further indiscretions in the future.

Despite my lifelong allegiance to the Democratic Party, North Carolina Republicans have always treated me with great kindness. None of them attempted to dig up or disseminate anything to discredit me. On the contrary, one of the most distinguished of them, Charles R. Jonas, Jr., who had managed Nixon's campaigns in North Carolina in 1968 and 1972, won my undying gratitude by paying me an exceedingly high compliment. When he was interviewed in respect to the *Observer* article, Jonas stated he had not been asked by anyone to dig up anything to discredit me. He added:

> That would be an impossible task. I think that Senator Ervin is one of a handful of people in the Senate whom it would be impossible to discredit. I think that is why he was chosen. He has a record of impeccable honesty and integrity. If I had to depend on any one person in the Senate to proceed fairly and in a way that would protect the innocent, it would be Senator Ervin.

Vice-President Spiro T. Agnew and Secretary of Agriculture Earl L. Butz undertook to assist White House aides in their effort to discredit the committee and its members. Agnew employed his flamboyant rhetoric most dexterously on this subject in the speech he made to the National Association of Attorneys General in St. Louis, on June 11, 1973.

After describing the Watergate hearings then in progress as a "beauty contest" with a "Perry Masonish impact" and asserting that the Senate Select Committee "can hardly hope to find the truth and can hardly fail to muddy the waters of justice beyond redemption," Agnew quoted a statement I had made at the opening of the hearings: "My colleagues and I are determined to uncover all the relevant facts, . . . and to spare no one, whatever his station in life may be." Agnew argued that my statement demonstrated that the hearings were "an adversary process, a trial situation," and in consequence all "persons accused or named by a witness" were entitled to the safeguards that the law secures to defendants being tried on criminal charges in courts.

In elaborating this thesis, Agnew declared, in substance, that the committee was denying basic rights to "all persons accused or named by a witness" in these ways:

—By not allowing their counsel to participate actively in all colloquies among the committee members, the staff, and the witnesses.

—By not allowing their counsel to cross-examine the witnesses giving testimony adverse to them.

—By not allowing them to call other witnesses or introduce other evidence to rebut the testimony of the witnesses giving testimony against them.

—By not allowing them to introduce evidence to impeach the credibility of the witnesses giving testimony against them.

—By receiving hearsay testimony.

—By not adhering to the rules of evidence which prevail in courts.

—By permitting the hearings to be televised.

Agnew conceded that in all likelihood the hearings would proceed despite the reservations he voiced, and summed up his condemnation of the committee by stating that "a great deal of what we see and hear in these hearings would be indignantly ruled out of any court of law in the United States."

I digress briefly to make certain observations. It is not the function of congressional hearings to determine the criminal guilt of any persons. They are conducted to determine the effectiveness of existing laws and the need for new laws and to inform the American people what is happening in our land. Virtually all of the evidence denounced by Agnew as hearsay would have been admissable in prosecutions for conspiracies in courts of law, under the rule that what one conspirator does and says to further the conspiracy is admissible against all conspirators.

Numerous persons were "accused or named" by witnesses in the Senate Watergate hearings. Since they had exercised their right under the committee rules to retain counsel to advise them when they testified, they were represented in the aggregate by numerous counsel.

If it had adopted the procedures advocated by Agnew, the Senate Select Committee would have had difficulty completing its task before the last lingering echo of Gabriel's horn trembled into ultimate silence.

Secretary Butz had much to say about the Senate Watergate investigation in speeches and interviews in North Carolina and elsewhere. He denounced it as a "very improper political inquisition," insinuated it was my investigation rather than the Senate's, charged me with conducting it merely to obtain publicity, and asserted I ought to call it off. On one occasion he was quoted as saying I was suffering from senility. When I was asked by the press if I had any comment to make on this report, I said: "Yes. A very short one. Secretary Butz is trying to abolish Watergate with billingsgate."

Even the Republican National Committee joined its journalistic allies to charge that Senator Talmadge, Senator Inouye, and I sought to prevent a full congressional investigation of allegations made in 1963 that Bobby Baker had been guilty of wrongful conduct while serving as Secretary of the Senate. To make this charge appear plausible and its refutation difficult and tedious, they cited numerous votes cast by Senator Talmadge, Senator Inouye, and me in 1963 upon many matters relating to five different measures.

Senator Talmadge, Senator Inouye, and I strongly supported a complete investigation by the Senate Rules Committee of the allegations against Bobby Baker, and voted accordingly. This is made indisputably clear by a detailed analysis of our votes, which I made and inserted in the *Congressional Record* for October 10, 1973. Incidentally, Bobby Baker was sent to prison by the United States District Court for the District of Columbia largely on the basis of evidence unearthed by the Senate Rules Committee in forty-five days of hearings.

I made this contemporaneous comment upon the charge against Senator Talmadge, Senator Inouye, and me:

> One can but admire the zeal exhibited by the Republican National Committee and its journalistic allies in their desperate effort to invent a red herring to drag across the trail which leads to the truth concerning Watergate. One must remember, however, that what happened in the Bobby Baker investigation 9 years ago does not diminish by a jot or tittle the right of Congress and the American people to know the truth in respect to the Watergate affair, or hide from intelligent people for an instant the tragic fact that the Watergate Affair was planned, financed, and procured by men chosen by the White House to exercise enormous governmental, political, and financial power in its behalf.

On July 24, 1973, George Bush, chairman of the Republican National Committee, asserted in a news conference on the basis of three affidavits that Carmine S. Bellino, chief investigator for the Senate Select Committee, had participated in the electronic bugging of certain Republican election officials and possibly the Republican candidate, Vice-President Nixon, during the presidential campaign of 1960.

Bush's charge distressed me very much for two reasons. First, I deemed it unjust to Bellino, who denied it and whom I had known for many years to be an honorable man and a faithful public servant; and, second, it was out of character with the high opinion I entertained of Bush. Copies of the affidavits had been privately submitted to me before the news conference, and I had expressed my opinion that there was not a scintilla of competent or credible evidence in them to sustain the charges against Bellino.

Senator Hugh Scott and other Republican senators requested the Senate Select Committee to investigate the charge. I appointed Senators Talmadge, Inouye, and Gurney to do this in behalf of the committee.

Senators Talmadge, Inouye, and Gurney conducted an extensive investigation over a period of two and a half months in which they interviewed twenty-five witnesses. After so doing, Senators Talmadge and Inouye concluded that "there is no direct, competent, or credible evidence to sustain the charges against Bellino." Senator Gurney filed a minority report which agreed "there is no direct evidence to sustain the charges of electronic surveillance by Bellino," but stated "there is however, some credible evidence of contemplated electronic surveillance."

A diligent effort was made in behalf of the White House to induce the Senate Select Committee to investigate allegations that J. Edgar Hoover, the former director of the FBI, who was then in his grave, had committed allegedly illegal or unethical acts at the instance of the White House during the presidencies of John F. Kennedy and Lyndon B. Johnson. I ruled that the committee had no jurisdiction to investigate these allegations because they had no relation to the presidential campaign or election of 1972. I made similar rulings in respect to allegations against Haldeman while acting as campaign manager for Nixon in his race against Edmund ("Pat") Brown for the governorship of California in 1962, and allegations that the Joint Chiefs of Staff had spied on Henry A. Kissinger and the National Security Agency. I made these rulings because I was determined the committee should not be diverted from its authorized task by extraneous matters.

Nevertheless some hard-core Nixon supporters among the commentators criticized the committee in general and me in particular for not investigating the allegations concerning J. Edgar Hoover's conduct during the Kennedy and Johnson administrations. They ignored the fact that the committee would have acted unconstitutionally if it had investigated matters the Senate had not authorized it to investigate.

Efforts were made to minimize the impact of Watergate by alleging improper actions of previous administrations. Even President Nixon participated to some extent in this. In reply to a question put to him at a televised press conference in San Clemente, California, on August 22, 1973, concerning the burglary of the office of Dr. Lewis J. Fielding, Daniel Ellsberg's psychiatrist, President Nixon said that burglarizing without court orders took place on a very large scale during the Kennedy and Johnson administrations.

On being questioned by a newsman concerning this statement, I said I had never heard of such burglaries in either the Kennedy or the Johnson administration, but even if they had occurred, they did not justify any burglaries committed during the Nixon administration. I added, "Murder and theft have been committed since the earliest history of mankind, but that fact has not made murder meritorious or larceny legal."

A few hard-core Nixon champions among commentators impugned the personal integrity of Democratic members of the committee. In so doing, they obeyed Mark Twain's humorous advice: "Truth is very precious; use it sparingly."

Efforts to discredit the Senate committee and minimize the impact of Watergate largely lost their effectiveness as the committee performed its allotted task. The explanation for this is simple. It is usually difficult for a person to judge the veracity of witnesses if he is compelled to base his judgment on their written or printed words. It is otherwise, however, if he sees and hears them testify in person. The Constitution of the United States recognizes and utilizes these truths by decreeing in the Sixth Amendment that in all criminal prosecutions in federal courts the accused shall enjoy the right to be confronted with the witnesses against him.

The million and a half communications the Senate Select Committee received from the people of our land illustrate these truths in trenchant fashion. Before the hearings began, the communications received by the committee were evenly divided between those who believed the committee would be an instrument for the discovery of truth and those who feared the committee would engage in a partisan witch hunt.

After millions of Americans saw and heard on television the witnesses testifying in person before the committee, the character of the communications being received by the committee was drastically altered, and those commending the comittee outnumbered those condemning it by more than nine to one.

In making it possible for these Americans to see and hear the witnesses, commercial television, which telecast a substantial part of the committee's public hearings, and public television, which telecast all of them gavel to gavel, performed services of incalculable value to the cause of truth.

3

EXECUTIVE
POPPYCOCK

IN its effort to hide the truth about Watergate, the White House
relied most strongly on the structure of the Nixon White House and
President Nixon's views of the powers of his office. Nixon had insulated
his nonofficial activities from exposure by isolating himself behind
Haldeman, and Haldeman had insulated his political activities from
exposure by isolating himself behind Gordon Strachan, who acted as
his intermediary with CREEP. In the jargon prevalent in the White
House and CREEP, "at that point in time" this placed Nixon and
Haldeman in positions of "deniability."

To President Nixon, the presidency was an imperial institution. He
maintained that when the Constitution divided the powers of the
federal government among Congress, the President, and the courts, it
vested in the President an executive privilege which is absolute in nature
and unreviewable by Congress or the courts.

This executive privilege, he asserted, conferred upon him as President
the absolute power to withhold from the Senate Select Committee the
testimony of his aides and former aides as well as that of himself, and
to deny it access to any documents or materials in the custody of the
White House. He even affirmed that if he voluntarily testified before
the Senate Select Committee, his act in so doing would inflict "irrep-

arable damage" on the constitutional principle of the separation of powers and "jeopardize the constitutional role of the President."

History has demonstrated the fallacy of President Nixon's views. President Thomas Jefferson furnished documentary evidence to the United States Circuit Court in Richmond in obedience to a subpoena *duces tecum* issued by Chief Justice John Marshall as Circuit Justice when he was presiding at the trial of Aaron Burr and his codefendants for treason. President Abraham Lincoln voluntarily appeared in person and testified before congressional investigating committees on two occasions during the Civil War. President Ulysses S. Grant testified by deposition in the trial of a criminal charge against his former Secretary of War. After his retirement from office, President Theodore Roosevelt voluntarily appeared and testified before a congressional committee investigating his campaign funds. On these occasions the constitutional principle of the separation of powers suffered no damage, and the constitutional role of the President was not jeopardized.

President Nixon undertook to buttress his views respecting executive privilege by a letter dated November 12, 1953, written by President Harry S. Truman after his retirement to Harold H. Velde, chairman of the House Un-American Activities Committee, in which he refused to appear before that committee in obedience to a subpoena and subject himself to inquiry concerning his official acts as President. This letter was not a precedent for President Nixon's views. Velde did not propose to interrogate Truman about criminal activities or unethical political transactions. Truman ended his letter to Velde with this statement: "If your intention, however, is to inquire into any acts as a private individual either before or after my Presidency and unrelated to any acts as President, I shall be happy to appear."

As chairman of the Senate Subcommittee on the Separation of Powers, I conducted extensive hearings on "Executive Privilege, the Withholding of Information by the Executive" in July and August 1971. As a result of the illuminating testimony taken at these hearings and my own study, I have certain abiding convictions respecting the nature and scope of executive privilege. I expressed these convictions in these words during the Senate Watergate investigation:

> At first blush the doctrine of the separation of the powers of government may seem to be a nebulous constitutional ambiguity. It is, however, simply an embodiment of a fundamental characteristic of the American constitutional system.

The Constitution of the United States divides the powers of government among the Congress, the President, and the Federal Judiciary for this two fold purpose: First, to preserve liberty by preventing the concentration in the hands of a single public official or group of public officials of the fundamental powers of government; and, second, to enable the Congress, the President, and the Federal Judiciary to perform their respective constitutional duties and functions without interference from each other.

To these ends, the Constitution vests in the Congress the power to make the laws; in the President the power to execute the laws; and in the Federal Judiciary the power to interpret the laws.

Each of them is forbidden to encroach upon the powers of the others, or to obstruct the others in the exercise of their powers.

Executive privilege is an incident of the doctrine of the separation of the powers of government. Under it, the President cannot be made to divulge certain confidential communications of an extremely limited nature.

Executive privilege is not an arbitrary power which confers upon the President something in the nature of a divine right to withhold from grand juries, courts, or authorized congressional committees whatever information, papers, or taped recordings he pleases.

The antiquated notion that the rulers of men possess and may exercise divine rights and arbitrary powers perished in America with the Revolution. The Constitution of the United States is a law for rulers and people alike at all times and under all circumstances. The President and all other public officers in our land are bound by oath or affirmation to respect and obey it.

When it is properly understood and applied, executive privilege serves a useful purpose. The Constitution and the laws impose upon the President certain official duties.

The President is entitled to receive from his aides in confidence full and uninhibited advice as to how they think he can best discharge those official duties. His aides might be deterred from giving such advice to him if they knew that its confidentiality would not be protected.

On the basis of these considerations, executive privilege permits the President to keep secret confidential communications between him and his aides and even confidential communications among his aides which are had for the purpose of aiding the President to perform in a lawful manner his official duties.

Further than this, executive privilege does not go. Since the official duties of the President as defined by the Constitution and the laws do not encompass illegal or unethical or political activities, executive privilege does not confer upon the President the arbitrary power to withhold information, papers, or taped recordings, which are relevant to alleged crimes being investigated by a grand jury or undergoing trial before a court, or which are relevant to illegal, unethical, or political activities being investigated by an authorized congressional committee.

The converse is true. Section 3 of Article II of the Constitution expressly declares that the President "shall take care that the laws be faithfully executed."

These words plainly impose upon the President a constitutional obligation to submit to grand juries, courts, and authorized congressional committees any information, papers, or taped recordings controlled by him which relate to illegal or unethical or political activities, and which are necessary to enable them to discharge their respective responsibilities as agencies of the Federal Judiciary and the Congress.

If this is not true, the President is above the Constitution, and his oath to support that instrument is a meaningless mockery.

While he acceded to some requests of the Senate Select Committee for information, President Nixon denied most of them. On such occasions he sought to make it appear he was rightly invoking executive privilege by claiming that the committee was seeking information relating to national security matters or official decision-making within the executive branch of the government.

The committee did not seek information of that nature. It confined itself to its allotted sphere, and only attempted to secure evidence shedding light on the questions whether illegal, improper, or unethical acts had been committed in respect to the presidential campaign and election of 1972 and whether any efforts had been made to cover them up.

Circumstances compel the inference that President Nixon had a deliberate purpose in denying the committee testimony of his aides and former aides, and to create public support for his so doing.

On March 12, 1973, he issued a statement designed to establish the proposition that the constitutional powers of the presidency would be irreparably damaged if his aides and former aides were compelled to testify before the committee. He also announced he would exercise his executive privilege and prevent his aides and former aides from obeying any subpoena commanding them to appear and testify before the committee. About the same time the White House suggested that if the Senate Select Committee and the Senate were unwilling to abide by this invocation of executive privilege, they should ask the Department of Justice to obtain an adjudication of its validity by prosecuting an aide or former aide who disobeyed a committee subpoena for contempt of Congress in the federal courts.

This White House suggestion was obviously based on its desire to frustrate the investigation by delaying the appearance of any Nixon aide before the committee until the matter of executive privilege could be resolved through protracted litigation.

As chairman of the Senate Select Committee, I was compelled to respond. What President Nixon asserted in his statement, I declared, in substance, "isn't executive privilege; it's executive poppycock. It's akin to the divine rights of kings, which passed out of existence in America in the Revolution."

I asserted I was going to give some free legal advice through the news media to President Nixon's aides, which they would do well to heed if they desired to stay out of jail. I assured them publicly, in essence, through the media that the Senate Select Committee was not going to postpone taking their testimony until justice made its long and tiresome journey on leaden feet through a criminal contempt prosecution. I said that if any aide refused to appear and testify before the committee in obedience to its subpoena, it would ask the Senate to invoke its powers as they are defined by the Supreme Court in *McGrain* v. *Daugherty* (273 U.S. 135), and *Jurney* v. *MacCracken* (293 U.S. 125). I pointed out that under these decisions the Senate could issue a warrant directing its sergeant at arms to arrest and bring before it any aide who disobeyed a committee subpoena, and that the Senate could convict him of contempt of the Senate and take appropriate action to compel him to testify.

I declared furthermore that the American people were interested in the revelation of the truth about Watergate and not in abstruse arguments about executive privilege, and that President Nixon would serve himself, his administration, and our country best by helping the committee to ascertain that truth.

4

CONSPIRATORIAL
CONVERSATIONS

DEAN had only one real contact with President Nixon between the time when the burglars were caught in the Watergate and February 27, 1973. This was on September 15, the day on which the grand jury indicted the original seven Watergate defendants.

As the presidential tape of September 15 subsequently disclosed, President Nixon, Haldeman, and Dean talked about many things at their secret meeting on that day additional to the proposed Patman investigation. For example, their conversation indicated they were pleased the indictments had stopped with the original seven; Haldeman said Dean "is one of the quiet guys that gets a lot done"; Dean said he had had "quite a three months" but that it had ended up "well at this point"; and President Nixon told Dean "the way you've handled it, it seems to me, has been very skillful, putting your fingers in the dikes every time that leaks have sprung here and sprung there."

As Dean afterwards testified before the Senate Select Committee, he and President Nixon met secretly in the Oval Office on February 27 and 28, 1973. On the first of these days, Dean said, the President told him Haldeman and Ehrlichman were spending too much time on Watergate, and instructed him to take responsibility for Watergate and to report directly to him on matters related to it. At the end of the first day's meeting, Dean asserted, the President told him he "had done an excellent job of dealing with this matter during the campaign," and he told the President he "had only managed to contain the matter during the campaign, but [he] was not sure it could be contained indefinitely." The President said further, Dean affirmed, "he would not permit the White House staff to appear before the Select Committee, rather he would only permit the taking of written interrogatories." Dean testified that in reply to a question from the President on this point he said "that written interrogatories were something that could be handled whereas appearances might create serious problems." The President added, Dean stated, "he would never let Haldeman and Ehrlichman go to the Hill." At the end of the two days of secret meetings Dean says he told the President he had been "a conduit for many of the decisions that were made and could be involved in an obstruction of justice." The President assured him he "had no legal problems."

During ensuing days, President Nixon held many secret meetings with Dean in the Oval Office. Sometimes others were present. The occurrence of these meetings was hidden from the public until June 25, 1973, when Dean shocked the nation by revealing what happened in them in a televised hearing before the Senate Select Committee.

I digress to observe that about a year later the testimony of Dean concerning what transpired at these secret meetings became virtually irrefutable when the House Judiciary Committee studied impeachment and the true import of the presidential tapes covering the secret meetings became available to it.

President Nixon held a secret meeting with Dean on March 13, 1973. They discussed in much detail the problems which the pendency of the Senate Judiciary Committee's hearings on L. Patrick Gray's nomination to be director of the FBI presented to the White House. After so doing, they talked about Watergate problems, and considered the possibility of using as red herrings to detract the nation's attention from Watergate certain charges that Dean said William C. Sullivan, a discharged FBI official, was willing to make against J. Edgar Hoover, the FBI, and Lyndon B. Johnson.

Although Dean informed the President he had no reason to think the prospective hearings of the Senate Select Committee "would get out of hand," President Nixon said "they're after Haldeman and Mitchell," and asked Dean if Haldeman's vulnerability to the committee was not Chapin, who had employed Segretti, and Strachan, who was Haldeman's aide.

Dean replied that Chapin "didn't know anything about the Watergate," and that although Strachan knew about Watergate and may have told Haldeman about it, he would "stonewall it" and say, "I don't know anything about what you are talking about." President Nixon then suggested that "the other weak link for Bob [Haldeman] is Magruder," because Haldeman had originally hired Magruder and Magruder "sure as hell knows Hunt."

After saying that the President's observation about Magruder applied to Mitchell also, Dean stated that the sole connection of Liddy and Hunt and their outfit with Watergate was intelligence gathering, and that both Magruder and Mitchell could claim that Liddy and Hunt and their outfit had embarked on an unauthorized prank of their own when they participated in Watergate.

In answer to an obviously rhetorical question on the part of President Nixon, Dean said it is "too late to go the hang-out road."

On March 15, 1973, President Nixon held a news conference in which he began to use the term "separation of powers" rather than the term "executive privilege." Although he asserted that Dean would furnish information to the Judiciary Committee considering Gray's nomination to be director of the FBI, he would not permit Dean to testify in a formal session or let any of the senators question him informally. He declared that he had "the constitutional responsibility to defend the separation of powers," and that he had to take this course because Dean had "a double privilege, the lawyer-client relationship, as well as the Presidential privilege."

Hunt's wife was killed in the crash of a Chicago-bound airplane on December 7, 1972, while she was carrying $10,000 in cash. Her death left Hunt much distraught with motherless children. As March 23, 1973, the date for the sentencing of the original seven Watergate defendants, approached, Hunt transmitted to Dean through intermediaries a secret demand that he be given $72,000 for living expenses for his family and $50,000 for attorney fees before his sentencing. This secret demand was accompanied by a secret threat from Hunt that if the money was not forthcoming, he might disclose some "seamy things" he had done for Ehrlichman while he was a consultant at the White House.

As he afterwards testified before the Senate Select Committee,

Dean talked to Ehrlichman about Hunt's demand and threat, and, at Ehrlichman's direction, discussed them by phone with Mitchell, who did not indicate whether Hunt would be paid. According to his subsequent testimony before the committee, Richard A. Moore, special counsel to the President, was informed by Dean of Hunt's demand and threat, and advised Dean to inform the President of it.

On the following day, March 21, Dean met secretly with President Nixon in the Oval Office. Dean opened the crucial part of the conversation with these words:

> I think there's no doubt about the seriousness of the problem we've got. We have a cancer—within—close to the Presidency, that's growing. It's growing daily. It's compounding, it grows geometrically now, because it compounds itself. That'll be clear as I explain some of the details of why it is . . . and there is no assurance that it won't bust.

After this preamble, Dean recited to President Nixon the matters stated in detail in the numbered paragraphs set forth below:

1. As head of the political arm of CREEP, Mitchell authorized his deputy chairman, Magruder, to employ Liddy to arrange for the burglary and bugging of the headquarters of the Democratic National Committee in the Watergate. He also procured Magruder an allotment of $250,000 for financing the operation out of campaign cash cached in safes of the finance arm of CREEP. Colson may have helped to push Magruder into the operation by calling him at the instance of Liddy and Hunt and urging him to "fish or cut bait" on their project.

2. With Hunt's aid, Liddy hired McCord and the four Cubans to break and enter the Democratic headquarters and bug telephones in it. While the bugged telephones were being monitored, the information thereby obtained was transmitted to Liddy, who gave copies of it to Mitchell and Haldeman's intermediary, Strachan. Strachan, in turn, probably gave some of it to Haldeman.

3. After McCord and the Cubans were caught in the Democratic headquarters and law enforcement officers connected Liddy and Hunt with them, certain CREEP officials and White House aides did various things to cover up the truth about Watergate and hide it from law enforcement officers, the news media, and the public. They apprehended

that its full disclosure might have a terrific impact on President Nixon's reelection.

4. To avoid this, Magruder and Herbert L. Porter, another CREEP official, committed perjury before the investigating grand jury, and Mitchell, Haldeman, Ehrlichman, Dean, and Kalmbach participated in one way or another in paying substantial sums of money to the seven original Watergate defendants for attorney fees and support money.

5. The demand for the money came originally from Liddy, who said he and his codefendants would "ride this out . . . if they all got counsel instantly," and the participating CREEP officials and White House aides made the payments "to take this through the election."

6. The money for the payments was supplied in part by Frederick C. LaRue, a friend of Mitchell and an official of CREEP, out of campaign funds controlled by CREEP, in part by Kalmbach out of additional funds raised by him, and in part by Haldeman who returned to CREEP $350,000 in campaign funds which he had reserved for polling purposes.

7. The moneys were transmitted to the seven defendants or their attorneys or families in various surreptitious ways by a retired New York police officer, Anthony T. Ulasewicz; and Dean was informed after the fact that Hunt's wife was carrying to somebody in Chicago for transmission to the Cubans, who were then in Miami, the $10,000 found on her after the fatal airplane crash.

8. The cover-up had thus far shielded the participating CREEP officials and White House aides. It was now in imminent peril, however, because of Hunt's demand for an additional $122,000 before his sentencing and this threat as to what he would do if it was not forthcoming: "I will bring John Ehrlichman down to his knees and put him in jail. I have done enough seamy things for him and Krogh that they'd never survive."

9. On its face, Hunt's threat referred primarily to Ehrlichman's possible complicity in the burglary of the office of Dr. Lewis J. Fielding, Daniel Ellsberg's psychiatrist, in Beverly Hills, California, in September 1971. Acting at the instance of Egil Krogh, a White House aide and head of the White House group known as the Plumbers, Liddy and Hunt had hired the Cubans to commit this burglary to obtain information relating to Ellsberg, which the White House sought.

10. Like the Segretti episode, this burglary had no direct con-

nection with the Watergate affair. But Hunt had been associated with Magruder in this affair, and Dean feared that any disclosures Hunt might make could endanger the entire cover-up and might result in the indictment of Mitchell, Haldeman, Ehrlichman, and himself for obstruction of justice. He believed Chapin and Krogh might also be subject to prosecution for violation of civil rights laws.

11. Dean anticipated, moreover, that when they were sent to jail by Judge Sirica, the other six original Watergate defendants would demand blackmail for their silence, and there would be "problems of continued blackmail" in the future.

After Dean related these things to President Nixon, and advised him that he, i.e., the President, would be hurt most by the crumbling of the cover-up, President Nixon and Dean discussed what options were open to the White House to prevent this from happening.

In doing this, they weighed prospective blackmail demands, the expectations of presidential clemency of Hunt and his associates, and Hunt's pending demand and threat. When President Nixon asked him how much money he would need to take care of prospective blackmail demands from the convicted Watergate defendants after they were imprisoned, Dean responded, "I would say these people are going to cost a million dollars over the next two years."

President Nixon thereupon assured Dean that he knew where he could get the million dollars in cash, and he and Dean then agreed that Mitchell ought to assume the responsibility of getting it disbursed. President Nixon asked Dean, in substance, if he could take care of the prospective blackmail demands if he got "the million bucks . . . and the proper way to handle it." When Dean replied in the affirmative, the President said, "It would seem to me that would be worthwhile."

Then they talked over the problems being posed for the White House by Hunt's impatient demand for clemency, and the prospective demands of Hunt's associates for it. When Dean observed that it would be politically impossible for the President to extend clemency to Hunt or the others, Nixon said, "You can't do it till after the '74 election, that's for sure." Dean replied that "even then you couldn't do it . . . because it may further involve you in a way you shouldn't be involved in this." President Nixon closed the colloquy on clemency with this statement: "No, it's wrong, that's for sure."

President Nixon made this inquiry of Dean: "Looking at the immediate problem, don't you have to handle Hunt's financial situation damn soon?" Dean responded: "I talked to Mitchell about that last night." President Nixon asserted: "You've got to keep the cap on the bottle that much in order to have any options. Either that or let it all blow right now." Nixon and Dean ended their discussion on Hunt's pending demand by agreeing that the "Hunt thing" was "worth buying time on at the moment."

After weighing all options, President Nixon declared, "It's better to fight it out and not let people testify," and Dean agreed. In so doing, Dean asserted, "Fight it at every corner, every turn; don't let people testify; cover it up is what we're really talking about; just keep it buried, and just hope we can do it."

At this point the President summoned Haldeman to the secret meeting, and a three-way discussion followed. After informing Haldeman he had been talking to Dean, who knew "about everything" and what "the potential criminal liabilities" were, President Nixon said he wanted Haldeman, Ehrlichman, Dean, and Mitchell to meet as soon as possible. He added, "Mitchell has to be there because he is seriously involved."

In explaining the necessity for the meeting, President Nixon said: "We've got to see how we handle it from here on. . . . We got to see what the line is. Whether the line is one of continuing to try run a total stonewall, and take the heat from that, having in mind there are vulnerable points."

Before the three-way discussion ended, President Nixon stated that Dean had the right plan before the election and handled "it just right" because he "contained it." He added: "Now after the election we've got to have another plan."

President Nixon asserted "there must be a four-way talk . . . of the particular ones we can trust." He added: "I don't want any criminal liability . . . for members of the White House staff, and for members of the Committee . . . I think Magruder is the major guy over there."

Haldeman observed "there is a possibility of cutting it at Liddy where you now are, but to accomplish that requires continued perjury by Magruder."

President Nixon replied, "Yeah. And it requires total control over all of the defendants." He asserted, further, that to "avoid criminal liability . . . we've got to keep [the] obstruction of justice thing off" Dean, Ehrlichman, Haldeman, Mitchell, Chapin "if possible," and Strachan.

Haldeman interjected, "And Magruder, if you can." President Nixon then stated that Dean's "point is that if Magruder goes down he'll pull everybody with him," and Haldeman responded, "that's my view."

President Nixon, Dean, and Haldeman proceeded to consider in detail the vulnerabilities of the White House to the aftermath of Watergate.

President Nixon dismissed quickly any hazard from blackmail demands from the original Watergate defendants arising after their imprisonment by Judge Sirica. He said, "It is going to require approximately a million dollars to take care of the jackasses that are in jail. . . . Let me tell you it's no problem. We could get the money. Mitchell could provide the way to deliver it."

President Nixon was much concerned by Hunt's demand for $122,000 before sentencing and his threat to expose the "seamy things" he had done for Ehrlichman and Krogh if the money was not forthcoming, and by Hunt's impatient demand for presidential clemency.

He said "Hunt might blow the whistle. . . . His price is pretty high. . . . As I pointed out to John [Dean] . . . at least we should buy the time on that."

After Haldeman wondered what the White House would need for blackmail "tomorrow and next year and five years from now," Dean reminded them of what they had done in this respect "just to get us through November 7th," and Haldeman acknowledged, "I recognize that's what we had to give to November 7th."

President Nixon then asserted "as far as what happened up to this time our cover . . . is just going to be the Cuban Committee did this for them up through the election."

Dean responded: "Yeah. We can put that together. That isn't, of course, quite the way it happened"; and President Nixon affirmed: "I know, but it's the way it's going to have to happen."

Dean told President Nixon and Haldeman that after Judge Sirica had sentenced the seven original Watergate defendants, the United States Attorney's Office would have the court immunize them from further prosecution and send them before the grand jury "to talk about anything further they want to talk about." Dean added: "They're going to stonewall it as it now stands. Except for Hunt. That is the leverage in his threat."

Haldeman said, ". . . this is Hunt's opportunity," and President Nixon declared, ". . . that's why you've got no choice with Hunt but the hundred and twenty or whatever it is." He then inquired of Dean: "Would you agree that that's a buy-time thing, you better damn well get that done, but fast?" Dean replied, "I think he ought to be given some signal anyway."

Dean said Mitchell had promised to call him about money tomorrow. When President Nixon asked him "if you had it, how could you get it to somebody," Dean responded: "I gather LaRue just leaves it in mail boxes and things like that, and tells Hunt to go pick it up."

In answer to President Nixon's inquiry as to what would happen if "Hunt blows the whistle," Dean said "It'll get Magruder," . . . "it would possibly get Colson," . . . and "it'll start the whole FBI investigation going again." He added that "Hunt can't get Mitchell." President Nixon then stated, in substance, that Hunt could get Ehrlichman on the Ellsberg thing, and Dean added, "Krogh could go down in smoke."

When President Nixon asked what would happen if Krogh claimed the Ellsberg affair was a "national security matter," Dean said "that won't sell . . . in a criminal situation."

President Nixon thereupon affirmed: "We have no choice on Hunt but to try to keep him."

They discussed clemency in detail. President Nixon said, "You know Colson has gone around on this clemency thing with Hunt and the rest," and Dean advised them Hunt was claiming he had a commitment from Colson that he would be out of prison by Christmas of 1973.

President Nixon declared "we're not going to be able to deliver on any kind of a clemency thing with Hunt and the rest. . . . We could get the money. There is no problem in that. We can't provide the clemency. . . . You could parole him [Hunt] for a period of time because of his family situation . . . , but you could not do [that for] the others."

President Nixon made it clear in this private meeting as well as on other occasions that he was strongly opposed to his aides' testifying before the Senate Select Committee.

In reply to an inquiry from him, Dean said, "We need to discuss" whether "we can get our story before a grand jury" and make it appear "they have really investigated the White House on this."

President Nixon suggested he could take the leadership in this by saying "I want another grand jury proceeding" and "I want everybody in the White House called." He added that would give a reason for his aides not to have to go up before the Senate committee, and put the investigation in secret sessions.

He manifested his satisfaction in these words: "I'm just thinking now of how the President looks. . . . We would be cooperating through a grand jury. Everybody would be behind us. That's the proper way to do this. It should be done through a grand jury, not up there in the kleig lights of the Committee."

Recognizing that the Senate Select Committee might proceed with its investigation notwithstanding the grand jury was functioning, President Nixon declared, "We would insist on executive privilege before the Committee," and "flat out" refuse to cooperate with it because the "matter [was] before a grand jury." He asserted that the White House could publicize its story by leaks it could control.

Haldeman originally voiced his opinion in favor of the proposed grand jury proceeding with these words: "So you are in a hell of a lot better position than you are up there."

Haldeman began to ask questions about what a witness could do before the grand jury. President Nixon and Dean both assured him that a witness could plead the Fifth Amendment or say he forgot.

Then Haldeman asked if a witness was not in a "very high risk perjury situation" before a grand jury.

President Nixon replied, "That's right. Just be damned sure you say I don't remember; I can't recall; I can't give any honest answer to that that I can recall."

Haldeman persisted: "You have the same perjury thing on the Hill, don't you?" President Nixon replied, "Oh, hell, yes."

Dean warned President Nixon and Haldeman that a grand jury would involve the criminal justice system, and that "once we start down any route that involves the criminal justice system, . . . you've got to have full appreciation there is really no control over that."

Dean stated, in substance, that a new grand jury would call Magruder again, and question him about all those meetings and the like, and Magruder would begin to change his story as to what he told the grand jury the last time. Dean added, "That way he's in a perjury situation."

Haldeman said, "That the best leverage you've got on Jeb—he's got to keep his story straight or he's in real trouble." Haldeman had a second thought: "Unless they get smart and give him immunity. If they immunize Jeb, then you have an interesting problem."

It is a surmise whether apprehensions inspired by these considerations prompted President Nixon to abandon the grand jury project. But abandon it he did with these words:

> Oh, well, if you open up the grand jury, it won't do any good; it won't be believed. And then you'll have two things going: the grand jury and . . . the other thing. . . . Then, however, we may say, Mitchell, et al. God, we can't risk that. I mean all sorts of shit'll break loose there. Then that leaves you to your third thing. The third thing is just to continue to hunker down and fight it.

When Dean expressed a fear that "something is going to break," President Nixon said, "When it breaks it'll look like the President is covering up."

Haldeman ended this private meeting by saying this to the President: "John Dean's point is exactly right, that the erosion here now is going to you, and that is the thing that we've got to turn off, at whatever . . . cost it takes."

This meeting ended at eleven-fifty-five on the morning of March 21. President Nixon held another secret conference on the Watergate affair with Haldeman, Ehrlichman, and Dean in the Oval Office late that afternoon.

Ehrlichman opened the discussion with an observation that the conferees went "round and round," "came up with all questions and no answers," and ended where they "started."

President Nixon responded "that's where we were this morning." He asked Ehrlichman if he had "anything additional to rush here."

Ehrlichman declared, "I just don't think that the immunity thing will wash." In making this declaration he was obviously referring to a proposal made by Dean outside the meeting that White House aides be given immunity from prosecution and sent to testify before the grand jury concerning their versions of Watergate.

President Nixon reminded Ehrlichman that the grand jury route had been his "idea of getting out of it," and inquired "what about" taking "the grand jury without immunity."

Ehrlichman replied, "I think that is still a possibility. It leads to some drastic results. . . . You end up with people in and out of the White House indicted for various offenses."

Ehrlichman advanced as another possible method of handling the problem the preparation of the White House's "view of the facts." He declared, "I think you could get out a fairly credible document that would stand up, and that will have the effect of trimming the scope" of the investigation. He added, "The big danger in the Ervin hearings, as I see it, is that they will . . . lead into areas . . . it would be better not to have to get into."

47

After this, President Nixon asserted, in substance, that they had two options. First, they could do nothing and seek to contain "the thing"; and, second, they could have Dean, as the White House counsel, prepare a written report presenting the Watergate affair in a light favorable to the White House.

The President then asked the group "as to what we should do now about" Hunt's current demand. Dean responded that Mitchell and LaRue were "aware of it," and "are in a position to do something."

To sustain his apprehension of the imminent peril of disclosure, Dean cited three factors. First, he said, "within this circle of people who have tidbits of knowledge are a lot of weak individuals and any one of those could cause it to blow." Second, he declared, the plaintiffs in the civil suit filed by Larry O'Brien, the Democratic chairman, against officers of CREEP were going to have rather intensive discovery proceedings, and "they may well work hand in glove with the Senate Committee." Third, he declared, "an attitude . . . has grown amongst all the people that have been involved in this thing to protect their own behinds." Dean called attention to these facts: "Dwight [Chapin], for example, now wants a lawyer; Kalmbach has hired himself a lawyer; Colson has retained a lawyer."

Dean suggested that President Nixon should declare that because of something just brought to his attention, he wanted to get all the information pertaining to the Watergate affair and lay it before the public"; that "it's not going to come out if people are going to take the Fifth Amendment before a grand jury"; that for like reasons "it's not going to come out" before a committee; and that in consequence he is going to appoint a special presidential panel to investigate and report back on the entire Watergate affair.

Dean further suggested that the President could select a panel composed of such officials as "the Deputy Attorney General, the head of the Criminal Division, [and] the head of the Civil Division"; require "everybody in the White House" to tell the panel "exactly what happened"; assure them that they would "not be prosecuted for it because" the point is merely "to get out all this information"; and to determine on the basis of what the panel discovers whether people can remain in the government or not."

Haldeman emphatically vetoed these suggestions of Dean with this statement: "The hue and cry would be that this is a super cover-up. Before they were just trying to cover up the information. Now they realize they've got guilty people, so they've immunized them so that they can't be prosecuted."

After being thus rebuked by Haldeman, Dean insisted that it might be better for them to take some affirmative action rather than to "just keep going" and "have the thing build up and all of a sudden collapse" with people getting "indicted" and "tarnished."

President Nixon thereupon commented, "After we've stonewalled it"; and Dean added, "After we've stonewalled it, and after the President's been accused of covering up that way."

President Nixon gave this emphasis to Dean's assertion: "That's the point."

Ehrlichman suggested there was another way. He stated, in substance, that Dean could make a written report to the President setting out that at his request he had investigated the Watergate affair.

In urging this course, Ehrlichman said it would put the President in a position where he could say in the event of a collapse at a later time: "Jesus, I had the FBI, and the grand jury and I had my own counsel. I turned over every rock I could find. And I rested my confidence in these people in good faith."

President Nixon interjected the idea that Dean should write the report in general terms, stating "that this man did not do it, this man did not do it, this man did do that." He explained that Dean would have to reveal the Chapin-Segretti affair.

President Nixon declared he could make the report available to the Senate Select Committee in this way:

> "Dear Senator Ervin," I'd say, "Here is the report, it is before your hearings. I want you to have it . . . and as I have said previously, . . . any . . . questions that are not answered here, any member of the White House staff . . . will be directed to answer."

In reply to an inquiry from Haldeman, the President stated, in substance, that the White House staff would answer any unanswered questions in an "informal way."

President Nixon then put this inquiry to Dean: "Getting back to this, John, you still sort of tilt to the panel idea yourself?"

Dean replied, "I see in this conversation the things . . . we've talked about before. But they do not ultimately solve what I see as the grave problem of a cancer growing around the Presidency, and that the cancer is going to continue to grow."

In response to another inquiry of the President, Dean said he really thought they had "to clean the cancer out now."

The ensuing colloquy illustrates President Nixon's intense aversion to having his aides appear before the Senate Select Committee in formal hearings as witnesses:

President Nixon: "You certainly don't want to do it at the Senate, do you?"

Dean: "No, sir. I think that would be an added trap."

President Nixon: "That's the worst thing."

Dean then asserted: "We've got to do it. You have to do it, to get the credit for it. That gets you above it. As I see it, that means people getting hurt, and I hope we can find the answer to that problem."

Ehrlichman posed the question as to what would happen if Dean rendered a report to the President setting out everything he knew about the Watergate affair, and the President sent the report to the Justice Department.

President Nixon asked whether the Justice Department would stop with Magruder, who had "a problem of action and perjury."

Haldeman stated initially that if they took this route, Magruder, Chapin, and Dean would almost certainly go to jail and he would probably do so.

After President Nixon questioned whether Haldeman and Dean would suffer this fate, Haldeman said Chapin and Strachan were "clean."

The President noted Dean's prediction that Magruder would "pull others down with him."

Dean characterized Hunt's current demand for money as black-mailing the White House, and declared, "It bothers me to do anything further now in the situation when Hunt's our real hang-up."

Haldeman stated that "the payment to Hunt" solves it; and President Nixon added, "The payment to Hunt does, yeah."

Dean observed that they needed somebody to assess the criminal liability because "maybe we are misassessing it."

Ehrlichman intimated that they might confide in Henry Petersen, head of the Criminal Division of the Department of Justice. He said, "You could say, 'Henry, I want to talk to you about questions that arise in the course of my investigation, but I have to swear you to secrecy.' If he'll take it on that basis."

Haldeman disapproved this suggestion with these words: "You immediately eliminate one of your options. You can, well, you can eliminate the option of the President being able to take the position he knew nothing about it."

In response to an inquiry of President Nixon, Dean said a statement by the White House would be a temporary answer to the problem.

President Nixon observed, in essence, that "a statement would . . . indicate the President has looked into the matter, has had his counsel report to him, and this [statement] is the result of that." He said this action would manifest "the offer of White House people to cooperate" with the Senate Select Committee, and "that we're not covering up." He admitted that such action "still leaves it, however, in the hands of the Committee." He surmised "the Committee will say 'No,'" and declared that in that event "we'll just stand right there" and "let the Committee do their damnedest."

Dean prophesied that they might have a new problem when Judge Sirica sentenced the original seven Watergate defendants on March 23. He said he thought the judge would state in a speech from the bench "that he is not convinced the case represents the full situation" and "that there are higher-ups involved in this." He added that the judge "may take some dramatic action" like appointing "a Special Prosecutor . . . to re-open the investigation."

President Nixon remarked, "In other words, we're damned by the courts before Ervin ever could get there."

This colloquy followed:

> ERLICHMAN: The only thing we can say is for Ziegler to say, "Look, we've investigated backwards and forwards in the White House, and we're satisfied on the basis of the report that nobody in the White House has been involved in the burglary, nobody had notice of it, knowledge of it, participated in the planning, or aided and abetted it in any way."
> PRESIDENT NIXON: Well, that's what you could say.
> EHRLICHMAN: And it happens to be true.
> PRESIDENT NIXON: Yeah.
> EHRLICHMAN: As for that transaction.
> PRESIDENT NIXON (laughs): Sure, as for that transaction.

Ehrlichman thereupon offered what he called "another concomitant to that." He said, "Supposing Mitchell were to step out on that same day and were to say 'I've been doing some investigation at 1701 and I find so and so, and so and so . . . I don't know what he would say, but maybe he'd want to make some kind of a disclosure."

This prompted President Nixon to propound a question, which nobody answered. He asked, "What the hell is he going to disclose that isn't going to blow something?"

The meeting thereupon adjourned with an agreement that the participants would meet the next morning.

LaRue later made certain revelations before the Senate Select Committe concerning what happened on the evening of March 21 shortly after this meeting adjourned.

Dean informed LaRue by phone that Hunt was demanding an immediate payment of $75,000 for use as attorney fees. After Dean refused to authorize him to make the payment, LaRue called Mitchell by phone, and Mitchell directed him to make the payment. LaRue took $75,000 in cash out of CREEP funds stored in his filing cabinet, placed it in a plain envelope, and sent it to Hunt's attorney, William O. Bittman, a Washington lawyer.

Mitchell, Haldeman, Ehrlichman, and Dean met secretly with President Nixon in the Oval Office on the morning of March 22 to devise a method for dealing with the Senate Select Committee.

After Ehrlichman stated, "Our brother Mitchell [has] brought us some wisdom on executive privilege," Mitchell called President Nixon's attention to the fact that some have waived executive privilege, and told him he believed "some of the current people at the White House should go up" to the Senate Select Committee "under controlled circumstances."

When President Nixon asked him how he would handle it, Mitchell replied, "I would lay out a formula, and negotiate it with Sam Ervin . . . I would also put together a damn good public relations team so that the facts can be adduced without putting on a political road show." He suggested further it might be "appropriate at this time to formulate John Dean's theory on the Segretti matter and the Watergate matter based on the documentation from the FBI."

Dean said, "I've done the Segretti thing. . . . We don't have any major problem with that." He added, "I haven't written" a report on Watergate, "and I really can't say if I can do it. . . . It's certainly something that should be done."

Haldeman recommended that Dean "ought to hole up for the week-end" and "get it done"; and President Nixon advanced the idea that Dean ought to seclude himself at Camp David over the weekend and "see what he could come up with." Ehrlichman urged as his "scenario" that Dean should present his report to the President as something the President had requested him to make.

President Nixon suggested that Dean could state in the report that pursuant to the President's request he was setting forth "the facts with regard to members of the White House staff as disclosed by the FBI reports and the grand jury testimony."

Ehrlichman and President Nixon indicated what the proposed Dean report was to declare. Ehrlichman said, "And the report says 'Nobody was involved' "; and Nixon asserted, "That's right."

In urging that some "present White House staff" should appear before the Senate Select Committee "under controlled circumstances," Mitchell argued that the White House was "being badly hurt" in the eyes of the public by the way executive privilege was being "handled."

Haldeman agreed that its insistence on an inflexible executive privilege was injuring the White House's standing.

He addressed this remark directly to President Nixon: "That's where you look like you are covering up right now. That's the only thing, the only active step you've taken to cover up the Watergate all along." President Nixon responded: "That's right."

Haldeman then told the President he was "just fine . . . on tradition and constitutional grounds and all that stuff," but that what he said on these subjects did not satisfy the "guy sitting at home, who watches John Chancellor say that the President is covering this up—this historic review blankets the wildest exercise of executive privilege in American history—and all that." Haldeman added that this guy says, "What the hell's he covering up. If he's got no problem why doesn't he let them go and talk?"

Haldeman further advised President Nixon: "They think you clanged down an iron curtain, and you won't let anybody out of here . . . that have ever worked here—scour lady on up."

Mitchell reinforced what Haldeman said about the White House's claim of an inflexible executive privilege by saying, "And it relates to the Watergate; it does not relate to Henry Kissinger or foreign affairs."

President Nixon observed: "All that John Mitchell is arguing, then, is that now we use flexibility in order to get on with the cover-up plan."

After these comments, those present discussed in detail how the appearance of current White House aides before the Senate Select Committee could be had under what Mitchell called "controlled circumstances."

I digress from the account of the secret meeting to relate events necessary to an understanding of the subsequent discussion of the conferees.

President Nixon had indicated in his news conference on March 15, 1973, that he might permit White House aides to give the Senate Judiciary Committee, which was considering the Gray nomination, answers to written interrogatories. At that time I had stated in answer to a newsman's inquiry that I would be unwilling for the Senate Select Committee to accept written answers to written interrogatories from White House aides for two reasons. The first reason, I said, was the impossibility of cross-examining written words on a piece of paper; and the second reason, I asserted, was the difficulty of distinguishing the written words of a truthful George Washington from those of a lying Ananias.

President Nixon told Mitchell, Haldeman, Ehrlichman, and Dean, "We want to see what can be worked out. We talked about informal sessions." He then asked, "Has Ervin's position been he insists on formal sessions?"

Mitchell and Dean replied, "We've never really gotten into that," and Haldeman said, "Ervin's response" to what the President had said in his news conference was "written stuff isn't any good. . . . You can't ask a piece of paper questions."

Ehrlichman suggested that the White House could open negotiations to obtain controlled circumstances for the appearance of White House aides before the Senate Select Committee by offering to furnish the proposed Dean report on Watergate to the committee if the White House and the committee could first agree on how witnesses would be treated by the committee.

Although he was interrupted before he completed his statement, Haldeman made this comment respecting the Senate Select Committee: "I was just thinking that, in the membership of the committee, we're in reasonably good shape. The members—the people that you have on the committee are not as bad as most, as some Senators who would turn [to] the use of TV afterwards for their own—."

Mitchell was insistent that the White House forthwith enter into negotiations with the Senate Select Committee for the appearance of White House aides before the committee under "controlled circumstances."

In reply to an inquiry of President Nixon, he suggested that Attorney

General Kleindienst talk to me as chairman of the committee about my "concept of the appearances of witnesses."

President Nixon augmented Mitchell's suggestion by stating, in essence, that Kleindienst should talk to "Baker and Ervin," and emphasizing that "we've got to . . . start the negotiation."

There was some discussion as to the White House aides who should go before the committee. Haldeman observed: "Everybody goes—including Ehrlichman and me; everybody except John Dean, who doesn't go because he's got the lawyer's privilege."

President Nixon and Mitchell agreed Dean should not go before the committee in either open or closed sessions as a witness.

Dean observed: "Everywhere they look they are going to find Dean." The President said "Sure," and stated that Dean had not done anything operational, but was merely getting all the facts as his councel at his direction. The President concluded: "Well, we've got to keep you out anyway."

Ehrlichman made this recommendation: "I think, John [Dean] could say to Ervin if that question comes up, 'I know the President's mind on this. He's adamant about my testifying, as such. At the same time he has always indicated that the fruits of my investigation will be known.'"

After much discussion, President Nixon, Mitchell, Haldeman, Ehrlichman, and Dean agreed on a way to deal with the Senate Select Committee.

Under it, Dean was to ask Attorney General Kleindienst to request Senator Baker, as vice-chairman, and me, as chairman, to meet with him and Dean, as the President's counsel, in an unpublicized fashion and place on Monday, March 26, "to discuss and explore a formula for providing the Committee the information it needs in a way that does not conflict with the President's general policies on executive privilege."

At a propitious time after their first meeting with us, Kleindienst and Dean were to seek to negotiate an agreement with Senator Baker and me under which the Senate Select Committee would take the testimony of White House aides in executive sessions in the absence of the press, radio, and television.

Dean assured President Nixon: "What it's doing, Mr. President, is getting you up above and away from it. And that's the most important thing."

President Nixon, Mitchell, Haldeman, Ehrlichman, and Dean discussed in detail arguments that Kleindienst and Dean could employ to persuade Senator Baker and me to accept their proposal.

Dean said he would remind me that the proposal harmonized with the Constitution and the position I took in the *Gravel* case, where he said I maintained "that legislative aides cannot be called to question for advice they give their Senator or Congressman."

I digress from my analysis of the tape recording this meeting to note that Dean was alluding to my role in *Gravel* v. *United States*, 408 U.S. 606 (1972), where the Supreme Court had upheld the argument made by Senator William B. Saxbe and me as attorneys for the Senate, as *amicus curae*, that Article I, Section 6, of the Constitution forbade a federal grand jury sitting in Boston to question Senator Mike Gravel's aide about any act occurring at a Senate subcommittee meeting while Senator Mike Gravel, as its chairman, was presenting to the subcommittee parts of the Pentagon Papers.

Dean indicated his hope that Kleindienst and he would be successful in the mission the conferees had assigned to them by voicing his appraisal of me. "Ervin away from his staff is not very much, and I think he might just give up the store himself right there and lock himself in. You know I've dealt with him for a number of years, and have seen that happen and have reached accord with him on legislation."

Although I will not challenge Dean's appraisal of me, I will make two observations that may be relevant to it. First, it is incompatible with that of my father and law partner, who was wont to say I had the trait one's friends called firmness and one's enemies called obstinacy; and, second, I am not conscious of having had any contact whatever with Dean prior to June 25, 1973, when he first appeared before the Senate Select Committee to testify about Watergate.

Despite Dean's professed optimism, President Nixon expressed the fear that I might reject the proposal by declaring "we are just going to have public sessions" and that Baker might sit there and "parrot Ervin's adamant thing, saying 'hell, no, there can't be anything except the public hearings.' "

This fear may have motivated this question which President Nixon put to Mitchell: "But I know we can't make a complete cave and have the people go up there and testify. You would agree on that?" Mitchell responded, "I agree."

President Nixon complained during the course of the meeting that Senator Baker would not communicate with the White House, and observed "Baker is not proving much of a reed up to this point." President Nixon interrupted the conference temporarily by phoning Attorney General Kleindienst and urging him "to babysit" Baker and give him "guidance."

Near the end of the secret meeting, President Nixon said, "We will survive it," complimented Dean on being a "son-of-a-bitching tough thing," and declared:

> I want you all to stonewall it, let them plead the Fifth Amendment, cover-up or anything if it'll save it—save the plan. That's the whole point. On the other hand, I would prefer, as I have said to you, that you do it the other way. And I would particularly prefer to do it that other way if it's going to come out that way anyway.

After this, President Nixon remarked to Mitchell, "Up to this point the whole theory has been containment, as you know, John," and Mitchell said, "Yeah."

The President then stated, "now we're shifting." After indicating his disapproval of President Eisenhower's treatment of his chief aide, Sherman Adams, President Nixon concluded: "But I don't look at it that way. That's the thing I am really concerned with. We're going to protect our people, if we can."

President Nixon and Mitchell obviously had convinced themselves that the Senate Select Committee would be serving its own interests by accepting the proposal on which the conferees had agreed.

Mitchell observed that acceptance of the proposal by the committee would expedite the hearings and meet all the complaints "they" had made "up to date." President Nixon observed: "They [would] get cross-examination," and Mitchell added, "They [would] get everything but the public spectacle."

Dean assured the President the proposal would put the White House "in the posture of everything short of giving them a public hearing," and show "you're not hiding anything."

The President agreed this would be so "particularly if we have the Dean statement" and it had been given to the Senate Select Committee.

When President Nixon asserted, "You really have to protect the Presidency," Mitchell assured him that the proposal Kleindienst and Dean were to make to Baker and me "does no violence to the Presidency at all." The President concluded: "The purpose of this scenario is to clear the Presidency. They say 'All right. Here's the report, we're going to cooperate with the Committee,' and so forth and so on. The main thing is to answer, and that should be a God damned satisfactory answer."

Kleindienst and Dean never presented the proposal of the conferees to Baker and me. This was so because intervening events brought into play the aphorism of Robert Burns: "The best laid schemes o' mice and men/Gang aft a-gley."

5

THE COVER-UP BEGINS TO UNRAVEL

THE cover-up of Watergate began to unravel with a letter that James W. McCord sent to Judge Sirica just before the District Court was scheduled to reconvene for the sentencing of the original Watergate seven.

By his letter, which was dated March 19, 1973, McCord told Judge Sirica these things about Watergate and aspects of the trial in which Hunt and the Cubans had pleaded guilty and he and Liddy had been convicted:

1. There was political pressure applied to the defendants to plead guilty, and remain silent.

2. Perjury occurred during the trial in matters highly material to the very structure, orientation, and impact of the government's case, and to the motivations and intent of the defendants.

3. Others involved in the Watergate operation were not identified during the trial, when they could have been by those testifying.

4. The Watergate operation was not a CIA operation. The Cubans may have been misled by others into believing that it was a CIA operation. I know for a fact that it was not.

5. His motivations were different from those of the others involved, but were not limited to or simply those offered in his defense during the

trial. This is no fault of his attorneys, but of the circumstances under which they had to prepare his defense.

McCord's letter also advised Judge Sirica that he believed retaliatory measures would be taken against him, his family, and his friends if he should disclose his knowledge of the facts "in this matter either publicly or to any government representative," and that in consequence he "would appreciate the opportunity to talk" to Judge Sirica "privately in chambers . . . following sentence."

When the District Court reconvened on Friday, March 23, Judge Sirica read McCord's letter in open court; postponed the sentencing of McCord to a later date; imposed a final sentence of from six years eight months to twenty years on Liddy; and gave Hunt a provisional maximum sentence of thirty-five years, and Barker, Gonzalez, Martinez, and Sturgis provisional maximum sentences of forty years each.

After imposing the provisional maximum sentences on Hunt, Barker, Gonzalez, Martinez, and Sturgis, Judge Sirica recommended their "full cooperation with the Grand Jury and the Senate Select Committee." In so doing, he said:

> I believe that the Watergate affair, the subject of this trial, should not be forgotten. Some good can and should come from a revelation of sinister conduct whenever and wherever such conduct exists. I am convinced that the greatest benefit that can come from this prosecution will be its impact as a spur to corrective action so that the type of activities revealed by the evidence at the trial will not be repeated in our nation.
>
> You must understand that I hold out no promises or hopes of any kind to you in this matter but I do say that should you decide to speak freely I would have to weigh that factor in appraising what sentence will be finally imposed in this case. Other factors will of course be considered but I mention this one because it is one over which you have control, and I mean each one of the five of you.

The act of Judge Sirica in reading McCord's letter to a crowded courtroom had the impact of a bombshell upon the news media, the public, and the White House.

About an hour after the District Court adjourned, Sam Dash, the committee's chief counsel, met with McCord at the instance of Bernard Fensterwald, McCord's newly retained attorney, in the latter's law office, and received the assurance that McCord would cooperate fully with the committee. In a secret meeting the following day McCord told Dash that Dean and Magruder had prior knowledge of the Watergate burglary.

On March 28, 1973, McCord testified for four hours in a closed session before the Senate Select Committee and top members of its staff, and declared that Colson, Dean, Magruder, and Mitchell had prior knowledge of the plan to burglarize and bug the Watergate.

Shortly thereafter Judge Sirica granted immunity to prosecution on additional federal charges to Liddy, Hunt, and McCord. When they were sent before the grand jury, which had been reconvened to resume its investigation of Watergate, Liddy refused to answer the questions of the grand jurors, but Hunt and McCord did testify. Liddy was given an additional sentence by Judge Sirica for refusing to testify before the grand jury.

Investigations in Washington leak like sieves. During all my years in the Senate I knew only one congressional committee that was "leak-proof." It was a committee of which I was a member, the Watkins committee, which investigated charges against Senator Joseph R. McCarthy in 1954.

After Hunt had testified before the grand jury and McCord had testified before the grand jury and the Senate Select Committee in closed sessions, there were multitudes of leaks to the news media insinuating that Colson, Dean, Magruder, Mitchell, and other CREEP officials and White House aides were implicated in various phases of the Watergate affair.

It is virtually impossible to trace the sources of leaks because those who are responsible for them will not confess their transgression and the newsmen who receive the leaks will not identify their benefactors.

Ron Ziegler, the White House press secretary, charged the Senate Select Committee with "irresponsible leaks of tidal wave proportions," and demanded that I put an end to them.

Members of the staff of the Senate Select Committee were undoubtedly responsible for many of these leaks. Some of them may have originated among the grand jurors investigating the Watergate. Some of them may have been planted at the instance of persons involved in the Watergate who were seeking to obtain immunity on the basis of the aid they could supposedly give to the prosecution. Moreover, many of the supposed leaks were in all likelihood merely some of the plethora of rumors and suspicions generated in the minds of third persons by the notoriety of Watergate.

Candor compels the confession that the Senate Select Committee was plagued by leaks during its entire existence. Hence Senator Baker may have been right when he made this humorous observation about the committee: "We didn't invent the leak, but we raised it to its highest art form."

I deplore leaks. I have never been able to understand why any man is so lacking in self-restraint that he lets anything that enters his mind forthwith tumble out of his mouth. There is a serious flaw in any person who purposely reveals information he is legally or morally obligated to keep in confidence before the appropriate time for its disclosure arrives.

Sam Dash and I diligently sought to stop leaks from the committee staff and discover their perpetrators. We met with no success in this effort.

On one occasion Senator James L. Buckley, whom I admire very much for his courage and intellectual integrity, urged me to put all members of the committee staff on oath and ask them if they were leaking to the news media information collected by the committee. I informed Senator Buckley that I would not accept his proposal for these reasons: first, it was incompatible with our system, which forbids calling on people for evidence to condemn themselves; second, it would be unproductive because perpetrators of leaks would deny their guilt; and, third, it would shatter the morale of the committee staff because it would be construed by innocent members of the staff as charging them with the offenses of the guilty.

Despite my dislike for leaks, I am constrained to admit that Neil MacNeil, of *Time* magazine, was not entirely in error when he stated to me that some leaks are good because they enable the news media to reveal hidden corruption and inefficiency in government. Hence, I admit that some of the leaks Ron Ziegler deplored may have hastened the prying open of the Watergate cover-up.

During the March 1973 hearings of the Senate Judiciary Committee on President Nixon's nomination of L. Patrick Gray, acting director of the FBI, for the permanent directorship of that agency, evidence was presented which damaged the White House's constant claim that presidential aides were innocent of wrongdoing in respect to Watergate and any suspected whitewash of it.

Much to the White House's chagrin, Gray released to the Senate Judiciary Committee raw FBI files which made these things clear:

1. Kalmbach, the President's personal attorney, and Chapin, the President's appointments secretary, did, in fact, arrange to pay Donald Segretti more than $30,000 out of the President's campaign funds for sabotaging the 1972 campaigns of candidates for the Democratic presidential nomination.

2. Haldeman, Ehrlichman, and Dean had undertaken, professedly on "national security grounds," to induce top officials of the CIA to persuade Gray, as acting director of FBI, to put an end to the FBI's attempt to trace four certified checks totaling $89,000, which had been issued by a Mexican bank and given to the Finance Committee to Reelect the President as a campaign contribution.

3. When the FBI investigated Watergate, Dean, as the President's counsel, sat in on all their interviews of presidential aides, and CREEP's attorneys sat in on all their interviews of CREEP employees.

4. As treasurer of the Finance Committee to Reelect the President, Hugh W. Sloan, Jr., had allegedly disbursed approximately $240,000 in cash to Magruder, Liddy, and Herbert L. Porter, another CREEP official, out of campaign funds secreted in safes in the office of the Finance Committee.

Gray testified personally before the Senate Judiciary Committee that he had permitted Dean to sit on the FBI's interviews of presidential aides because he believed the FBI could not have obtained such interviews otherwise; that he had delivered copies of FBI's interviews of various persons to Dean during the course of the investigation; and that Dean had probably lied to the FBI by saying he did not know whether Hunt had an office in the Executive Office Building.

The inference is inevitable that the testimony before the Senate Judiciary Committee made Gray's confirmation improbable, prompted Chapin's early retirement from the White House, and induced the President's ultimate withdrawal of the Gray nomination. About this time Colson severed his official connection with the White House and returned to the private practice of law.

The Mexican checks and a related check, the Dahlberg check, were of crucial importance in the Watergate investigation. For this reason, it is essential to know the history of these checks. This history was disclosed by the evidence that had been previously presented by the prosecution to Judge Sirica and the petit jury in the trial of the seven original Watergate defendants and the testimony subsequently received by the Senate Select Committee.

Some Texas supporters of Nixon, who desired to conceal their identities, procured from the Banco Internacional of Mexico City four cashier's checks totaling $89,000. The checks were issued to Manuel Ogarrio, a Mexican lawyer, who endorsed them in blank. On April 5, 1972, Robert H. Allen, a fund-raiser for Nixon in Texas, had these Mexican checks delivered to the finance arm of CREEP in Washington. Several days later Dwayne O. Andreas, a Minneapolis businessman, who also desired to conceal his identity, gave $25,000 in cash for Nixon's campaign to Kenneth H. Dahlberg, the finance chairman of Nixon for the Midwest. Dahlberg used the $25,000 to procure a cashier's check from a bank in Boca Raton, Florida, which he delivered to the finance arm of CREEP.

Instead of entrusting them to a bank in Washington or elsewhere for collection, the finance arm of CREEP transmitted the four Mexican checks and the Dahlberg check through the agency of Liddy to Bernard L. Barker, who deposited them for collection in his account at the Republic National Bank of Miami.

After their collection by this bank, Barker withdrew in cash the proceeds of the Mexican and Dahlberg checks totaling $114,000 in various installments between April 21 and May 8, 1972. More than $10,000 of the withdrawals consisted of new $100 bills.

In mid-May Barker remitted $112,000 of these moneys in cash through the agency of Liddy to the finance arm of CREEP, which forthwith stored them in cash with other cash in the safes in its Washington office.

As treasurer of the finance arm of CREEP, Sloan made cash disbursements out of these safes. In late May and early June 1972 he removed cash totaling $24,000 from them, and gave it to Liddy as final payments on the sums aggregating $199,000 in cash which he gave Liddy at Magruder's directions.

When he testified before the Select Committee in June 1973, Sloan told it in response to an inquiry by Senator Gurney that the $24,000 was "evidently . . . used for the Watergate operation," and that he suspected that it included "some of those same physical $100 bills" that the finance arm of CREEP had received from Barker through the agency of Liddy.

Sloan's suspicion was conclusively corroborated by the FBI, which traced by their serial numbers to their source the forty-five new $100 bills possessed by the four Cubans at the time of their arrest.

The Republic National Bank of Miami informed the FBI it kept no record of the serial numbers of the new $100 bills it delivered to Barker with the proceeds of the Mexican and Dahlberg checks. The FBI ascertained, however, that the Federal Reserve Bank which served the Miami area shipped to the Republic National Bank of Miami on April 19, 1972, numerous new $100 bills, that the Federal Reserve Bank kept a record of the serial numbers of these new $100 bills, and that the serial numbers of the forty-five new $100 bills possessed by the four Cubans at the time of their arrest disclosed that they were among the numerous $100 bills the Federal Reserve Bank shipped to the Republic National Bank of Miami on April 19, 1972.

These facts made indisputable the conclusion that the four Cubans had $4,500 of President Nixon's campaign funds in their possession when they and McCord were apprehended by the Washington police burglarizing the offices of the Democratic National Committee in the Watergate.

After Gray's testimony before the Senate Judiciary Committee, Judge Sirica's reading of the McCord letter in open court, and McCord's testifying in secret sessions before the Senate Select Committee, the White House's problems, both existing and prospective, intensified.

Some of these problems became publicly known as they arose. Others remained hidden until they were disclosed by testimony taken by the Senate Select Committee. Some were not revealed in their true dimensions until the existence and contents of President Nixon's tapes were exposed to view.

Circumstances compel the inference that the White House was clinging to its hope that it might persuade the Senate Select Committee to allow presidential aides to testify before it informally in closed sessions in the absence of the press, radio, and television.

Instead of approaching the committee directly, the White House sent up some trial balloons on the subject through its press secretary, Ron Ziegler. He stated, in essence, in press briefings during the last days of March and the first days of April that the White House had always been willing to cooperate with the committee in devising a procedure for the appearance of presidential aides before it which did not "infringe on the doctrine of the separation of powers," and that in consequence the White House might permit these aides to testify before the committee "informally."

In reply to inquiries from newsmen, I asserted that presidential aides "are not royalty or nobility who can be excused from testifying under oath and in public"; that I was unwilling for presidential aides to visit us by night like Nicodemus of old and whisper in our ears things the public was not allowed to hear; and that "I would accept nothing less than the sworn testimony of presidential aides in public sessions."

I also reiterated my prior threat that I would ask the Senate to direct its sergeant at arms to arrest and bring before the Senate for appropriate action any presidential aide who refused to appear before the committee in obedience to a subpoena and testify.

In the hope of setting the matter at rest, I called for April 2 one of the two press conferences I held during my years in the Senate.

In this press conference, I stated that in claiming he had an absolute power to deny the committee the testimony of his aides President Nixon was "shooting the so-called executive privilege doctrine way out past the stratosphere" and doing "a terrible disservice to the high office of the presidency." I added that executive privilege does not apply to illegal or unethical behavior, such as the Watergate burglary and bugging.

In answer to a question put to me by one of the newsmen, I said, "The President is conducting himself in such a manner as to reasonably engender in the minds of the people the belief he is afraid of the truth."

When I suggested that President Nixon was overlooking decisions of the Supreme Court defining the powers of authorized congressional committees to compel the production of evidence, another newsman asked me if the President was not a lawyer and did not obtain his legal education at Duke University Law School in North Carolina. I answered, "Yes," and stated that I was going to suggest to the Duke Law School, a great institution of legal learning, that it recall its illustrious graduate and give him a refresher course in the law of evidence.

I digress to note that several days later a profound constitutional scholar called my office and left this message for me: "Your suggestion does not go far enough. You ought to recommend that Duke Law School recall the President and give him a profound and protracted course in constitutional law, and in so doing lay stress on the powers and duties of the Presidency."

Carolyn Lewis, one of the most brilliant representatives of television on Capitol Hill, asked me in jesting guise if I was going to heed Ziegler's request and put an end to leaks. I responded, in substance, that anyone who stopped leaks to the news media on the Washington scene would merit immortality for the earth's greatest achievement since the morning stars sang together for glory at the Creation.

I ended my news conference by declaring that "every person—be he Republican or Democrat or Mugwump—should cooperate with the Committee" in its effort to reveal the truth about the allegations concerning Watergate.

In reporting my news conference, the *Washington Post* said: "Ervin presently has the backing of at least five of the other six members of the Watergate Committee to force a showdown with the White House on executive privilege."

Shortly thereafter, the White House made its first direct approach to the committee on the subject by requesting Senator Baker and me to meet in secret with Ehrlichman and discuss what rules would govern the appearance of presidential aides before the committee if the President decided to permit them to appear.

This meeting occurred in Blair House on the afternoon of April 9. In response to Ehrlichman's inquiries, I informed him that the committee would subpoena such presidential aides as it believed had any knowledge relating to the Watergate affair, and stated in detail what the Committee would require of them. In so doing, I said the committee would require presidential aides and all other witnesses appearing before it to testify on oath in public sessions, and would permit press, radio, and television to cover the public hearings and report whatever occurred in them. I assured him the White House would be permitted to invoke any claim of executive privilege in respect to the testimony of any presidential aide, but the committee would determine the validity of any such claim.

Senator Baker advised Ehrlichman that his views were in complete accord with those expressed by me.

The Senate Select Committee subsequently adopted Rules of Procedure which conformed to these views and which are worthy of emulation by other congressional investigating committees for their efficiency and fairness.

The White House was disappointed in its expectation that Dean would furnish President Nixon with a written report on Watergate that he could use to persuade the committee to exonerate his aides of wrong-doing, or at least to limit the scope of its investigation.

According to his testimony before the committee, Dean, Magruder, and Liddy met with Mitchell, who was then Attorney General, in his office in the Justice Department on January 27 and February 4, 1972.

On the first occasion, Dean testified, Liddy explained to Mitchell, as the prospective chairman of the Political Committee to Reelect the President, what Dean called a mind-boggling plan for obtaining intelligence concerning what the Democrats intended to do in the approaching presidential campaign.

In depicting what he called Liddy's "sales-pitch" to Mitchell, Dean testified to the committee as follows:

> [His] plans called for mugging squads, kidnapping teams, prostitutes to compromise the opposition, and electronic surveillance. He explained that the mugging squads could, for example, rough up demonstrators that were causing problems. The kidnapping teams could remove demonstration leaders and take them below the Mexican border and thereby diminish the ability of the demonstrators to cause problems at the San Diego convention. The prostitutes could be used at the Democratic convention to get information as well as compromise the persons involved. I recall Liddy saying that the girls would be high class and the best in the business. When discussing the electronic surveillance, he said that he had consulted with one of the best authorities in the country and his plan envisioned far more than bugging and tapping phones. He said that, under his plan, communications between ground facilities and aircraft could also be interrupted. . . . I cannot recall for certain if it was during this meeting or at the second meeting in early February that he suggested the potential targets. The targets that I recall he suggested were Mr. Larry O'Brien, the Democratic headquarters, and the Fontainebleau Hotel during the Democratic Convention. Mr. Liddy concluded his presentation by saying that the plan would cost approximately $1 million.

At the conclusion of Liddy's presentation, Dean testified, Mitchell "took a few long puffs on his pipe," told Liddy "the plan . . . was not quite what he had in mind and the cost was out of the question, and suggested to Liddy he go back and revise his plan, keeping in mind that he was most interested in the demonstration problem."

I digress to state that at the time of this meeting the Republican Party was planning to hold its National Convention in San Diego, California.

In describing to the Senate Select Committee the meeting on February 4, 1972, Dean testified:

> Magruder had scheduled another meeting in Mr. Mitchell's office on a revised intelligence plan. I arrived at the meeting very late, and when I came in, Mr. Liddy was presenting a scaled down version of his earlier plan. I listened for a few minutes and decided I had to interject myself into the discussion. Mr. Mitchell, I felt, was being put on the spot. The only polite way I thought I could end the discussions was to interject that these discussions could not go on in the Office of the Attorney General of the United States and that the meeting should terminate immediately. At this point the meeting ended. I do not know to this day who kept pushing for these plans. Whether Liddy was pushing or whether Magruder was pushing or whether someone was pushing Magruder.

At the urging of President Nixon and Haldeman, Dean testified, he went to Camp David on the afternoon of March 23, 1973, and began to write the proposed report. He testified that before he had completed it, on March 28, Haldeman summoned him to return to Washington. When he entered Haldeman's office in the White House, he testified, Haldeman told him "Mitchell and Magruder were waiting for me" in a nearby office and "wanted to talk to me about my knowledge of the meetings in Mitchell's office."

"I told Haldeman," Dean testified, that Mitchell and Magruder "were both aware of the situation and I was not going to lie if asked about those meetings," and "Haldeman said that he did not want to get into it, but that I should go in and work it out with Mitchell and Magruder."

During his ensuing meeting with Mitchell and Magruder, Dean testified, they asked him to agree to corroborate in any appearance he might make before the grand jury or the Senate Select Committee the testimony they had previously given to the grand jury to the effect that the meetings with Liddy in Mitchell's office in January and February 1972 had dealt solely with the election laws. When he failed to agree to do so, Dean testified, Mitchell and Magruder said if he testified other than the way they had "it would only cause problems."

What Haldeman said to him just before his conversation with Mitchell and Magruder, Dean testified, indicated that Haldeman was "in the process of uninvolving himself, but keeping others involved." As a consequence of Haldeman's remark and earlier advice given him by Ehrlichman as to how he should testify if called before the grand jury, Dean testified, he decided to refrain from completing his report or giving it to the White House.

On August 15, 1973, President Nixon publicly stated that on March 30 he had been told that Dean could not complete his proposed report on Watergate and that he thereupon relieved Dean of responsibility to report to him on Watergate-related matters and assigned that task to Ehrlichman.

6

WATERGATE
WOES

THE White House was also beset by other problems. The news media became increasingly critical of President Nixon's failure to take positive action respecting Watergate. His ratings in the polls began to topple. Senators and representatives started to demand that responsibility for investigating and prosecuting the criminal aspects of Watergate be taken from the Department of Justice, which was legally subservient to the President, and given to a special prosecutor, who was legally as well as actually independent of the White House.

Republicans in high places expressed their misgivings publicly. Senator Hugh Scott, the Republican Senate Leader, said Republican senators were worried by the political impact of Watergate; George Bush, the chairman of the Republican National Committee, asserted that Watergate must be "promptly and fully cleared up" in the interest of the party; Senator Robert W. Packwood described Watergate as "the most odious issue since Teapot Dome"; and Senator Barry Goldwater declared that Republican candidates would be endangered in 1974 if President Nixon did not act to clear up Watergate immediately.

During April 1973 President Nixon, Haldeman, and Ehrlichman had frequent communications by telephone and in personal meetings in which they secretly discussed various problems posed to the White House by Watergate. What they said at these times reflected serious concern about Magruder, Hunt, Mitchell, Colson, and Strachan.

Knowing that Hunt and others could furnish evidence sufficient to establish his guilt in the burglary and bugging of the Watergate and subsequent cover-up operations, Magruder decided to confess to the prosecutors that he had committed perjury in testifying in grand jury proceedings and at the January trial that Liddy and his confederates had been engaged in a lark of their own, and to plead guilty and seek a light sentence. He retained James J. Bierbower, an able trial lawyer, to represent him.

Since the White House believed Magruder was about to talk to the prosecutors, Ehrlichman undertook to ascertain what he was going to reveal to them.

After Larry O'Brien, the Democratic National Chairman, sued officials of CREEP for damages for the break-in and the bugging, CREEP retained two attorneys, Paul L. O'Brien, and Kenneth W. Parkinson, to defend the civil action.

On April 5 Ehrlichman had a secret conversation with Paul O'Brien. He disclosed to Ehrlichman what Magruder had told him he was prepared to testify, and Ehrlichman reported to President Nixon what O'Brien told him. As narrated by Magruder to O'Brien, related by O'Brien to Ehrlichman, and relayed to President Nixon by Ehrlichman, Magruder was expecting to testify in judicial proceedings as follows:

In January and February 1972 Magruder, Dean, and Liddy met with Mitchell, as President Nixon's prospective political campaign manager, in the Attorney General's office in the Department of Justice. At those times Liddy presented to Mitchell elaborate plans for exercising surveillance over Democratic installations and officials in the forthcoming presidential elections. After Mitchell withheld his approval from these plans, Colson urged Magruder by phone to expedite Liddy's intelligence project, and Strachan informed him in person that President Nixon wanted it implemented. On March 30, 1972, Magruder met with Mitchell and LaRue at Key Biscayne, Florida, and presented Mitchell with a reduced Liddy plan for bugging the Democratic National Committee offices in the Watergate, the Fontainebleau Hotel in Miami, and Senator George McGovern's headquarters in Washington. Mitchell approved this plan and authorized a budget of $250,000 for its implementation. Magruder informed Sloan that Liddy was allowed to draw this amount in CREEP funds. He also informed Strachan of these events to enable him to alert other officials in the White House. After the burglary and bugging, he gave wiretap records to Strachan for transmission to Haldeman. After Liddy, Hunt, McCord, and the four Cubans were indicted in September 1972, payments of CREEP funds were made to them, and possibly offers of presidential clemency were made to Liddy, Hunt, and McCord.

On April 8 Ehrlichman reported to President Nixon by phone that he had had a meeting with Dean and that it "went fine."

When the President asked what Dean thought Magruder would do, Ehrlichman replied, "Nobody knows." The President indicated that the prosecutors would ask Magruder these questions: "Who told you? Did you clear this with anybody? Who gave the final approval?" The President added that if Magruder was "going to pull the plug, he's going to pull it on Mitchell rather than on Haldeman." Ehrlichman agreed.

Ehrlichman predicted that if Magruder testified, "they'll get him for both . . . perjury and Watergate." The President asserted, "That's what I would think. He had better plead the Fifth Amendment. I don't think he's got any other choice."

They talked about Mitchell, who they agreed was "going to be put to the prod on this one." Ehrlichman told the President that Dean "thinks John Mitchell is living in a dream world right now," and "thinks this is all going away."

When the President asked him "what Dean thinks about it," Ehrlichman replied, "Dean says it isn't going to go away. It's right on top of us and that the smartest thing that he, Dean, could do is go down there and appear cooperative."

The President said, "Right."

The White House remained concerned in respect to what Magruder might tell. At Ehrlichman's insistence, Lawrence Higby, an assistant to Haldeman, telephoned him on April 13, and queried him about it. Higby bugged the conversation without Magruder's knowledge.

Magruder told Higby he had perjured himself many times to conceal Watergate, and knew he was going to prison. He informed Higby further that he was going to be guided by his lawyer's advice, that his lawyer had not yet decided whether he should testify or plead the Fifth Amendment, and that he was going to tell "the truth full and completely" if he testified. Higby told Magruder he couldn't see how he had anything to gain "by turning on the White House or by turning on Bob [Haldeman]." Magruder responded he was "not going to turn on anybody."

Magruder then advised Higby that if he testified his evidence would implicate Mitchell, Dean, and Strachan, but that neither President Nixon nor Haldeman would be involved by it in any way. Although Strachan got information about "everything" from him and "knows," Magruder said: "I'm sure he did nothing with it. . . . It was all junk." Magruder predicted to Higby "nobody of any substance will be hurt other than Big John [Mitchell]."

Ehrlichman advised the President that Higby's tape of Magruder's remarks "closed all his doors" and "beats the socks off him if he ever gets off the reservation."

Although the facts underlying their fear were still virtually unknown to the public and largely unknown to the press and the prosecutors, President Nixon, Haldeman, and Ehrlichman became afraid that the Watergate cover-up was on the verge of falling apart.

It is clear in retrospect why this should have been so. Hunt, who had been immunized against further prosecution except for future perjury, was scheduled to testify before the grand jury within a few days.

Magruder's lawyer was engaged in plea bargaining with the prosecutors. He was trying to secure an agreement with them under which Magruder would plead guilty to an agreed count, testify to what he knew about Watergate, and receive in return a comparatively light sentence.

Ehrlichman sought to learn from Kalmbach what he might say about his activities in raising money at his and Dean's instance and disbursing it in surreptitious ways, through the agency of the retired New York policeman Anthony T. Ulasewicz, to the original Watergate defendants and their families. Apparently, Kalmbach gave Ehrlichman no information beyond saying he had retained James H. O'Connor as his counsel.

Colson and Strachan were expected to be called before the grand jury in the immediate future.

Dean had become something of a problem to the President, Haldeman, and Ehrlichman. As he had stated privately to the President, Dean believed he was in danger of being indicted for what he had done "to contain Watergate." He had engaged the services of one of the area's wisest criminal lawyers, Charles N. Shaffer, to aid him in the early days of April, and had notified both President Nixon and Haldeman of that action. Shaffer was assisted by Robert C. McCandless.

They were seeking to negotiate immunity for Dean with the prosecutors. To that end, they had promised the prosecutors that Dean would talk to them under an arrangement whereby the prosecutors pledged themselves to use what Dean told them solely to determine whether they should recommend immunity for Dean.

Apparently Dean was steadfast in his loyalty to the President at this time and was determined not to reveal to the prosecutors any communications between the President and himself.

President Nixon had repeatedly stated both privately and publicly that Dean, as counsel for the President and the White House as well as by virtue of executive privilege, was forbidden to divulge any communications between him and the President or between him and the President's aides.

I digress for an observation. Notwithstanding President Nixon's apparent notion that the attorney-client privilege constitutes an absolute cloak of secrecy, it can be invoked only to bar disclosure of a communication between a lawyer and his client if it is for a lawful purpose or in furtherance of a lawful end.

Circumstances compel the inference that although he had complete confidence that Dean would not tell prosecutors or courts anything involving him, President Nixon was apprehensive that Dean might implicate Haldeman and Ehrlichman if he talked to prosecutors or testified in judicial proceedings. He may have based his apprehension on Dean's statements in prior secret meetings that he believed Haldeman and Dean to be indictable for what they did in the aftermath of Watergate, as well as on Dean's advice to Haldeman and Ehrlichman that his lawyer had told him they were targets of the prosecutors.

At any rate, on April 11, Ehrlichman phoned Attorney General Kleindienst that no White House aide should be granted immunity, and Kleindienst informed Assistant Attorney General Peterson of this phone call.

Two questions arise: Did Ehrlichman make this phone call at the President's direction? If so, did the President intend to deter Dean from talking to the prosecutors or testifying in a judicial proceeding?

The denial of immunity is an effective way to deter a person from talking or testifying if he has to incriminate himself in so doing.

On April 14, 1973, President Nixon busied himself with Watergate-related matters from 8:55 A.M. until 11:35 P.M. During these hours these events occurred:

President Nixon, Haldeman, and Ehrlichman held three secret meetings totaling 5 hours and 37 minutes. President Nixon and Haldeman held one secret meeting totaling 18 minutes. At President Nixon's direction, Haldeman talked by phone with Magruder, and Ehrlichman interviewed Mitchell and Magruder in person. Haldeman and Ehrlichman reported to President Nixon what they learned by so doing. After 11 P.M., President Nixon called Haldeman and Ehrlichman separately by phone, and conversed with them for periods totaling 45 minutes.

What was said by the President, Haldeman, and Ehrlichman on these occasions was contemporaneously and surreptitiously recorded on President Nixon's tapes, and was revealed to the House Judiciary Committee during its impeachment inquiry in 1974. The words which President Nixon imprinted with his own voice on these tapes cannot be reconciled with the assurances he gave the American people in person and through Ziegler, his press secretary, over a period of many months that he wanted the truth about Watergate revealed and condemned any efforts to cover it up.

As his tapes reveal, President Nixon did not dillydally on April 14 as he had done so often in his previous secret conferences with aides. Maybe he was spurred to decision by two statements Ehrlichman made, one while he was reporting on his conversation with Colson and Colson's law partner and attorney, David Shapiro, concerning Hunt's probable testimony, and the other while the conferees were discussing whether the President should fire Dean.

Ehrlichman reported that Hunt was going to testify before the grand jury two days later. He added, Colson "wants you to be able to say afterwards that you cracked the case" and "declares that the next 48 hours are the last chance for the White House to get out in front of this and that once Hunt goes on that's the ball game."

President Nixon asked Ehrlichman: "What do Colson and Shapiro think we ought to do—get busy and nail Mitchell in a hurry?" Ehrlichman said, "Yes. They feel that after he testifies . . . the whole thing is going to fall in short order."

When the conferees were discussing whether Dean should be fired because of his involvement in the aftermath of Watergate, Ehrlichman stated he did not know what the decision on Dean should be, but that the President should "look again at the big picture." Ehrlichman added, "You are now possessed of a body of fact." President Nixon agreed: "That's right." Ehrlichman then asserted, "You can't just sit there." The President admitted, "That's right." Ehrlichman ended this phase of the conversation by saying, "You've got to act on it. You've got to make some decisions, and the Dean thing is one of the decisions that you have to make."

Ehrlichman said he had gotten his information concerning what Hunt might testify from Shapiro, who had talked to him.

President Nixon observed that "Hunt's testimony on pay-off, of course, would be important," and inquired, "Is he prepared to testify on that?" Ehrlichman indicated that Hunt was, and added that he was going to implicate O'Brien and Parkinson "by hanging them up on obstruction of justice." The President noted that in that event Hunt would raise a problem with regard to Kalmbach, who would have "possible vulnerability as to whether he was aware" of the motive for the payments to the original Watergate defendants. Ehrlichman undertook to reassure the President by stating, "Dean says very flatly that Kalmbach did not know the purpose of the payment and has no problems."

The President then put this question to Ehrlichman: "So basically then Hunt will testify that it was so called hush money. Right?" Ehrlichman replied he believed so. Haldeman suggested that Hunt could serve the same purpose by denying it was hush money and saying it was given to those he "had recruited for this job" because of concern for their families. The President said: "That's right; that's what it ought to be; and that's got to be the story." Ehrlichman observed that story was "the only defense they have"; and Haldeman declared, "That was the line they used around here. That we've got to have money for their legal fees and family."

President Nixon mentioned that Dean had told him a few weeks before "about the problem of Hunt's lawyer" needing "sixty thousand or forty thousand dollars or something like that." Haldeman advised him that Mitchell had taken care of that problem through LaRue, but that Dean had talked to LaRue and LaRue had stated to Dean that he "intends to tell the truth if he is called to testify."

An enigmatic interchange ensued. The President asked, "What instructions?" Haldeman replied, "I don't know any of that." When the President said, "But his instructions will be, LaRue, I was helping to get—" Ehrlichman interrupted him by saying, "The way Dean talks LaRue wasn't even thinking about the message." Haldeman added, "I don't think LaRue cares. I think LaRue figures that the jig is up."

Haldeman also gave this information to the President and Ehrlichman:

CREEP was given $1.6 million in cash, which had remained unexpended from prior campaigns. Believing it could not spend this much money in ways which were not traceable, CREEP sent $350,000 of it to Haldeman, ostensibly for use in polling. A portion of it, $22,000, was disbursed to cover the cost of newspaper advertisements which Colson prepared and which purported to be those of private citizens extolling President Nixon for his action in Vietnam. When the original Watergate defendants began to clamor for money, Haldeman returned the remaining $328,000 through the agency of Strachan to CREEP.

The conferees closed the discussion concerning the money with these statements:

> PRESIDENT NIXON: The bad part of it is . . . the obstruction of justice thing which it appears to be. . . . And yet, they ought to go up fighting . . . I think they all ought to fight. That this was not an obstruction of justice; we were simply trying to help these defendants.
> EHRLICHMAN: I agree.
> PRESIDENT NIXON: I know if they could get together on the strategy, it would be pretty good for them.
> EHRLICHMAN: Well, I think, undoubtedly, that will shake down.

His tapes indicate that the President was troubled by the possibility of Hunt's testifying that Colson had assured him of presidential clemency if he remained silent. He disclosed that he had told Colson that the tragic death of Hunt's wife "was a terrible thing . . . and that we will take that into consideration," and that Colson had assured Hunt's lawyer, Bittman, that he, Colson, knew of "Hunt's concern about clemency" and would "go to bat for him" and believed his views "would be listened to."

The President then asked Ehrlichman if Colson had stated whether Hunt was going to testify about a "promise of clemency." Ehrlichman replied he did not ask Colson and Colson did not say at the time of his recent talk with him and Shapiro. He added, however, that on a prior occasion Colson had assured him he had not promised presidential clemency to Hunt.

The President voiced his concern for Colson by saying, "You see you can make a hell of a circumstantial case on Colson. . . . Colson is closest to this crew of the robbers than anybody else." He suggested that Hunt might incriminate Colson by testimony relating to the phone call Colson made to Magruder in his and Liddy's presence in respect to Liddy's intelligence plan. Ehrlichman informed the President that he had asked Colson specifically about that event, and Colson had asserted that when "they said intelligence he meant one thing and apparently they meant another."

In reply to the President's question as to whether Hunt was prepared to testify concerning his "other activities," Ehrlichman stated he "couldn't derive that" from his conversation with Colson and Shapiro.

I digress from the analysis of the tapes of April 14 to interpolate clarifying facts. Mitchell steadfastly claimed he had no complicity in Watergate. His talkative wife, Martha, repeatedly told the press that someone was trying to make her husband "the goat" in the Watergate incident. Haldeman, Ehrlichman, and Dean discussed secretly among themselves on several occasions the advisability of the White House pinning responsibility for Watergate on Mitchell.

The tapes of April 14 disclose that President Nixon, Haldeman, and Ehrlichman were convinced that Magruder's forthcoming testimony would result in Mitchell's speedy indictment by the grand jury and his ultimate conviction by a petit jury.

The President concluded that the White House's Watergate woes would end abruptly if Mitchell could be pressured into confessing publicly and promptly that he was "morally and legally responsible" for Watergate. Ehrlichman asserted that such action by Mitchell would "redound to the Administration's advantage," and Haldeman affirmed "that that's the only way to beat it now."

President Nixon directed Ehrlichman to contact Mitchell as soon as the meeting adjourned, and to urge him to acknowledge his responsibility to the prosecutors at once.

President Nixon was convinced that the White House's Watergate troubles would vanish if Mitchell confessed or was convicted of complicity in the affair. This was evidenced by his tape of this telephonic conversation he had with Haldeman on April 15:

PRESIDENT NIXON: If they get a hell of a big fish that is going to take a lot of the fire out of this thing on the cover up and all that sort. If they get the President's former law partner and Attorney General, you know. Do you agree?

HALDEMAN: Yeah. What I feel is people want something to be done to explain what to them is now a phony looking thing. This will explain it.

PRESIDENT NIXON: Explain that they did it, and then of course the cover up comes up and they did that too.

HALDEMAN: And it all makes sense; it is logical, believable because it's true.

PRESIDENT NIXON: Right.

HALDEMAN: It seems to me that there is at least a strong possibility, if not probability or certainty, that public reaction is going to be, well, thank God that is settled; now let's get away from it.

PRESIDENT NIXON: That's right.

HALDEMAN: I think people want solutions; they don't want problems. . . . They want it explained, and they want to get off of it. . . . What do you say when they indict Mitchell and Mitchell doesn't plead guilty? You obviously can't say I'm sorry.

PRESIDENT NIXON: It is not proper for me to comment on that because there has been an indictment. . . . I think we should not judge this case until it has been heard in the judicial process.

HALDEMAN: What you can do is express your faith in the system. You know there is a lot to be gained from this if the damn system comes out right.

The tapes of April 14 show that Ehrlichman met with Mitchell in Ehrlichman's office in the White House between the first and second meetings, and taped the ensuing conversation between them without Mitchell's knowledge.

Ehrlichman's tape reveals a protracted and heated discussion between him and Mitchell. In urging him to acknowledge responsibility for Watergate, Ehrlichman told Mitchell in detail he was "in a situation of jeopardy," insinuated he could not escape from it, and declared that by acknowledging his responsibility he would serve the institution of the Presidency by putting Watergate "behind us."

When Ehrlichman mentioned John Dean in his argument, Mitchell made these illuminating remarks: "Poor John is the guy that just got caught in the middle; like so many others that were first of all trying to keep the lid on it until after the election. And in addition to that, to keep the lid on all the other things that were going on over here [in the White House] that would have been even worse I think than the Watergate business."

In refusing to confess any responsibility for Watergate, Mitchell told Ehrlichman:

> Let me tell you where I stand. There is no way that I'm going to
> do anything except staying where I am because I'm too far out. The
> fact of the matter is that I got euchred into this thing, . . . by not
> paying attention to what these bastards were doing, and well you
> know how far back this goes. This whole genesis of this thing was
> over here [at the White House], as you're perfectly well aware."

When Ehrlichman asserted he was not aware of that, Mitchell indicated that Watergate really had its origin in an intelligence plan called Sandwedge which John J. Caulfield had discussed with Haldeman and Dean in 1971.

When he reported his meeting with Mitchell to President Nixon and Haldeman in their second secret meeting of the day, Ehrlichman stated in detail what Mitchell had said, and observed he "lobbed mud balls at the White House at every opportunity."

Although Mitchell's refusal to acknowledge responsibility for Watergate undoubtedly disappointed them, it did not reduce President Nixon, Haldeman, and Ehrlichman to a state of despondency. As the presidential tapes of April 14 and succeeding days show, they believed the grand jury would indict Mitchell before the Senate Select Committee could begin its hearings on the scheduled date, May 17, and were convinced the Senate committee would be unable to hold any hearings before all motions, trials, and appeals in the Mitchell case were finally determined because of the danger that publicity engendered by hearings would prejudice Mitchell's right to a fair trial and the government's ability to prosecute him successfully. President Nixon estimated on one of his tapes that the Mitchell case could not be finally concluded in less than four years.

While they were talking about Mitchell, President Nixon said he needed somebody to "give me a report . . . on this thing" [i.e., Watergate]. When Haldeman asked him if events had not overtaken that project, the President said no, because when they get Mitchell "they're going to say what about Haldeman, what about Chapin, and what about Colson and the rest." He added that he needed a report saying "there are no other higher-ups," which would "put a cap on it" and "then face the Segretti crap." Ehrlichman, who said he had prepared a written report of seven or eight pages, stated that "in forcing this out Dean remains a problem" and read to the President what he had "come to" on that matter.

The tapes of April 14 disclose that President Nixon, Haldeman, and

Ehrlichman discussed in detail whether Dean should be fired because of his involvement in what they called the aftermath of Watergate. The President said: "I have made a decision. He's to go."

The President said, "Dean is not like Mitchell in the sense that Dean only tried to do what he could to pick up the pieces and everybody else around here knew it had to be done"; and Ehrlichman remarked "there were eight or ten people around here who knew about this, knew it was going on. Bob [Haldeman] knew, I knew, all kinds of people knew." After saying "Well, I knew it, I knew it," the President declared, "I must say, though, I didn't know it, but I must have assumed it. I thank you both for arranging it that way, and it does show the isolation of the President, and here it's not so bad."

Ehrlichman said, "The point is that if . . . the wrongdoing which justified Dean's dismissal is his knowledge that that operation was going on, then you can't stop with him. You've got to go through the whole place wholesale." When the President said, "Fire the whole staff," Ehrlichman replied, "Exactly."

The President may have summed up his reason for his decision to fire Dean in this statement:

> I think he [Dean] made a very powerful point to me that of course you can be pragmatic and . . . cut your losses and get rid of 'em. Give 'em an hors d'oeuvre and maybe they won't come back for the main course. Well, out, John Dean. On the other hand, it is true that others did know."

Ehrlichman assented by saying, "We've made Dean a focal point in the Gray process, . . . and he will become a focal point in the Ervin process."

Haldeman closed this phase of the discussion by saying that if Dean is dismissed "he'll still be a focal point" and that "what Dean did, he did with all conscience in terms [of] the higher good."

According to the tapes of April 14, President Nixon believed Haldeman's problem was Strachan rather than Segretti, and he was anxious to know what Magruder was going to say about Strachan and what Strachan was going to say about the materials Magruder claimed he had given to him to carry to Haldeman. The tapes reveal that he requested both Haldeman and Ehrlichman to contact Magruder.

During their separate meeting on April 14, Haldeman reported to the President that he had interviewed Magruder by phone and had learned these things:

Magruder had agreed to tell the grand jury everything he knew about Watergate, and plead guilty to an appropriate count. He said he would implicate Mitchell, Dean, Strachan, and Porter. He said he would implicate Strachan merely by testifying he gave wiretap materials to him for delivery to Haldeman. He stated further, however, he was "sure Gordon [Strachan] never sent them to Bob [Haldeman] because they were all trash" and "the tragedy of this whole thing is that it produced nothing."

Magruder "doesn't say anything now directly—but did in the earlier stuff that Strachan knew about it before hand. That Strachan knew they were bugging the Watergate. Strachan says he didn't."

President Nixon inquired of Haldeman: "What would Strachan say?" Haldeman replied, "Strachan has no problem with that. He will say that after the fact there are materials that I can now surmise were what he is referring to but they were not at the time identified in any way as being the result of wiretaps, and I did not know they were. They were among tons of stuff."

The President asked Haldeman, "What will you say . . . if they claim that the reports (i.e., the reports of the wiretaps) came . . . to your office?" Haldeman replied, "This doesn't even have to come out." The President said, "But they will ask it in the grand jury." Haldeman observed: "The grand jury is secret. The only way it will come out is if they decide to indict Strachan and put him on trial."

The tapes reveal that President Nixon phoned Haldeman at 11:02 P.M. on April 14 and suggested that "John [Ehrlichman] should put" Strachan "through a little wringer" to prepare him for testifying.

Pursuant to the President's direction, Ehrlichman interviewed Magruder and his lawyers. He taped what they said without their knowledge. He reported to the President and Haldeman in respect to this interview at the third secret meeting they held on April 14.

His report concerning what Magruder said he was going to testify to before the grand jury was similar to that which Haldeman had previously made to the President. But he added that Magruder had told him these additional things:

Magruder and LaRue went to Key Biscayne "around the end of March" to present to Mitchell a new Liddy proposal which involved bugging Watergate, the McGovern headquarters, and the Fontainebleau Hotel. Mitchell orally approved it. "Nobody felt comfortable in this thing but we were sort of bulldozed into it."

At this point the President interjected: "By Colson?" Ehrlichman responded, "That's the inference," and resumed his recital of what Magruder had told him. It was as follows:

Magruder gave Strachan a copy of the written budget allocating $250,000 for the implementation of the Liddy proposal, which Mitchell had approved. The budget was "very specific in terms of the kinds of equipment to be used." Magruder told Strachan he was going to implement the proposal, and stated "I read his non-response as OK from higher-up." He added, "I am not able to say of my own knowledge that there was any knowledge of anyone higher-up."

The wiretaps obtained from the original burglary and bugging were "junk." When reports of them were given him, Mitchell called Liddy and "chewed him out." As a consequence, Liddy organized the second break-in without Magruder's or Mitchell's knowledge.

The prosecutors are "hot after Colson," but the only thing Magruder knew they had on him was his phone call concerning Liddy's project.

Dean devised a cover story in concert with these other people, and enlisted Bart Porter who went to the grand jury and perjured himself to go along with the cover story. Dean prepared Magruder and others to testify before the grand jury, and relayed to people at CREEP what was being said by witnesses to the grand jury.

"Haldeman's very much of a target of the United States Attorney."

As he concluded his report concerning what Magruder had said, Ehrlichman stated that one of Magruder's attorneys told him "he did not think they had anything" on Haldeman, that "this thing is rapidly deteriorating," but that "in all of this I don't see any evidence of the involvement of the President."

After Ehrlichman completed his recital of what Magruder had said, the President expressed the opinion that the prosecutors would get Dean "for the aftermath and the obstruction," and directed Haldeman and Ehrlichman to inform Colson and Strachan about Magruder's forthcoming testimony before the grand jury.

During the course of their secret meeting, the President asked Haldeman and Ehrlichman this question: "You don't think this would lead to an indictment of Colson, do you?"

Ehrlichman replied that Dean believed everyone "in the place is going to be indicted," and Haldeman responded that Dean thought "Mitchell, Haldeman, Ehrlichman, Colson, Dean, Strachan, Kalmbach, Kalmbach's go-between, Kalmbach's source, LaRue, Mardian, Parkinson, Bittman, and Hunt were technically indictable in the cover-up operation." Haldeman added that Dean had suggested that all of them should make a guilty plea and be given immediate clemency. Ehrlichman commented, "No way," and the President observed, "You know damn well it is ridiculous to talk about clemency."

At various periods during the secret meetings of April 14, President Nixon discussed with Haldeman and Ehrlichman his concern respecting what he called public relations, especially in respect to the grand jury and the Senate Select Committee.

The President's comments on the committee were ambivalent. Although Ziegler had counseled stonewalling, the President said, "I believe that cooperation with the Committee might at least indicate no cover-up," and "that's what I'm trying to do." The conferees then discussed negotiating with the Senate committee, and making a court test of its powers in case a satisfactory agreement with it was not reached.

Later the President declared he was opposed to cooperating with the Senate committee unless he "could get a resolution of the entire Republican Caucus in the Senate." And finally, he told Ehrlichman: "I think you ought to meet with Ervin and cut the deal. And then even though there isn't much of a compromise, you would say, 'we worked on a compromise under which there is executive privilege.'"

For the sake of continuity, I deviate from the analysis of the tapes to note that Senator Baker and I met with Ehrlichman, at his request, in secret at Blair House shortly after this, and he importuned us to soften the requirements we had explained to him in our April 9 meeting. We advised him that we could not do so, and gave him a copy of the committee's *Rules of Procedure,* which had just been approved and printed.

Although they provided for preliminary executive sessions in appropriate cases to determine whether a prospective witness knew anything relevant to what the committee was authorized to investigate, the rules expressly stipulated that every witness possessing such knowledge would be required to testify on oath in public sessions, and that press, radio, and television would be permitted to cover the hearings.

At Ehrlichman's entreaty, Baker and I agreed that the committee would allow each witness so testifying to close his testimony with a brief statement not subject to interruption or cross-examination. Maurice Stans was the only witness who exercised this privilege. He closed his testimony with these words: "All I ask, Mr. Chairman, is that when you write your report you will give me back my good name."

The tapes of April 14 demonstrate that President Nixon, Haldeman, and Ehrlichman considered and rejected various proposals as to what the White House might do or say to improve its public image.

At one point Haldeman observed: "If the situation's going to get worse, then you may have to do something. If this is as bad as it's going to get, maybe you're better off not doing anything."

When the multitude of words on these lengthy tapes are weighed and reconciled, they disclose that the President, Haldeman, and Ehrlichman finally agreed on these things: first, Ehrlichman should forthwith convey to Attorney General Kleindienst the information which had been gathered about Mitchell and Magruder to show that the White House had conducted an investigation and communicated its findings to the grand jury and the Department of Justice before any indictments were returned; and, second, the White House should make a public announcement concerning Watergate.

The reason for these decisions may be found in these words, which one of his presidential tapes shows he spoke to Dean at their last secret meeting in the Oval Office on April 16: "On the PR side I sure as hell am not going to let the Justice Department step out and say look we dragged the White House in here. I've got to step out and do it."

Immediately after the conferees decided he should transmit the fruits of the White House's investigation to the Attorney General, Ehrlichman called Kleindienst by phone, and told him what the White House had learned about Mitchell and Magruder, and that Magruder would implicate Dean, LaRue, and Porter as well as Mitchell.

It is worthy of note that in so doing Ehrlichman was merely conveying to the Department of Justice information which the President, Haldeman, and he knew it was bound to receive from Magruder and LaRue anyway.

When the President called Ehrlichman at 11:22 P.M. on April 14 to converse further about Watergate-related matters, Ehrlichman told him he was going to talk to Dean "to try to get him . . . to get off this passing the buck business," but he did not know "how far I can go." The President said, "John, that is not going to help you," and added that Dean "has to look down the road to one point that there is only one man who could restore him to the ability to practice law in case things go wrong. He's got to have that in the back of his mind."

. . .

Magruder met with the prosecutors on April 14, and Dean began meeting with them on April 15. Dean told them the White House Plumbers had hired Liddy and Hunt to burglarize the office of Daniel Ellsberg's psychiatrist, Dr. Fielding, in Beverly Hills in September 1971 in an unsuccessful effort to get information about Ellsberg, and that he and Ehrlichman had delivered a part of the materials removed from Hunt's safe in the Executive Office Building after the Watergate break-in to Acting FBI Director Gray with the direction they should never see "the light of day." This portion of these materials included the cablegrams Hunt was altering to defame President Kennedy.

After declining as "inappropriate" Ehrlichman's request for a meeting with him, Dean met secretly with President Nixon in the Oval Office about nine o'clock on the evening of April 15. The White House afterwards asserted it had no tape of this meeting.

Dean testified about it before the Senate Select Committee in June 1973. In so doing, he said:

He told the President he "had gone to the prosecutors" that day and informed them of his own involvement and that of others in the Watergate affair.

He assured the President that he had had no discussions with the prosecutors concerning his conversations with him or anything in the area of national security. The President told him he could not talk about national security areas or conversations he had had with him because they were privileged. The President asked him a number of leading questions, which made him "think the conversation was being taped" and "a record was being made to protect" the President. The President asserted that when he had said in March "$1 million was nothing to raise to pay to maintain the silence of the defendants . . . he had, of course, only been joking." Near the end of the meeting, the President said in an almost inaudible tone, "he was probably foolish to have discussed Hunt's clemency with Colson."

On the following day, April 16, President Nixon and Dean met secretly in the Oval Office in the morning and in the Executive Office Building in the afternoon. President Nixon's tapes show these things occurred at the morning meeting:

The President asked Dean to sign two writings so he could have them in hand for future contingencies. One was in the form of a letter to the President from Dean resigning his position as a member of the White House staff, and the other was in the form of a letter to the

President from Dean requesting an indefinite leave of absence from his position. The President said he would use the letter of resignation only in case Dean pleaded guilty, and the letter requesting the leave of absence only if Dean was "going in on some other basis."

Dean stated he ought not to go unless Haldeman and Ehrlichman went, and refused to sign either writing. The President informed Dean that Haldeman and Ehrlichman were willing to sever their connection with the White House if he deemed it appropriate, and Dean agreed he would write his own letter on the subject and tender it to the President later in the day. The President said, "I pray to God we don't . . . have to use these things."

After discussing with Dean the payment made in March to satisfy Hunt's demand for money for counsel fees, President Nixon observed, "But you had knowledge; Haldeman had knowledge; and Ehrlichman had knowledge. And I suppose I did. I am planning to assume some culpability on that." Dean commented, "I don't think so." The President declared, "You were simply helping the defendants get their fees."

During the course of the meeting, President Nixon told Dean to "tell the truth," and added, "that son of a bitch Hiss would be free today if he hadn't lied about his espionage."

In other connections, the President instructed Dean "to testify, if you do, . . . that the President told you nothing is privileged that involves wrongdoing." He also admonished Dean not to tell his lawyers or anybody else about the electronic surveillance of newsmen and employees of the National Security Council at the time the White House suspected that such employees were leaking information relating to the SALT talks to the press. He assured Dean the surveillance in this instance related to national security.

The President asked Dean what he would testify "if this thing breaks" and they ask you "What did you report to the President?" Dean replied, "I would refuse to answer any questions as to anything unless you waive." The President declared, "On that point, I would not waive."

Despite this statement, President Nixon said, "You could say I reported to the President," and he "has authorized me to say . . . I told him . . . that nobody in the White House was involved." Dean demurred as to his revealing what he said to the President. He added, "I think that's privileged," but "I think you say anything you want to say about it."

The President said, "I can say that you did tell me that nobody in the White House was involved, and I can say that you came in . . . and said 'I think the President needs to hear more about this case. And it was the time I started my investigation.' " Dean said, "That was the Wednesday before they were sentenced."

The President instructed Dean: "Get your chronology of that Wednesday you came in and told me. . . . That's when I became interested . . . in the case, and I said 'now, God damn it, I want to find out the score.' And I set in motion Ehrlichman, Mitchell and a few of— not Mitchell, but others. Okay." Dean said, "Sure."

The President and Dean agreed that Dean should say he did not tell the President about the post-Watergate affair before that time (i.e., March 21) because he did not know about it until then.

The President asked Dean whether he thought "the thing is likely to break today." Dean replied, "No, I don't." The President then put this question to Dean: "But don't you agree with me that the President should make the first announcement and not the Justice Department? Dean responded, "Yes, I do . . . on his own staff." The President exclaimed, "Oh, hell, I'm going to make the announcement with regard to Magruder, too. God damn it, it's our campaign. I'm not going to have the Justice Department [get credit for it]. . . . We triggered this whole thing. . . . You helped trigger it." Dean declared, "I put everybody's feet to the fire because it just had to stop." The President asked, "What got Magruder to talk?" and added, "I would like to take the credit."

At a later stage of their conversation, President Nixon assured Dean "I'm not going to let the Justice Department break this case," and Dean said, "You've got to break it."

The President expressed concern about the prosecutors asking Dean why he did not tell him earlier about the post-Watergate thing. Dean stated, "That's a PR situation, Mr. President. The United States Attorneys are not going to ask me questions as to what I said to the President or didn't say."

The President said, "I would hope you could help on the P.R. . . . I would like for you to say, and you're free to talk about it. You're to say, 'I told the President about this. I told the President first that there was no involvement in the White House. Afterwards, I told the President [about the post-Watergate thing]. And the President said, look, I want to get to the bottom of this thing, period.' "

The President continued: "See what I'm driving at—not just the White House. You continued your investigation, and so forth. The

President went ahead, investigated in his own way, which I have done . . . Believe me. I put a little pressure on Magruder, and a few of these clowns. And, as a result of the President's action, this thing has been broken."

Dean asserted, "That's right."

The President continued: "Because also I put pressure on the Justice Department."

President Nixon blamed Mitchell and Colson for "the clemency stuff." Dean stated, in substance, that Ehrlichman was responsible for anything Colson may have said to Hunt on the subject. Dean asserted that Colson presented Hunt's story to Ehrlichman in his presence and Ehrlichman instructed Colson: "Give him the inference he's got clemency, but don't give him any commitment."

Dean gave the President this consolation in respect to the Senate Select Committee: "I think if there are indictments down there in that courtroom none of the individuals should go up and testify [before the Senate Select Committee]. I think the Watergate is just going to be totally carved out of the Ervin hearings."

The President accepted this consolation by saying, "That's the Watergate, right. Then the other stuff is not that important, Segretti and all that."

Dean said, "That stuff is not that important."

When they met in the Executive Office Building on the afternoon of April 16, Dean presented to President Nixon a letter from him to the President, which he had composed since their morning meeting and offered to sign:

> You have informed me that Bob Haldeman and John Ehrlichman have verbally tendered their requests to be given an immediate and indefinite leave of absence from your staff. By this letter I also wish to confirm my similar request that I be given such a leave of absence from the staff.

Dean asserted, in substance, he did not "want to go" if Haldeman and Ehrlichman remained in the White House because his leaving under that circumstance would make him a scapegoat.

The President and Dean talked inconclusively about the letter and other Watergate problems, and separated without any decision being made.

7

NO SURCEASE
FROM
WATERGATE

THE President's announcement on Watergate was the subject of intensive discussion, writing, and rewriting in the White House. Its exact wording was approved at a secret meeting of the President with Haldeman, Ehrlichman, and Ziegler, which was held in the Oval Office between 3:50 and 4:35 P.M. on April 17, 1973.

A few minutes later President Nixon read his announcement to the White House press corps. After doing so, he departed hastily without submitting himself to questioning. The announcement consisted of three sections.

The first section, which related solely to the Senate Select Committee, contained several assertions in the nature of a preamble. These assertions were as follows:

For several weeks representatives of the committee and the White House "have been talking about ground rules which would preserve the separation of powers without suppressing the facts. . . . An agreement has been reached which is satisfactory to both sides. . . . The Committee rules, as adopted, totally preserve the doctrine of separation of powers. . . . They provide that the appearance by a witness may, in the first instance, be in Executive Session, if appropriate. . . . Executive privilege is expressly reserved and may be asserted during the course of the questioning as to any question." Although "much has been made of the issue as to whether the proceedings could be televised," the President has never considered that to be "a central issue, especially if the separation of powers problem is otherwise solved," as he "now thinks it is."

After these assertions, the first section concludes that all members of the White House staff will appear voluntarily before the Senate Select Committee when requested by it, testify on oath, and answer fully all proper questions.

The second section, which covered judicial proceedings arising out of Watergate, was as follows:

> On March 21st, as a result of serious charges which came to my attention, some of which were publicly reported, I began intensive new inquiries into this whole matter.
>
> Last Sunday afternoon, the Attorney General, Assistant Attorney General Petersen, and I met at length in the EOB to review the facts which had come to me in my investigation and also to review the progress of the Department of Justice investigation.
>
> I can report today that there have been major developments in the case concerning which it would be improper to be more specific now, except to say that real progress has been made in finding the truth.
>
> If any person in the Executive Branch, or in the government is indicted by the grand jury, my policy will be to immediately suspend him. If he is convicted, he will, of course, be automatically discharged.
>
> I have expressed to the appropriate authorities my view that no individual holding, in the past or at present, a position of major importance in the administration should be given immunity from prosecution.
>
> The judicial process is moving ahead as it should; and I shall aid it in all appropriate ways and have so informed the appropriate authorities.

By the third section of his announcement, President Nixon gave the people this solemn assurance: "As I have said before and I have said throughout this entire matter, all government employees and especially White House staff employees are expected fully to cooperate in this matter. I condemn any attempts to cover-up in this case, no matter who is involved."

After President Nixon completed the reading of the announcement, Ron Ziegler told the White House press corps that all previous White House statements on Watergate were now "inoperative."

The face-saving motive, which prompted President Nixon to saturate the first section of the announcement with verbiage about the separation of powers, was obvious. He was trying to camouflage his abrupt retreat from his prior deliberate claim that as President he was vested with an absolute executive privilege empowering him to withhold the testimony of his aides and former aides from the Senate Select Committee.

The press characterized the announcement as a drastic switch in the President's position and an effort on his part to avoid a direct confrontation with the Senate Select Committee on the executive privilege issue.

At the time the President read his announcement to the White House press corps I was en route to North Carolina to address the student body and the public at Davidson College.

On my arrival at Davidson, I found a large group of newsmen waiting to interview me on the announcement. One of them postulated that President Nixon had surrendered to me on executive privilege, and asked me if I had any comment to make on that premise. By way of response, I said, "When I win, I crow softly, if at all; and when I lose, I weep gently, if at all. I do not consider President Nixon's change of mind a surrender to me. I consider it a victory for constitutional government in America."

In response to other inquiries, I pointed out that there was no great significance in the provision of the committee's rules of procedure allowing the interposition of objections to the admission of evidence on the ground of executive privilege. It was, I said, simply a specific application of the well-established principle of evidence and fair play that anyone who was aggrieved by it could object on any ground to the introduction of testimony he deemed incompetent for any reason.

I pointed out further that under its rules of procedure, the committee would be the judge of whether a presidential aide could refuse to answer questions. In elaborating on this, I said, "Somebody has to rule on that point. These guidelines expressly say the Committee is going to do the ruling. If the Committee rules adversely to the witness on any question of privilege, the Committee shall require the witness to testify."

Events immediately preceding and succeeding the release of the announcement robbed the White House of the surcease from Watergate it was designed to ensure. Some of these events were public in nature. Others were hidden for many months on President Nixon's tapes.

These were undoubtedly days of dread for the White House. The prosecutors, Earl J. Silbert, Seymour Glanzer, and Donald E. Campbell, were sending E. Howard Hunt, James W. McCord, Gordon C. Strachan, Richard A. Moore, Dwight L. Chapin, Herbert W. Kalmbach, Frederick C. LaRue, Herbert L. (Bart) Porter, John N. Mitchell, Charles W. Colson, and others before the grand jury. They were continuing to bargain with their attorneys for the testimony of Magruder and Dean. But their efforts to induce the inscrutable Liddy to talk failed.

Some of the witnesses had little personal knowledge of Watergate. Others were uncooperative or even downright recalcitrant. While they received much information from Magruder, Dean, and their attorneys in bargaining sessions, the prosecutors were unable to translate it into testimony for the grand jury because of the difficulty of nailing down an agreement with Magruder and because of the denial of immunity for Dean. As a consequence, the prosecutors fell substantially short of prying open and presenting to the grand jury the truth respecting the Watergate affair.

Notwithstanding the secrecy the law imposes on testimony before the grand jury, prolific leaks from the grand jury room fed an avid press and grapevine with Watergate-related items. As one of his secret tapes discloses, President Nixon importuned Assistant Attorney General Petersen to stop these leaks. With a sense of futility born of much experience on the Washington scene, Petersen merely observed that leaks of forbidden information to the press are "part and parcel of the Washington business."

The White House was constrained to deny publicly that it had offered executive clemency to the original Watergate defendants for their pleas of guilty and silence, that the President had prior knowledge of Watergate, and that any of the key presidential aides were involved in it.

The White House had other public woes. Senator Weicker issued a press release setting out that at Dean's request Acting FBI Director Gray had burned politically sensitive files that had been taken from Hunt's safe in his office in the Executive Office Building shortly after the burglars had been caught in the Watergate. This press release precipitated Gray's resignation, and the increasingly unfavorable publicity concerning Magruder forced him to relinquish the post of director of Policy Development for the Department of Commerce to which he had been appointed after the election.

Dean and Mitchell issued separate press releases stating they did not intend to be made scapegoats for Watergate.

Dean's statement, which was issued on April 19, prompted a secretive White House act. Immediately after its issuance Stephen Bull, a presidential aide, checked with the secret service agents in charge of President Nixon's secret taping system to determine whether Dean knew of its existence, and was informed by them that he did not.

On the same day Attorney General Kleindienst publicly announced he was withdrawing from the Watergate investigation and entrusting its supervision solely to Petersen because of his own close relationship to some of those whose names were being linked in the press with the burglary.

Four days before Kleindienst's announcement, however, to wit, on Sunday, April 15, Kleindienst and Petersen made secret visits to the White House, and gave President Nixon information in private as to what Magruder and Dean had said to the prosecutors up to that time.

This account is based in part on a White House edited transcript of a Nixon tape, and in part on evidence afterwards given by Petersen to the Senate Select Committee and the grand jury. The crucial information they gave the President was as follows:

Magruder had told the prosecutors that Mitchell had authorized a budget of $300,000 for the burglary and bugging of the Watergate; that he, Magruder, had given copies of the budget and the intercepted wiretaps, which Liddy called the Gemstone files, to Strachan for delivery to Haldeman; and that after the burglars were caught in the Watergate, Dean had coached him and Porter to testify falsely before the grand jury. Dean had told the prosecutors that, acting on Ehrlichman's instructions, he had ordered Hunt to flee the Washington scene when the press announced the four Cubans had documents referring to him in their possession at the time of their arrest, and that he and Ehrlichman had delivered to Gray for the purpose of destruction files that had been removed from Hunt's safe in the Executive Office Building shortly after the burglary.

A conversation between the President and Petersen followed. Petersen stated that "school was going to be out as far as Haldeman was concerned" if Strachan would testify he had delivered to Haldeman the papers entrusted to him by Magruder. He told the President, "I cannot guarantee you that we have a criminal case at this point, but I can guarantee you that" Haldeman and Ehrlichman "are going to be a source of vast embarrassment to the Presidency, and for that reason I think the best thing that you could do would be to get rid of them immediately." Petersen urged the President, however, to keep Dean on the White House staff for the time being because he was "the first man to cooperate with us."

The President protested the innocence of wrongdoing on the part of Haldeman and Ehrlichman, asserted Magruder and Dean were simply trying to exculpate themselves, and secured a promise from Petersen of sufficient advance warning of any forthcoming public action by the Department of Justice to give him time to take appropriate action.

President Nixon urged that the prosecutors exercise caution in considering immunity for Magruder and Dean.

He told Petersen, in substance, that the first time he heard anything disconcerting about Watergate was on March 21, 1973; that on that day Dean came in and told him "about these things"; that he sent Dean to Camp David and told him to "sit down and write this out"; that Dean "came back and told him he was not able to do it"; that it was "no wonder he was not able to do it" because "it was a report which would implicate him"; and that he then asked Ehrlichman to get him the facts.

Petersen subsequently testified that he knew it "was commonplace in the press that Dean had" given the President a report on Watergate, and in consequence he put this question to him at this point: "Didn't Dean ever give you a report of all of this?" The President replied that Dean had never given him a report.

Petersen's recommendation that he forthwith dismiss Haldeman and Ehrlichman undoubtedly shocked President Nixon profoundly. As appears by a taped phone conversation between him and Ehrlichman on the preceding day, the President considered Haldeman the "closest man to him," and Ehrlichman stated that separating the President and Haldeman would be "like separating Siamese twins."

From April 15 through April 29 President Nixon spent substantial energy and time secretly discussing Watergate-related problems with Haldeman and Ehrlichman and with Assistant Attorney General Petersen. All told, he had six secret meetings and nineteen secret phone conversations on these problems with Petersen. This account of these secret communications is based on White House–edited transcripts of tapes.

Since many of the secret discussions of the President with Haldeman and Ehrlichman related to Dean, it is illuminating to observe how the words on the President's tapes of April 17 appraised Dean's role in the Watergate affair.

For two hours and forty-five minutes on that day President Nixon, Haldeman and Ehrlichman discussed Ehrlichman's so-called action plan, which was designed to minimize the harm of anything Dean might reveal to the prosecutors concerning Watergate.

In the last analysis, Ehrlichman's action plan was two-pronged. First, it contemplated that the President would summarily dismiss Dean; and, second, that in so doing the President would issue "an historical explanation" stating, in substance, that the President had entrusted the White House's investigation of Watergate solely to Dean, that the President had relied upon Dean to furnish him with a true report concerning the affair, and that the President was dismissing Dean because he had proved to be unreliable.

In urging the President to adopt and implement the action plan immediately, Ehrlichman indicated it had Colson's blessing. He cited Colson's argument that "the City of Washington . . . knows that Dean had little or no access to you." President Nixon interjected: "True, that's quite right. Dean was just a messenger."

Ehrlichman resumed Colson's argument "that knowledge imputed to us [that is, Haldeman and Ehrlichman] is knowledge imputed to you [that is, the President], and that if Dean testifies "that he imputed great quantities of knowledge to us, and is allowed to get away with that, that will seriously impair the Presidency ultimately" because it would be very easy to argue that all you have to do is read Dean's testimony—look at the previous relationships—and there she goes."

Ehrlichman added that Colson said the key was that Dean should not get immunity. The President stated, "Well, he told me that, and I couldn't agree more."

But President Nixon refused to adopt Ehrlichman's action plan. He suggested that if he dismissed Dean that day Dean would go out and charge that the President was covering up for Haldeman and Ehrlichman because he knew what they knew. He reminded Haldeman and Ehrlichman that Dean did not report to him. "I was a little busy," the President added, "and all of you said, 'Let's let Dean handle that and keep him out of the President's office.'"

Haldeman and Ehrlichman reminded the President that he had stated in August 1972 that Dean had reported to him that nobody in the White House was involved in Watergate. The President assured them the report was not in writing, Dean did not make it to him orally, and he had never seen Dean about this matter until about March 1973, when Ehrlichman advised him to talk to Dean.

Later that afternoon President Nixon was discussing Watergate problems with Secretary of State William P. Rogers. Haldeman and Ehrlichman entered the meeting. Ehrlichman informed Rogers that Dean reported to him because under "the organizational set-up" he was "one of the two conduits that" Dean "had to the Boss." When Rogers asked Haldeman how Dean contacted the President, Haldeman replied, "He dealt with one of us." The President informed Rogers: "Dean was handling it for the White House. Our people were aware that he was."

As Petersen reported to Nixon in one of their secret meetings, the attorneys for Dean gave some information on this aspect of Watergate to the prosecutors while they were seeking immunity for their client. They told the prosecutors they wanted a deal, that Dean acted as an agent, and did not do anything except what Haldeman and Ehrlichman told him to do. According to Petersen, they added that if the prosecutors insisted on trying Dean rather than giving him immunity, their defense would be to try Haldeman and Ehrlichman for Watergate and President Nixon for areas outside Watergate.

During his secret meetings and secret phone conversations with President Nixon, Petersen revealed to him what prospective witnesses were telling the prosecutors, what actual witnesses were testifying before the grand jury, and virtually all the activities, plans, and problems of the prosecutors.

To induce Petersen to do this, President Nixon gave him repeated assurances that he was sincerely trying "to get to the bottom of this," that he was "after the truth, even if it hurts me," and that he was "going to do the right thing." He expressly promised Petersen that "anything you tell me will not be passed on."

By his own words on President Nixon's secret tapes, Petersen expressed his acceptance of Nixon's assurances and promise, his complete confidence in Nixon's intellectual integrity and sincerity, and his conviction that as President, Nixon was entitled to demand and receive the information he was giving him. After all, it is to be noted, one of the principal duties of the President under the Constitution is to take care that the laws be faithfully executed.

Petersen disclosed to President Nixon, however, by words imprinted on the tape of April 27, 1973, that Silbert and his assistants were not "at ease with my reporting to you."

This tape reveals another constitutional conviction of Petersen's, which he undoubtedly deemed theoretical rather than practical in the contemporary context. While they were discussing what proved to be an unfounded rumor that Dean had "made statements to the prosecuting team implicating the President," Petersen informed President Nixon that he had said to the prosecutors: "We have to draw the line. We have no mandate to investigate the President. We investigate Watergate." Petersen added: "I don't know where that line draws, but we have to draw that all the time."

In elaborating this view, Petersen said to the President: "My understanding of our responsibilities is that if it comes to that I would have to come to you and say, 'We can't do that.' The only people who have jurisdiction to do that is the House of Representatives, as far as I'm concerned."

President Nixon approved Petersen's opinion by declaring "That's right."

In saying these things, Petersen was obviously manifesting his acceptance of a constitutional theory entertained by some distinguished scholars who claim that the President of the United States cannot be prosecuted for crime unless he has first been impeached by a majority of the House of Representatives and removed from office by two-thirds of the Senate.

I reject this theory on the basis of an extreme illustration. If he is exempt from criminal prosecution until he has been impeached by the House and removed from office by the Senate, the President can constitutionally forestall his impeachment and removal from office, and thus evade responsibility for his criminal acts by perpetrating unpunishable homicides upon a sufficient number of those representatives and senators who think he merits impeachment and removal.

As the tapes indicate, Petersen was desirous of protecting the presidency. To this end, he repeatedly urged Nixon to sever the connection of Haldeman, Ehrlichman, and Dean with the White House before the grand jury returned any indictments against any CREEP officials or White House aides. He anticipated an early return of such indictments.

On April 27 Petersen emphasized the desirability of the President asking Haldeman, Ehrlichman, and Dean for their resignations or giving them leaves of absence without further delay by saying: "The problem is one of timing. In my humble judgment the question of timing is working first to your detriment with respect to your image before the press and public; and secondly, I think it is working toward the detriment of the investigation because it is giving all of these people an attitude of hope that I think is unwarranted."

In commenting to Ehrlichman and Ziegler on his secret communications with Petersen, President Nixon said, "I've got Petersen on a short leash."

Notwithstanding his promise to Petersen that "anything you tell me will not be passed on," President Nixon forthwith relayed to Haldeman and Ehrlichman everything Petersen told him.

After Petersen had advised him how essential Strachan's testimony was to any effort by the government to establish any receipt by Haldeman of copies of the Watergate budget and wiretaps, President Nixon opened a discussion of this matter by observing to Haldeman and Ehrlichman: "Strachan has got to be worked out. I don't know how that's going to work out." Both Haldeman and Ehrlichman thereupon informed the President that they had talked to Strachan, and he had assured them he would say Haldeman was never involved in any way. Petersen subsequently told the President that Strachan refused to cooperate with the prosecutors.

After the President had informed Ehrlichman of what Petersen said Dean told the prosecutors about him, Ehrlichman sought out Colson and White House aide Kenneth W. Clawson, and sought and received from them assurances that they would contradict any evidence by Dean that Ehrlichman had instructed him to direct Hunt to flee the Washington scene shortly after the burglars were apprehended in the Watergate.

After Petersen disclosed to him that LaRue was talking freely to the prosecutors and that Kalmbach was scheduled to be called before the grand jury at an early date, President Nixon instructed Haldeman to convey that information to Kalmbach; and Ehrlichman contacted Kalmbach, told Kalmbach that Dean and the prosecutors were "out to get" him and Haldeman, and asked Kalmbach, in essence, not to incriminate them when he testified before the grand jury.

Despite his public announcement of April 17, his secret tapes show that President Nixon never lost his reluctance to have his aides appear before the Senate Select Committee, which he sometimes called in private "the damn Ervin Committee."

He told Petersen the committee "should drop the . . . investigation the day the grand jury took it up seriously," the committee "would be highly irresponsible to move forward," and the prosecutors ought to demand that the committee refrain from acting so that both the government and Mitchell would be ensured a fair trial. He insisted that Mitchell's attorneys ought to raise "holy hell" with the committee to accomplish the same end.

President Nixon also told Petersen he did not "want the damn Ervin Committee to go forward" if Magruder pleaded guilty and became a witness for the government, and asked him if "we can try to enjoin the Committee." Petersen replied, "I don't think so. Judge Sirica's even instructed all these people to cooperate with the Committee." He added, "And if we file an injunction action, . . . we're going to have another constitutional confrontation between the judiciary and the Committee."

Petersen assured the President, however, that he would ask "Senator Ervin . . . to hold off public sessions that might interfere with the right of fair trial for the others" as soon as he was able to secure a guilty plea from Magruder.

Numerous statements of President Nixon on his tapes indicate he was still wedded to the idea that the grand jury would soon return indictments against Mitchell or Magruder and make "the Ervin thing moot."

As the White House–edited transcripts of Nixon's tapes demonstrate, his conversations with Haldeman, Ehrlichman, and Petersen engendered in President Nixon's mind not only the conviction that "Dean is the only one who can sink Haldeman and Ehrlichman," but also the determination to deter Dean from testifying against them by thwarting his efforts to obtain immunity from prosecution.

President Nixon, Haldeman, and Ehrlichman agreed to insert the President's "view that no individual holding, in the past or at present, a position of major importance in the administration should be given immunity from prosecution" in his public announcement of April 17 for the specific purpose of discouraging the Department of Justice from granting immunity to Dean.

To be sure, the President did not confess this to Petersen, but, on the contrary, put the repeated importunities he made to Petersen on April 17 and 27 to deny immunity to Dean on the high plane that he had strong feelings against an offending high official going scot-free. Indeed, he asserted, "I am not trying to protect anybody. I want the damn facts [to come out]. If you can get the facts from Dean . . . I don't care."

Petersen had informed President Nixon, however, that he did not believe the prosecutors could get the facts from Dean unless immunity was extended to him. In elaborating this belief, he had told the President that although the prosecutors were trying to persuade Dean to plead guilty to a single felony count and become a witness for the government, his attorneys were steadfastly declaring that if he was not given total immunity, Dean would plead not guilty, and go on trial.

To impress Petersen with the firmness of his view, President Nixon told Petersen: "I just want you to know that if you give immunity, I will have to talk." Petersen responded: "OK. Let me put it this way. I will not do this without your knowledge. If it is necessary for me to do that, I will come to you first, and we can reach an agreement that you will disavow it, and [declare] that was the decision of the prosecutor. I don't want to make that decision, Mr. President. I don't want to immunize John Dean. I think he is too high in the echelon."

Petersen agreed with President Nixon that if immunity was granted to Dean "it's going to look awful," but he added, "the thing that scares the hell out of me is . . . suppose Dean is the only key to Haldeman and Ehrlichman and the refusal to immunize Dean means that Haldeman and Ehrlichman go free."

In their last recorded discussion of this subject, President Nixon said, "I do not want the impression left that by saying 'Don't grant immunity to a major person' . . . I am trying to block Dean giving evidence against Haldeman or Ehrlichman." Petersen responded, "I understand that," and added that the prosecutors had come to this conclusion respecting Dean: "If he's going to have any credibility at all, he'll have the most credibility if he goes in and pleads and testifies as a co-defendant against Ehrlichman and Haldeman as opposed to someone who has been given immunity and is testifying against them."

Dean was denied immunity from prosecution, and he refused to plead guilty or testify for the government.

The White House tapes subsequent to April 14 contain some frank comments by Ehrlichman on payments by "our guy" to the seven original Watergate defendants, their families, and attorneys, and an intriguing version of what President Nixon said to Dean on March 21, 1973, when Dean presented to him Hunt's demand for additional payments.

On April 15 President Nixon had an illuminating conversation with Ehrlichman concerning the payment of money by "our guys" to the Watergate defendants. The President asked Ehrlichman, "What was involved? I mean, from our side, our guys."

Ehrlichman replied, "Well, you had defendants who were concerned about their families. You had lawyers who were concerned about their fees. You had a campaign organization that was concerned about the success of its campaign, . . . and didn't want these fellows to say anything in public that would disrupt the campaign." In reply to an inquiry by the President, Ehrlichman expressed the opinion that it is legitimate to want people not to say anything in public that would disrupt the campaign or embarrass people.

The President asked, "Cover up, you mean?" Ehrlichman said, "It would impeach the campaign in effect. But at the same time a lot of the same people who had that legitimate motive had an illegitimate motive because they were involved in protecting their own culpability and here we're talking about LaRue, Magruder, Mitchell possibly."

The President asked, "If they wanted the defendants to shut up in court?" Ehrlichman replied, "Certainly, certainly."

Ehrlichman added, "If I were Dean, I would develop a defense that I was being manipulated by people who had a corrupt motive for ostensibly a benign motive."

Two days later President Nixon, Haldeman, and Ehrlichman met in secret to consider Watergate-related problems. The President brought up the subject of his prior discussion with Ehrlichman by asking, "You say that our purpose was to keep them from talking to the press?"

Ehrlichman responded, "Well, that was my purpose—and before I get too far out on that I want to talk to an attorney and find out what the law is—which I have not yet done." The President exclaimed, "Right!" Haldeman interjected, "That's just what I want to do, too." The President exclaimed, "Right. Good!"

During the course of the ensuing conversation, Haldeman admitted that Dean had "really turned into an unbelievable disaster for us," and Ehrlichman characterized him as a "piranha."

According to the transcript of the Nixon tape of April 17, President Nixon and Haldeman discussed on that day what had been said in the Oval Office on March 21, 1973, when Dean told the President that Hunt was threatening to reveal all the "seamy things" he had done for Ehrlichman if he was not paid $122,000 for lawyer fees and family support before he was sentenced.

When Haldeman remarked, "I was in here when he told you," the President said, "Good. What did we say?"

Haldeman stated, in substance, that they said, "We can't do anything about it. . . . We don't have any money, and it isn't a question to be directed here. This is something [which] relates to Mitchell's problem." Haldeman added that Ehrlichman has no problem with the Hunt thing because he declared, "If you're going to get into blackmail, to hell with it."

President Nixon said, "Thank God you were in there when it happened." He then put this question to Haldeman: "But you remember the conversation?" Haldeman replied, "Yes, sir." Nixon asked, "I didn't tell him to get the money, did I?" Haldeman answered, "No." Nixon asked, "You didn't either, did you?" Haldeman responded, "Absolutely not! I said [to Dean] . . . this is something you've got to work out with Mitchell—not here. There's nothing we can do about it here."

According to Haldeman, Dean suggested it could require a million dollars to keep "these guys" silent; and the President ended the conversation on the subject by saying, "That's ridiculous," it may require "two, or ten, and eleven [million]," and "once you start down the path with blackmail it's constant escalation."

The President stamped with approval what Haldeman said by saying, "Yes. That's my only conversation with regard to that."

The President then asked Haldeman to explain the circumstances surrounding his returning to LaRue the remainder of the $350,000 entrusted to him. "Dean said," Haldeman asserted, "they need money for the defense, for their fees." He added, "And it was always put that way. That's the way it was always discussed."

The President commented, "Right. That's why I want that line. I think that's most important."

In their secret talk on April 27 President Nixon and Petersen discussed Hunt's demand as well as payments to Hunt's attorney Bittman, Dorothy Hunt, and the Cubans. The President assured Petersen that when Dean told him of Hunt's demand on March 21, he advised Dean that "we can't do it," and that Dean went on to Ehrlichman with Hunt's demand and Ehrlichman said, "No dice."

Petersen told the President that they could have made the payments openly. He added, "Once you do it in a clandestine fashion it takes on elements of cover-up and obstruction of justice."

Although it was not publicly known at the time, the White House was much disturbed in April 1973 by the possibility that the burglary of Dr. Fielding's office might be revealed.

This account of the matter is based on testimony presented afterwards to the Senate Select Committee and the record in the case against Daniel J. Ellsberg.

Newspaper publications of portions of the Pentagon Papers and of details of the SALT talks during 1971 outraged President Nixon, and he authorized the establishment by Ehrlichman of a secret White House investigatory unit to stop security leaks and to investigate other sensitive security matters.

Pursuant to this authority, Ehrlichman named his chief assistant, Egil Krogh, Jr., and White House aide David R. Young, Jr., co-chairmen of this special unit, and ordered them to report to him. Since their function was to stop "leaks," they were called the Plumbers.

Daniel J. Ellsberg, who was charged with disseminating copies of the Pentagon Papers to the press, had received treatment from Dr. Lewis J. Fielding. The White House was anxious to obtain information from Dr. Fielding concerning Ellsberg in the hope it could be used to discredit him.

FBI agents sought such information from Dr. Fielding on two occasions. Being faithful to his Hippocratic oath, Dr. Fielding refused to discuss his patient with them. In consequence, Krogh and Young proposed to Ehrlichman that a covert operation be undertaken to obtain Dr. Fielding's files relating to Ellsberg, and Ehrlichman approved the proposal on the expressed condition that it should not be traceable. Krogh and Young employed Liddy and Hunt to carry out the covert operation. Krogh paid Liddy $5,000 to finance the venture with money advanced to him by Joseph Baroody, a Washington public relations consultant, at Colson's request, and Baroody was later repaid that sum out of a contribution made by a dairy organization to President Nixon's campaign for reelection.

Ehrlichman subsequently stated that he talked to President Nixon about the need for Liddy and Hunt to visit California in connection with the Ellsberg investigation, and that the President declared Krogh should do anything necessary to ascertain Ellsberg's motive in disseminating the Pentagon Papers.

On the night of September 3–4, 1971, Liddy and Hunt kept watch outside Dr. Fielding's residence and office in Beverley Hills while their hired accomplices, Bernard L. Barker, Felipe De Diego, and Eugenio R. Martinez, burglarized and ransacked Dr. Fielding's office. They were unable to find any files relating to Ellsberg.

When he talked to his aide, Richard A. Moore, in a secret meeting on April 19, President Nixon said, so Moore testified, that this "investigation of Ellsberg had been done because [J. Edgar] Hoover [director of the FBI] could not be counted on doing it because Mr. Hoover was a close friend of Mr. Ellsberg's father-in-law."

After Dean had talked to the prosecutors, Petersen had a secret phone conversation with President Nixon on April 18 in which he advised the President that the prosecutors had been informed that Liddy and Hunt had burglarized Dr. Fielding's office at the instance of the Plumbers.

According to Petersen's subsequent testimony to the Senate Select Committee and the grand jury, President Nixon thereupon advised Petersen: "I know about that. That is a national security matter. You stay out of that. Your mandate is to investigate Watergate." After receiving this order, as he afterwards testified, Petersen called Silbert and told him that the President had ordered the prosecutors to stay out of the Fielding burglary.

Petersen was much troubled by President Nixon's order relating to the burglary of Dr. Fielding's office. Ellsberg was then on trial before United States District Judge W. Matthew Byrne and a jury in California on criminal charges arising out of his alleged action in respect to the Pentagon Papers.

Petersen believed it the duty of the Department of Justice to inform Judge Byrne of the burglary of Dr. Fielding's office, and threatened to resign if this was not done.

At the insistence of Kleindienst and Petersen, President Nixon consented to having the Department of Justice send a memorandum relating to the burglary to Judge Byrne with the suggestion that he hold it in camera.

Judge Byrne ignored the suggestion, read the memorandum in open court, directed that it be supplied to Ellsberg's attorneys, and ordered that an investigation be made to determine whether Ellsberg's constitutional rights had been violated. After so doing, he publicly disclosed that at the request of the White House he had met with Ehrlichman on April 5 and 7 during the pendency of the Ellsberg case, and Ehrlichman had indicated to him that the President was considering him for appointment as permanent director of the FBI.

Pursuant to an order of Judge Byrne's requiring the government to investigate and report to him whether it had subjected Ellsberg to electronic surveillance, William D. Ruckelshaus, who had just been appointed acting director of the FBI, sent Judge Byrne a memorandum revealing that the FBI had wiretapped Ellsberg's conversations, and Petersen sent him a memorandum disclosing that the Department of Justice did not know what had become of the records of those wiretaps.

Upon receipt of these memorandums, Judge Byrne permanently dismissed the case against Ellsberg on the ground of government misconduct. In so doing, he cited as the basis of his decision the government's failure to produce the records of the wiretaps.

Shortly after the dismissal of the Ellsberg case, it was discovered that the records of the wiretaps had been removed from the FBI and deposited in Ehrlichman's safe in the White House.

After Dean began to talk to the prosecutors, the White House decided to prepare itself to meet any disclosures he might make with respect to his secret meetings with President Nixon. As a consequence, Haldeman received from presidential aide Stephen B. Bull, who apparently had supervision of President Nixon's secret tapes, twenty-two tapes of presidential conversations recorded in February, March and April 1973, and listened to them. After so doing, he discussed the March 21 tape with the President and was directed by him to listen to it again and determine what answers should be given to questions arising out of the discussion it recorded.

As April neared its end, the public Watergate woes of the White House intensified. There was a marked increase in press charges that high-ranking officials of CREEP and the White House were implicated in a massive cover-up of the Watergate affair. Some Republican congressional and party leaders added their voices to those who were insisting that President Nixon take aggressive action to discover and disclose the truth respecting Watergate. Demands increased in Congress and bar groups that the Watergate investigation should be taken from the Department of Justice and entrusted to a special prosecutor independent of the White House.

8

PRETENSES AND
OTHER THINGS

PRESIDENT Nixon concluded that the time for dramatic action on his part had arrived. On the morning of April 30 the White House announced through press secretary Ziegler that Haldeman, Ehrlichman, Dean, and Attorney General Kleindienst had resigned. Ziegler also stated that President Nixon had appointed Secretary of Defense Elliot L. Richardson Attorney General.

On the evening of the same day, President Nixon delivered to the American people a televised speech on Watergate. The speech was cleverly contrived to present the speaker to the nation as a dedicated, harassed, and overburdened President, who had been engrossed throughout the presidential campaign of 1972 in efforts to obtain prosperity and peace with honor in Southeast Asia for Americans and peace for the world, who by reason of such efforts had been justifiably ignorant at all times before March 21, 1973, of the true nature of the Watergate affair and the possibility of any involvement of any of his political or governmental aides in it, who had learned for the first time since March 21, 1973, as a result of new investigations supervised by him, that some of his political or governmental aides may have participated in the Watergate break-in and in subsequent efforts to hide the identities and activities of those responsible for it from law enforcement officers, the press and the public, and who was now determined that the truth relating to the Watergate affair be fully brought out no matter who was involved, and to do everything in his power to ensure that the guilty were brought to justice.

To sustain these propositions, President Nixon made these specific statements to the nation in his televised speech:

On June 17, 1972, while he was in Florida trying to get a few days' rest after his visit to Moscow, he learned for the first time of the Watergate break-in from news reports and immediately ordered an investigation by appropriate government authorities. After indictments were returned against the seven original Watergate defendants on September 15, 1972, he was repeatedly told by those conducting the investigation that there was no reason to believe that members of his administration were in any way involved.

As a result of these assurances, he discounted as false the articles in the press which appeared to implicate members of his administration or officials of the Committee for the Reelection of the President in illegal activity during and preceding the 1972 presidential election, and in efforts to cover up that illegal activity.

In March 1973 new information came to him for the first time indicating "that there was a real possibility that some of these charges were true and suggesting further that there had been an effort to conceal the facts both from the public" and from himself.

As a consequence of this new information, he "personally assumed the responsibility for coordinating intensive new inquiries into the matter," and "personally ordered those conducting the investigations to get all the facts and to report them directly" to him.

He was determined that the truth should be fully brought out—no matter who was involved. To this end, he "again ordered all persons in the government or at the Reelection Committee" to "cooperate fully with the FBI, the prosecutors, and the grand jury." And since ground rules had been adopted preserving "the basic constitutional separation of powers between Congress and the Presidency," he also "directed that members of the White House staff should appear and testify voluntarily under oath before the Senate Committee investigating Watergate."

"Today in one of the most difficult decisions" of his presidency, he accepted the resignations of two of "his closest associates in the White House—Bob Haldeman, John Ehrlichman"—whom he described as "two of the finest public servants it has been my privilege to know." He wanted "to stress that in accepting these resignations" he meant "to leave no implication whatever of personal wrongdoing on their part."

The newly appointed Attorney General Elliot L. Richardson had been given "absolute authority to make all decisions bearing on the prosecution of the Watergate case and related matters," including "the authority to name a special supervising prosecutor for matters arising out of the case . . . if he should consider it appropriate."

Although he had always previously insisted on running his own campaigns for office, he decided as the 1972 campaign approached that the concerns of the presidency should "come first and politics second" because "1972 was a year of crucially important decisions, of intense negotiations, of vital new directions, particularly in working toward the goal which had been" his "overriding concern throughout" his "political career—the goal of bringing peace to America and peace to the world."

For this reason, he removed to the maximum extent possible the campaign decisions and operations of 1972 from the President's office and the White House, and delegated them to the Committee for the Reelection of the President. As a consequence of this delegation of the management of his campaign and his preoccupation with the crucial concerns of the presidency, he had no information of any "alleged improper actions" involving any of his political and governmental aides which may have occurred in connection with the presidential election of 1972 prior to March 21, 1973.

As the man at the top, however, he accepted responsibility for any "alleged improper actions" which may have occurred within the White House or within his campaign organization in connection with his campaign for reelection, and refused to adopt the cowardly course of blaming them on those to whom he had delegated the authority to run the campaign. After all, they were his subordinates, whose zeal may have exceeded their judgment and "who may have done wrong in a cause they deeply believed to be right."

Although he accepted nominal responsibility for any "alleged improper actions" incident to his campaign for reelection in 1972, he was not really accountable for them because he was totally ignorant of what was being done in it, and because "both of our great political parties have been guilty of shady tactics in times past" on the theory that the good end they had in view justified the evil means they employed.

He pledged to the American people from the presidential office that he would do everything in his power to ensure that the guilty were brought to justice and that such abuses as may have occurred in the election of 1972 were "purged from our political processes in the years to come."

It is noteworthy that President Nixon did not specify any "shady tactic" approximating Watergate which had occurred in times past in American politics.

On May 9, 1973, the Senate Judiciary Committee opened its hearings on the nomination of Elliot L. Richardson as Attorney General. He assured the committee he would appoint a special prosecutor, who would have "all the independence, authority, and staff" he needed. On the same day, President Nixon publicly announced that the special prosecutor would enjoy the complete cooperation of the executive branch.

As a result of the resignations of Haldeman, Ehrlichman, and Dean, President Nixon named General Alexander M. Haig, Jr., his chief of staff; Melvin R. Laird, his counselor for domestic affairs; and Leonard Garment, presidential counsel. He also appointed J. Fred Buzhardt his special counsel on Watergate, and Professor Charles A. Wright, of the University of Texas Law School, his part-time legal consultant.

As the time for the hearings of the Senate Select Committee approached, President Nixon issued guidelines for past and present members of his staff who might be called as witnesses by the committee.

It was a far cry from these guidelines, which were apparently designed to shield him, to President Nixon's original arbitrary claim that as President he had the absolute power to withhold from the committee all of the testimony of his aides.

These guidelines, which were promulgated on May 3, specified that White House aides should invoke executive privilege only in connection with conversations involving the President, conversations among themselves involving communications with the President, and presidential papers, which were broadly defined as "all documents produced or received by the President or any member of the White House staff in connection with his official duties."

The aides were also "restricted from testifying as to matters relating to national security."

The Constitution is not a schizophrenic instrument that speaks with a forked tongue. Hence, there was a rank absurdity in President Nixon's long-held claim that although it expressly imposes upon the President the duty to take "care that the laws be faithfully executed," the Constitution impliedly vests in him an arbitrary executive privilege to frustrate the performance of this duty by his subordinates by withholding from them his aides' testimony revealing criminal conduct.

Insofar as I have been able to ascertain, President Nixon did not publicly abandon this absurd claim until May 22, 1973.

At the time of the organizational meeting of the Senate Select Committee in February 1973, the cover-up of Watergate was intact. The task of assembling a competent and sufficient staff was a tedious undertaking, which was not fully accomplished until mid-April.

Notwithstanding its smallness in the days following the organizational meeting, the staff diligently pursued leads suggested by press articles and rumors, and, in so doing, made multitudes of inquiries without substantial success.

After McCord wrote his famous letter to Judge Sirica, talked to chief counsel Dash, and testified before the Senate Select Committee behind closed doors, the prospect for discovering the truth about Watergate brightened.

McCord's personal knowledge, however, was largely limited to the break-in and the bugging. In addition to his personal knowledge, he had acquired much information from Liddy, Hunt, and others concerning the planning of the burglary and the bugging, and the payment of "hush money" and offers of clemency for the silence of the original Watergate defendants.

This information indicated that Mitchell, Dean, and Magruder had participated in varying ways in meetings with Liddy in which the break-in and the bugging of the Watergate were planned.

While precedents permitted congressional investigating committees to receive hearsay evidence, the Senate Select Committee was unwilling to rely on such evidence to establish the crucial facts relating to Watergate, and initiated an intensive investigation to discover testimony corroborative of McCord's revelations.

By interviewing the secretaries to CREEP and at the White House, as well as Department of Justice officials and Hugh W. Sloan, Jr., former treasurer of CREEP, and subpoenaing and studying many records, the staff assembled much testimony supportive of what McCord had revealed. Despite this, the committee was still short of direct evidence sufficient to settle the all-important question whether the

Watergate break-in and cover-up were the products of conspiracies among persons in the higher echelons of CREEP and the White House. So the committee turned to a consideration of the desirability of using its immunity powers.

Conspiracies are formed, and to a large degree executed in secret. For this reason, it is often impossible to establish the existence of a conspiracy without the testimony of a conspirator or to obtain the testimony of a conspirator without granting him immunity from prosecution.

The statute authorizing congressional committees to compel witnesses appearing before them to give testimony incriminating themselves and to grant them immunity for so doing was co-authored by Senator John L. McClellan, Senator Roman L. Hruska and me, and was enacted by Congress on October 15, 1970. This statute empowers a congressional committee to grant a witness a limited immunity, which is known as use immunity. In explaining use immunity, Judge Sirica said:

> Rather than barring a subsequent related prosecution, it acts only to suppress, in any such prosecution, the witness' testimony and evidence derived directly or indirectly from that testimony. Evidence obtained wholly independently of immunized testimony may serve as a basis for prosecuting the witness for activities and transactions including those covered in his own statements. (361 F.Supp. 1270, 1274)

After due deliberation, the committee decided that the only way to remove the secrecy in which Watergate was still substantially shrouded was to immunize some of the principal suspects.

Early in May the committee ascertained that Magruder and Dean were willing to testify before it if they were first granted use immunity, and that in combination they possessed personal knowledge sufficient to enable them to reveal virtually the entire Watergate affair to the committee. As a consequence, the committee invoked the procedure which secured use immunity to Magruder and Dean.

Samuel Dash's energy was boundless. In addition to handling administrative matters, researching legal questions, and supervising interviews of prospective witnesses by staff members, he met with me virtually every day to discuss committee problems and keep me abreast of the evidence being unearthed. The staff computerized evidence as it was gathered and thus made it instantly retrievable.

By herculean around-the-clock efforts, the staff had discovered by mid-May much of the evidence necessary for presentation of the break-in, bugging, and cover-up phase of the Watergate investigation, and the committee was ready to open its public hearings.

Since the committee was composed of seven senators accustomed to making their own decisions, it was only natural for differences of opinion to arise among them from time to time as to how the committee ought to proceed.

To facilitate efficient and harmonious action, the committee held frequent meetings in the seclusion of my Senate office, where its members discussed freely and frankly the problems confronting them and reached by common consent or majority vote decisions respecting them. Afterwards Senator Baker and I jointly announced these decisions to the press, and the committee performed its public duties in an atmosphere of substantial unity.

There was originally a difference of opinion among members as to how the evidence relating to the break-in, the bugging, and the cover-up of Watergate ought to be presented. Senators Talmadge and Gurney proposed the committee should concentrate on whether President Nixon was involved in any way in the Watergate affair, and undertake to solve this question speedily by calling as its first witnesses Haldeman, Ehrlichman, and Mitchell.

With the strong support of chief counsel Samuel Dash, I strenuously opposed this proposal. Although conscious of its good faith, I believed the proposal reflected an impatience to obtain results too quickly, and that there was a far more effective way to elicit and disclose the truth in respect to Watergate.

In my judgment, it was not possible for the committee, the Congress, and the nation to comprehend fully how Watergate could have happened and its true proportions been concealed for approximately a year without an understanding of the hierarchical structures of the White House and CREEP.

Besides, to borrow one of President Nixon's favorite expressions, the interviews of Mitchell, Haldeman, and Ehrlichman by the staff indicated that they intended to "stonewall" Watergate; and I was convinced it was unwise to call them to the witness stand before Magruder, Dean, and other witnesses had given testimony implicating them and affording a substantial foundation for their cross-examination by a committee lawyer or member who might believe their "stonewalling" was obscuring the truth.

Fortunately, a majority of the committee supported my views, and the testimony relating to this phase of the investigation was presented to it and the public in a methodical way that illuminated clearly the identities and activities of those involved in the Watergate affair.

To avoid fragmentation of the narrative, I defer discussion of the committee hearings to comment on two matters that overlapped their early days. The first was an effort to delay or stymie the hearings; the other was a manifestation of President Nixon's propensity to giving his version of Watergate without taking an oath or subjecting himself to cross-examination.

In conformity with his pledge to the Senate Judiciary Committee, Elliot L. Richardson designated Archibald Cox, a member of the faculty of the Harvard Law School, Special Prosecutor in the Watergate case. Shortly afterwards, Richardson issued guidelines stipulating these things: first, the special prosecutor would have jurisdiction over crimes arising out of the Watergate affair and the 1972 presidential election as well as allegations involving the President and his staff; second, the Attorney General would not countermand or interfere with the special prose-cutor's actions or decisions; and, third, Cox would not be removed as special prosecutor except for extraordinary improprieties on his part.

On May 23, the Senate Judiciary Committee approved Richardson's nomination as Attorney General as well as his naming of Cox as Special Prosecutor and the guidelines executed by him.

Archibold Cox, who was a Democrat, had served as Solicitor General under Presidents Kennedy and Johnson. I entertained high respect for his character and capability, and deemed his selection by Richardson wise.

Soon after qualifying as Special Prosecutor, Cox visited me and asked me in my capacity as chairman of the Senate Select Committee to post-pone all further committee hearings until the grand jury investigating Watergate returned indictments, an event which he estimated would occur in about ninety days. He feared pretrial publicity generated by committee hearings might prevent fair trials of the persons to be indicted and thus permit them to go unwhipped by justice.

In rejecting Cox's request, I made these observations:

—By a unanimous vote, the Senate had directed the committee to conduct the investigation and complete it by February 28, 1974. It had given the committee no authority to postpone doing these things.

—After indictments were returned, the special prosecutor would ask for additional postponement until trials were completed in respect to them—events which could require years, since justice all too often travels on leaden feet.

—Since there was a nationwide interest in Watergate, there would be much publicity concerning it until the truth was revealed, and for that reason there was a greater chance for indicted persons to get fair trials "in an atmosphere of judicial calm" after rather than before the committee hearings.

—Since the courts could secure fair trials to indicted persons by careful selection of trial juries, or delaying trials, I did not accept Cox's pessimistic fears as valid.

—In any event, I believed that it was more important for the committee to inform Congress and the American people what high officials entrusted by the President with enormous governmental and political power had done than it was for the courts to send a few people to jail.

After I rejected his request, Cox importuned the Senate Select Committee by letter to overrule me and cancel its public hearings for several months. In a meeting behind closed doors on June 5, the committee voted unanimously to deny this request, and resumed public hearings.

The Senate Select Committee had applied to Judge Sirica for orders authorizing use immunity for Jeb Stuart Magruder and John W. Dean. On June 6 Cox moved Judge Sirica to annex to his immunity orders for these persons restrictions forbidding radio and television coverage of their testimony. He insisted as a basis for his motion that "widespread pretrial publicity might prevent bringing to justice those guilty of serious offenses in high government offices."

The constitutional and legal issues incident to the motion have been brilliantly expounded in Judge Sirica's opinion, which is reported in 361 Federal Supplement 1270, and a book entitled *The Power to Probe*, by James Hamilton, an able member of the legal staff of the Senate Select Committee. Hence, I shall not discuss them here. It suffices to note that Judge Sirica denied Cox's motion because, under the existing facts, the statute regulating the granting of use immunity to witnesses in congressional hearings required the court to issue immunity orders without restrictions and without regard to its own opinion as to their wisdom.

Although I staunchly opposed Cox's efforts to delay the committee hearings and to forbid their being televised, I understood why his conscience impelled him to make them. I am constrained to say, however, that if he had succeeded in keeping the committee hearings from being televised, his action would have deprived the American people of the most effective means for determining for themselves the truth about Watergate, and would have left them in a state of discord far more intense than that which actually resulted.

After qualifying as Special Prosecutor, Cox assembled a legal staff that was impressive for its youthfulness and brilliancy. The average age of its thirty-two members was thirty-two years. Seventeen of them were graduates of Harvard Law School, and seven of the eight lawyers constituting his senior legal staff had held important posts under previous Democratic administrations.

After thoroughly briefing Cox's staff in respect to what they had unearthed about Watergate, Silbert and his assistants, Glanzer and Campbell, who resented the appointment of the Special Prosecutor, retired from further participation in the Watergate investigation.

During his tenure as Special Prosecutor, Cox discharged his duties ably, courageously, and faithfully.

Aside from the right to refuse to give self-incriminating testimony and to refrain from revealing certain well-defined privileged communications, every competent person in America is obligated by law to testify before courts and other public bodies constitutionally empowered to seek the truth in respect to matters under inquiry by them.

In May, reports circulated in Washington that the prosecutors, who were presenting testimony to the grand jury investigating Watergate, had advised the Department of Justice that the evidence assembled by them made it desirable to call President Nixon as a witness. About the same time a newsman asked me if I would call the President to testify before the Senate Select Committee. I replied I would do so if I felt such action to be necessary. I added that I knew of "no law that says the President is exempt from the duties which devolve on other citizens."

These events may have induced the White House to announce through Ziegler that it would be "constitutionally inappropriate" and "do violence to the separation of powers" for President Nixon to give any oral or written testimony to either the Watergate grand jury or the Senate Select Committee.

According to a Washington rumor, the Department of Justice, which all too often makes its ruling on constitutional and legal questions harmonize with the political desires of the White House, advised the White House that the President could not be required to answer questions except by a summons issued by the House of Representatives in an impeachment proceeding.

The White House did not give any rational explanation for its assertion that it would be "constitutionally inappropriate" and "do violence to the separation of powers" for the President to testify. By so doing, the White House emulated the preacher who was fired by a backwoods church and who inquired of the chairman of its board of deacons why the church had taken such action. The preacher asked, "Don't I argufy?" The chairman answered, "You sure do argufy." The preacher asked, "Don't I sputefy?" The chairman replied, "You sure do sputefy." The preacher inquired, "Then why did the church fire me?" The chairman responded, "Because you don't show wherein."

Since both the grand jury and the committee were sitting within two miles of the White House, his appearance before them would not have inconvenienced President Nixon or slowed the wheels of government. Indeed, it might have not only aided the search for truth but furthered the President's constitutional obligation to "take care that the laws be faithfully executed."

The President is the servant of the Constitution and not its master. There is nothing explicit or implicit in that instrument which exempts him from a duty the law imposes on all competent human being in our land.

In addition to observing that the occupant of the presidential office is not royalty, I pointed out that when he was presiding over the trial of former Vice-President Aaron Burr for treason in the United States Circuit Court at Richmond, Virginia, in 1807, Chief Justice John Marshall, America's ablest jurist of all time, ruled that he had jurisdiction to issue a subpoena requiring President Thomas Jefferson to produce a letter relevant to the issues in the case, and that Jefferson acquiesced in the ruling by producing the letter.

Prior to May 22, the White House was buffeted by such publicly made allegations as these:

During the summer of 1970 a White House aide, Tom Charles Huston, prepared and President Nixon approved, at least temporarily, a massive intelligence plan which purported to authorize the Central Intelligence Agency, the Federal Bureau of Investigation, the Defense

Intelligence Agency, and the National Security Agency, acting without judicial warrants, to commit burglaries and other illegal acts to spy on any persons they deemed to be included within a category vaguely defined as internal security targets.

During the week following June 13, 1971, the day of the publication of the first installment of the Pentagon Papers by The *New York Times*, the White House organized a vigilante group of White House aides popularly known as the Plumbers to probe and plug leaks of governmental data to the press, and the Plumbers hired Liddy and Hunt to burglarize the office of Dr. Lewis J. Fielding in September 1971 for the purpose of obtaining files disclosing Dr. Fielding's opinion as to the mental or emotional state of his patient, Daniel L. Ellsberg, who had allegedly disseminated the Pentagon Papers to *The New York Times* and the *Washington Post*.

On June 23, 1972, six days after the burglars were caught in the Watergate, and during ensuing days, the White House, acting through Haldeman, Ehrlichman, and Dean, sought to persuade the CIA to help block an FBI investigation of $89,000 in Nixon campaign money that was supposedly "laundered" in a Mexican bank.

During the summer of 1972 President Nixon's personal attorney, Herbert W. Kalmbach, solicited $230,000 for payments to the original Watergate defendants.

Although he was unwilling to testify on oath and submit himself to cross-examination in respect to such matters, President Nixon issued a 4,000-word statement on May 22 giving his version of these and other Watergate-related accusations.

In it he conceded for the first time that there had been "wide-ranging efforts" in the White House to cover up the Watergate affair. In denying any personal involvement on his part, he specifically stated:

—I had no prior knowledge of the Watergate operation.
—I took no part in, nor was I aware of any subsequent efforts that may have been made to cover up Watergate.
—At no time did I authorize any offer of Executive Clemency for the Watergate defendants, nor did I know of any such offer.
—I did not know, until the time of my own investigation, of any effort to provide the Watergate defendants with funds.
—At no time did I attempt, or did I authorize others to attempt, to implicate the CIA in the Watergate matter.
—It was not until the time of my own investigation that I learned

of the break-in at the office of Mr. Ellsberg's psychiatrist, and I specifically authorized the furnishing of this information to Judge Byrne.

—I neither authorized nor encouraged subordinates to engage in illegal or improper campaign tactics.

President Nixon admitted in his statement that he had approved wiretapping the conversations of Daniel L. Ellsberg and others to discover the identities of persons leaking information affecting national security, that he had temporarily sanctioned the Huston intelligence plan to ascertain the identities of domestic subversives and foreign agents, and that he had authorized the creation of the Plumbers to learn in the interest of national security the motives that had prompted the past actions of Ellsberg and might influence his future conduct.

President Nixon asserted in his statement that these projects were unrelated to Watergate and the presidential election of 1972. While this was true, these projects involved efforts by persons connected with the White House to gather information desired by the White House by surreptitious methods similar to those employed in Watergate. Hence, evidence of them was relevant in law and logic to prove the identities, the knowledge, the intent, and the motives of those responsible for Watergate.

The President also asserted in his statement that he did not contemplate that the Plumbers would use illegal means to accomplish their mission, and that he withdrew his approval of the Huston plan after five days because J. Edgar Hoover condemned it as illegal. While his assertion relating to the Huston plan was subsequently corroborated by Mitchell, it is noteworthy that Tom Charles Huston testified before a House committee that the President did not formally withdraw his approval of the plan at any time.

President Nixon further declared in his statement that someone, whom he did not name, had suggested to him that the FBI investigation of the Mexican bank transaction impinged on a covert action of the CIA in Mexico, and that he had instructed Haldeman and Ehrlichman to contact the CIA about it before he discovered the suggestion to be unfounded.

Ziegler delivered copies of the President's May 22 statement to the newsmen covering the White House, and immediately after such delivery Garment and Buzhardt undertook to answer the questions the statement provoked in their minds. By this process the White House made certain that no newsman could put an inquiry to President Nixon concerning the events covered by the statement.

When I was in Winston-Salem, North Carolina, on May 31, 1973, a newsman asked me what I thought of the Huston intelligence plan, and I stated I thought it revealed a "Gestapo mentality." I still maintain this was a sound appraisal of a scheme designed to confer on a federal investigatory officer the arbitrary power to commit an illegal burglary to spy on any human being within the borders of the United States whom he might consider in the exercise of his unbridled discretion to be an "internal security target."

Everything activated by Watergate was not somber. My wife and I resided in an apartment in the Methodist Building in Washington. Inasmuch as we shared the view that public servants ought to be accessible to the public, our telephone was listed in the Washington telephone directory. From time to time our nocturnal repose was shattered at two or three o'clock in the morning by telephone calls from concerned citizens who had imbibed too freely of potent beverages and wanted to discuss with me at those untoward hours what they called affairs of state. We endured these tribulations with fortitude in order to preserve my accessibility to my constituents.

After I became chairman of the Senate Select Committee, our listed telephone rang at all hours of the night with calls from all areas of the nation, including distant Alaska and Hawaii. Some of the calls came from representatives of the news media seeking information. Others came from curious-minded individuals who merely desired to converse with someone who had suddenly acquired notoriety. Some came from persons who can be best described as unusual.

One of the last group called me from someplace in Kentucky every night and talked to me by long-distance telephone thirty or forty minutes. He assured me he was a minister of the Gospel, that he was in daily communication with the Almighty in respect to Watergate, and that the Almighty had instructed him to relay to me each day what the Almighty had told him that day about Watergate.

If I had given full credence to what my informant said the Almighty told him about Watergate, I would have lost my faith in the theological doctrine of the omniscience of God. This is so because my informant said the Almighty told him the chief culprit in Watergate was one of the innocents, Vice-President Spiro T. Agnew.

On one occasion I asked my informant if he would make a supplication to the Almighty in my behalf. After assuring me he would be pleased to do so, he inquired, "What do you want me to ask the Good Lord?" I replied, "Please ask him to make his revelations about Watergate directly to me. Since the Good Lord has to look after this earth, all its inhabitants, and the entire universe, he couldn't possibly spend as much time talking to me about Watergate as you do." Although my request seemed to offend my informant, it did not deter him from calling me again the next night.

When he called, he said he wanted the Senate Select Committee to call him as its first witness in the hearings, which were scheduled to begin in a few days. He added that he had just talked to the Almighty about this, and that the Almighty had told him to tell me to call him first. I advised him I hated to disobey the Almighty's instruction, and we'd be delighted to welcome the Almighty as the lead-off witness, but we couldn't permit the informant to enact the role because he didn't know anything about Watergate except what the Almighty had told him and somebody might object to his testimony because it was hearsay.

After he had hung up and I had sat down, our phone rang again. My wife answered it, and discovered that my Kentucky informant was calling again. When he ascertained her identity, he told her he believed it would be all right with the Almighty for him to relay to her what He had said that day about Watergate and let her recount it to me.

My wife, who is always patient, listened to him until he hung up. She then said, "We'll get an unlisted telephone tomorrow." We did. Our repose in the future was more peaceful than it had been in the recent past.

9

SENATE
COMMITTEE
HEARINGS

IN the light of the public investigations of the Senate Select Committee, the impeachment deliberations of the House Judiciary Committee, and the criminal trials of the prominent suspects conducted before Judge Sirica and the jury by the staff of Special Prosecutor Leon Jaworski, it is difficult to realize in retrospect that in May 1973 the truth respecting Watergate was still substantially unknown.

Investigative reporters, such as Carl Bernstein, Bob Woodward, Seymour Hersh, and Clark Mollenhoff, had dug up much information about Watergate. This information was fragmentary, however, and like an unassembled picture puzzle with crucial pieces missing. Besides, it must be remembered, the existence of President Nixon's tapes had not yet been revealed.

The Senate Select Committee opened its hearings on May 17, 1973, in the spacious and marble-columned Senate Caucus Room on the third floor of the Old Senate Office Building, which in times past had been the site of the Teapot Dome, the Kefauver crime, the Army-McCarthy, and the McCarthy censure hearings.

Newspapers, magazines, radio, and television covered the public hearings in unprecedented fashion. In so doing, they enacted admirably the role of the free press under the First Amendment.

The national television networks, ABC, CBS, and NBC carried the public hearings live in their entirety, largely on a rotating basis, from the opening day through September 26. The public television networks telecast all the public hearings live gavel to gavel, and rebroadcast them in the evenings.

As a consequence, millions of Americans saw and heard the witnesses as they testified, judged for themselves their respective credibilities, and formed their own judgment as to what Watergate was all about. The thousands of communications they sent the committee proved there is a tremendous reservoir of intellectual honesty and morality in America.

In conformity with custom, the Senate Select Committee received the opening statements of its members before taking the testimony of its first witness. I quote excerpts from these statements in the order in which they were made. As chairman, I said in part:

> We are beginning these hearings today in an atmosphere of the utmost gravity. The questions that have been raised in the wake of the June 17 break-in strike at the very undergirding of our democracy. If the allegations made to this date are true, then the burglars who broke into the headquarters of the Democratic National Committee at the Watergate were in effect breaking into the home of every citizen of the United States. And if these allegations prove to be true, what they were seeking to steal was not the jewels, money, or other property of American citizens, but something much more valuable— their most precious heritage: The right to vote in a free election. . . . The clear mandate of the unanimous Senate resolution provides for a bipartisan investigation of every phase of political espionage and illegal fund-raising. Thus it is clear that we have the full responsibility to recommend any remedial legislation necessary.
>
> In pursuing its task, it is clear that the committee will be dealing with the workings of the democratic process under which we operate in a nation that is still the last, best hope of mankind in his eternal struggle to govern himself decently and effectively.
>
> We will be concerned with the integrity of a governmental system designed by men who understood the lessons of the past and who, accordingly, established a framework of separated governmental powers in order to prevent any one branch of the Government from becoming dominant over the others. The Founding Fathers, having participated in the struggle against arbitrary power, comprehended some eternal truths respecting men and government. They knew that those who are entrusted with power are susceptible to the disease of tyrants, which George Washington rightly described as "love of power and the proneness to abuse it." For that reason, they realized that the power of public officers should be defined by laws which

they, as well as the people, are obligated to obey, a truth enunciated by Daniel Webster when he said that "whatever government is not a government of laws is a despotism, let it be called what it may."

To the end of insuring a society governed by laws, these men embodied in our Constitution the enduring principles in which they so firmly believed, establishing a legislature to make all laws, an executive to carry them out, and a judicial system to interpret them. Recently, we have been faced with massive challenges to the historical framework created in 1787, with the most recent fears having been focused upon assertions by administrations of both parties of executive power over the Congress—for example, in the impoundment of appropriated funds and the abuse of executive privilege. Those challenges, however, can and are being dealt with by the working of the system itself—that is, through the enactment of powerful statutes by the Congress, and the rendering of decisions by the courts upholding the lawmaking power of the Congress.

In dealing with the challenges posed by the multitudinous allegations arising out of the Watergate affair, however, the Select Committee has a task much more difficult and complex than dealing with intrusions of one branch of the government upon the powers of the others. It must probe into assertions that the very system itself has been subverted and its foundations shaken.

My colleagues on the committee and I are determined to uncover all the relevant facts surrounding these matters, and to spare no one, whatever his station in life may be, in our efforts to accomplish that goal. At the same time, I want to emphasize that the purpose of these hearings is not prosecutorial or judicial, but rather investigative and informative.

I was followed by Senator Baker, who, as vice-chairman, rendered alert and cooperative service to the committee at all times. In reiterating the query "What did the President know and when did he know it?" Senator Baker expressed the anxiety of multitudes of Americans. In his opening statement, he said:

The very integrity of our political process itself has been called into question. . . . This committee is not a court, nor is it a jury. We do not sit to pass judgment on the guilt or innocence of anyone. The greatest service this committee can perform for the Senate, the Congress, and for the people of this nation is to achieve a full discovery of all the facts that bear on the subject of this inquiry. This committee was created by the Senate to do exactly that. . . . Virtually every action taken by this committee since its inception has been taken with complete unanimity of purpose and procedure. The integrity and fairness of each member and of its fine professional staff have been made manifest to me, and I know they will be made manifest to the American people during the course of this proceeding. This is not in any way a partisan undertaking, but, rather, it is a bipartisan search for the unvarnished truth.

Throughout the hearings Senator Talmadge exhibited an uncanny capacity to put to witnesses questions that went to the heart of the issues. In his opening statement, he declared:

> The vote of the Senate was nonpartisan, being unanimous. This committee has been organized on a nonpartisan basis . . . In my judgment, this committee must get the facts, the full facts, and all the facts on a totally objective, nonpartisan basis, and let the chips fall where they may.

Senator Talmadge was followed by Senator Gurney, a strong conservative, who had suffered disabling wounds and received decorations for valor while serving with the American army in the European theater in the Second World War. His vigorous cross-examination of some of the witnesses materially aided the committee in its search for truth. In his opening statement, he said in part:

> This committee begins today historic hearings which may well turn out to be the most significant hearings ever conducted by any committee of Congress. . . . Between the work of prosecutors, grand jury, excellent investigative reporting, and this committee, Watergate is going to be cleaned up. . . . What is of great concern is the effect that Watergate may have on the American Presidency. . . . The sense of history rides with these hearings. And this thought should guide our work to the ends that it be thorough, yes, completely thorough, but always careful, deliberate, responsible, statesmanlike to the end that the system of government and justice of a free and democratic society, these United States, will work its will in a fair and impartial and objective manner.

Senator Inouye was born in Hawaii of Japanese ancestry. I have never known a more patriotic American. He served in Italy with an American unit recruited in Hawaii during the Second World War, lost his right arm as a result of wounds, and was awarded the Distinguished Service Cross for extraordinary heroism in action. He is exceedingly alert, and has a fine sense of humor. During an executive session of the Senate Select Committee, a member made a motion and I said, "All who favor the motion raise their right hands." Senator Inouye said, "Mr. Chairman, are you trying to disfranchise me? I have no right hand." I said, "You may raise your left."

Senator Inouye made these observations in his opening statement:

> The hearings which we begin today may be the most important held in this century. At stake is the very integrity of the election process. . . . These hearings should serve to enlighten and reform. They should lay the groundwork for a reaffirmation of faith in our American system.

Senator Weicker served the committee with great energy and diligence. In his opening statement he made these trenchant remarks:

> A few men gambled that Americans wanted the guilt of efficiency rather than the turbulence of truth. And they were stopped a yard short of the goal by another few, who believed in America as advertised. So the story to come has its significance not in the acts of men breaking, entering, and bugging the Watergate, but in the acts of men who almost—who almost—stole America.

Senator Montoya exhibited a remarkable judicial temperament during the hearings. In his opening statement, he said:

> We hope to alert the conscience and the vigilance of our citizens, . . . restore their faith in our electoral process, . . . and insure against any future sinister invasions of the sanctity of our democratic institutions.

The staff was extremely diligent in interviewing prospective witnesses and assembling documentary evidence. As a consequence, the Senate Select Committee took the testimony of sixty-three witnesses in fifty-three days of public hearings during the period beginning on May 17 and ending on November 15, 1973. Each of these witnesses made an opening statement without interruption, and was then subjected to questioning by the chief counsel or one of his assistants, the minority counsel or one of his assistants, and the seven committee members.

The first phase of the public hearings dealt with the planning and perpetrating of the break-in and the bugging of the offices of the Democratic National Committee in the Watergate and the ensuing cover-up of the activities and identities of the responsible CREEP officials and White House aides, and was completed during the first thirty-nine days of hearings.

The second phase of the public hearings focused on political espionage and political "dirty tricks," and occupied nine days of hearings. The third phase of the public hearings probed allegations of illegal campaign contributions, and exhausted the last five days of the hearings.

For reasons that will be revealed later, the Senate Select Committee held no other public hearings. At various times during the remainder of 1973 and until its expiration on June 30, 1974, the committee took the testimony of numerous witnesses respecting political contributions made by the dairy industry, the mysterious $100,000 contribution which the agents of the tycoon, Howard Hughes, delivered to President Nixon's intimate friend, Charles G. ("Bebe") Rebozo, and related matters.

Most of the witnesses appearing before the committee were forthright and helpful. The faulty recollections, which some of them professed, indicated, however, an acceptance of the doctrine that sometimes a good "forgettery" may be better than a good memory—a doctrine which his secret tape of March 21, 1973, shows that President Nixon expounded to Haldeman and Dean when he undertook to explain to them how White House aides could testify about Watergate-related matters. The professed ignorance of a few witnesses concerning crucial events which they had full opportunity to know, and which normal curiosity on their part would have caused them to know, indicated that they knew the maxim "Where ignorance is bliss, 'tis folly to be wise."

In addition, the committee collected substantial documentary evidence, largely in the form of memorandums addressed to Haldeman by White House aide Fred Malex, relating to the "Responsiveness Program," the program under which federal programs were diverted from their true purposes to further the reelection of President Nixon.

The Senate Select Committee was also involved in much litigation with various persons who did not want the truth about Watergate revealed. Since Samuel Dash's book *Chief Counsel* and James Hamilton's book, *The Power to Probe*, ably delineate the issues involved in this litigation, I omit all reference to it except some subsequent comments on the committee suit seeking access to presidential tapes and papers.

Despite the unceasing efforts of the White House to stymie the investigation and the inability of the Senate Select Committee to obtain access to President Nixon's secret tapes after it had discovered their existence, the committee conducted a thorough investigation, which revealed the truth concerning both the first and second Watergate conspiracies. The printed record of its activities total 16,091 pages. Approximately 11,700 of them are required to detail the oral and documentary testimony it received.

Consideration of space and time preclude any detailed recital of this great mass of evidence. The specific nature of much of it and what it established in respect to the first Watergate conspiracy has been disclosed on previous pages.

Before recounting some of the highlights of the testimony, I will state with succinctness what it revealed with respect to the second conspiracy.

The arrest of McCord and the four Cubans in the Watergate created consternation in CREEP and the White House. Thereupon various officers and employees of CREEP and various White House aides undertook to conceal from law enforcement officers, prosecutors, grand jurors, courts, the news media, and the American people the activities and identities of those officers and employees of CREEP and those White House aides who had participated in any way in the Watergate affair.

Various officers and employees of CREEP and various White House aides engaged in one or more of these acts to make the concealment effective and thus obstruct the due administration of justice:

1. They destroyed the records of CREEP antedating the burglary and the bugging.

2. They induced the acting director of the FBI, who was a Nixon appointee, to destroy the State Department documents which E. Howard Hunt had been falsifying.

3. They obtained from the acting director of the FBI copies of scores of interviews conducted by FBI agents in connection with their investigation of the burglary and the bugging, and were enabled thereby to coach their confederates to give false and misleading statements to the FBI.

4. They sought to persuade the FBI to refrain from investigating the sources of the campaign funds that were used to finance the burglary and the bugging.

5. They intimidated employees of CREEP and employees of the White House by having their lawyers present when these employees were being questioned by agents of the FBI, and thus deterred these employees from making full disclosures to the FBI.

6. They lied to agents of the FBI, prosecutors, and grand jurors who undertook to investigate the burglary and the bugging, and to Judge Sirica and the petit jurors who tried the seven original Watergate defendants in January 1973.

7. They persuaded the Department of Justice and the prosecutors to take out-of-court statements from President Nixon's chief campaign fund-raiser, Maurice Stans, White House aides Charles Colson, Egil Krogh, and David Young, and Charles Colson's secretary, instead of requiring them to testify before the grand jury investigating the burglary and the bugging in conformity with the established procedures governing such matters, and thus denied the grand jurors the opportunity to question them.

8. They persuaded the Department of Justice and the prosecutors to refrain from asking Donald Segretti, their chief hired saboteur, any questions involving Herbert W. Kalmbach, President Nixon's personal attorney, who was known by them to have paid Segretti for "dirty tricks" he perpetrated upon honorable men seeking the Democratic presidential nomination, and who was subsequently identified as one who played a major role in the secret delivery of "hush money" to the seven original Watergate defendants.

9. They made cash payments totaling hundreds of thousands of dollars out of campaign funds in surreptitious ways to the seven original Watergate defendants as "hush money" to buy their silence and keep them from revealing their knowledge of the activities and identities of the officers and employees of CREEP and the White House aides who participated in Watergate.

10. They gave assurances to some of the original seven Watergate defendants that they would receive presidential clemency after serving short portions of their sentences if they refrained from divulging the activities and identities of the officers and employees of CREEP and of the White House aides who had participated in the Watergate affair.

11. They made arrangements by which the attorneys who represented the seven original Watergate defendants received their fees in cash from moneys that had been collected to finance President Nixon's re-election campaign.

12. They induced the Department of Justice and the prosecutors of the seven original Watergate defendants to assure the news media and the general public that there was no evidence that any persons other than the seven original Watergate defendants were implicated in any way in any Watergate-related crimes.

13. They inspired massive efforts on the part of segments of the news media friendly to the administration to persuade the American people that most of the members of the Select Committee named by the Senate to investigate Watergate were biased and irresponsible men motivated solely by desires to exploit the matters they investigated for personal or partisan advantage, and that the allegations in the press that presidential aides had been involved in Watergate were venomous machinations of a hostile and unreliable press bent on destroying the country's confidence in a great and good President.

One shudders to think that the Watergate conspiracies might have been effectively concealed and their most dramatic episode dismissed as a "third-rate" burglary conceived and committed solely by the seven original Watergate defendants had it not been for the courage and penetrating understanding of Judge Sirica, the thoroughness of the investigative reporting of Carl Bernstein, Bob Woodward, Seymour Hersh, Clark Mollenhoff, and other representatives of a free press, the devotion to their First Amendment responsibilities of the *Washington Post, The New York Times, Time* magazine, *Newsweek*, and other publications, the labors of the Senate Select Committee and its excellent staff, and the dedication and diligence of Special Prosecutors Archibald Cox and Leon Jaworski and their associates.

10

THE NIXON
WHITE HOUSE

For convenience of narration, I state from time to time that the White House or CREEP took actions of questionable legality or morality. In so doing, I do not refer to the many men and women employed in the White House or at CREEP who did their work during the days of Watergate with fidelity to law and ethics. I refer to the handful of men responsible for the questionable actions.

In explaining why Watergate happened, Dean said: "The Watergate matter was an inevitable outgrowth of a climate of excessive concern over the political impact of demonstrators, excessive concern over leaks, an insatiable appetite for political intelligence, all coupled with a do-it-yourself staff, regardless of the law."

The explanation for the existence of this climate may be found in the character of President Nixon. It is noteworthy that none of the men who pleaded or were adjudged guilty of obstruction of justice in the Watergate affair had ever had any experience in government or politics apart from his association with Nixon.

During Nixon's administration our country was torn asunder by the war in Vietnam. President Nixon and some of his closest White House aides viewed those who demonstrated against our participation in the war and the drafting of men for service in it as enemies of Nixon and

America, and not as free Americans exercising the right of dissent guaranteed them by the First Amendment.

As time passed, they developed a siege mentality, and added to their category of Nixon's enemies editors, journalists, labor leaders, lawyers, and others whose only offense was that they opposed the Nixon administration policies.

As counsel to the President, Dean drew up a confidential memorandum "on dealing with our political enemies," and Colson prepared a list of twenty persons who he thought ought to be dealt with as enemies on a priority basis. According to Dean's confidential memorandum, the White House was to use "available federal machinery," such as Internal Revenue Service tax audits, denial of federal grants, and criminal prosecutions and civil suits to harass persons opposed to the Nixon administration. The memorandum was devised to enable the White House, in Dean's inelegant phrase, to "screw" its enemies.

Dean brought copies of his confidential memorandum, Colson's priority list of Nixon's enemies, and the Huston plan with him when he left the White House, and they were offered in evidence during the Select Committee's hearings. The part of the Huston plan relating to foreign intelligence, however, was withheld by the committee.

According to testimony received by the committee, the White House frequently attempted to induce the Internal Revenue Service to institute punitive tax audits against persons inimical to the Nixon administration. On one occasion, so Dean said, the White House caused the Internal Revenue Service to institute a punitive tax audit against a reporter because he wrote an article critical of Nixon's friend, Rebozo.

This intriguing question arises: Did Dean's confidential memorandum relating to "dealing with our enemies" reflect the mind and heart of President Nixon?

During the consideration of impeachment, the impeachment inquiry staff deciphered President Nixon's secret tape of September 15, 1972, fully and completely and presented a transcript of it to the House Judiciary Committee. This transcript revealed that when they met in the secrecy of the Oval Office on that day, President Nixon, Haldeman, and Dean made these statements:

> PRESIDENT NIXON: I would not want to be in Edward Bennett Williams' position after this election. . . . We're going after him.
> HALDEMAN: That is a guy we've got to ruin.

PRESIDENT NIXON: You want to remember, too, he's an attorney for the Washington Post.

DEAN: I'm well aware of that.

PRESIDENT NIXON: I think we are going to fix the son of a bitch. Believe me. We are going to. We've got to, because he's a bad man.

DEAN: Absolutely . . . I've tried to . . . keep notes on a lot of the people who are emerging . . . as less than our friends.

PRESIDENT NIXON: Great.

DEAN: Because this is going to be over someday, . . . We shouldn't forget the way some of them have treated us.

PRESIDENT NIXON: I want the most comprehensive notes on all of those that tried to do us in. . . . They didn't have to do it. . . . I mean if . . . they had a very close election everybody on the other side would understand this game. But now they are doing this quite deliberately and they are asking for it and they are going to get it. We have not used this power in this first four years. . . . We have never used it. We haven't used the Bureau and we haven't used the Justice Department, but things are going to change now. . . . They're going to get it right.

DEAN: That's an exciting prospect.

PRESIDENT NIXON: It's got to be done. It's the only thing to do.

HALDEMAN: We've got to.

PRESIDENT NIXON: We've been just God damn fools. For us to come into this election campaign and not to do anything with regard to the Democratic Senators who are running, and so forth. That'd be . . . absolutely ridiculous. It's not going . . . to be that way any more. . .

PRESIDENT NIXON: . . . .The Post is going to have damnable . . . problems out of this one. They have a television station.

DEAN: That's right, they do.

HALDEMAN: They have a radio station, too.

PRESIDENT NIXON: Does that come up too? The point is, when does it come up?

DEAN: I don't know. But the practice of non-licensees filing on top of licensees has certainly gotten more active in the area.

PRESIDENT NIXON: And it's going to be God damn active here . . . the game has to be played rough.

Edward Bennett Williams was apparently a bad man who needed ruining in the eyes of Nixon and Haldeman simply because he was an able lawyer who happened to be attorney for the *Washington Post* and the Democratic National Committee.

The Nixon White House undertook to use the Internal Revenue Service to aid its friends as well as to punish its enemies, and to divert federal contracts, grants, and loans under its Responsiveness Program from their true statutory purposes to further President Nixon's re-election. Besides it used much energy to devise ways to intimidate news media it deemed unfavorable to President Nixon by threats such as antitrust suits.

The Nixon White House's insatiable appetite for intelligence was manifested in many ways. The Special Services was established in the Internal Revenue Service to do something alien to tax-gathering, i.e., to investigate individuals and organizations deemed hostile to the Nixon administration. Employees of the National Security Agency suspected of leaking data and journalists suspected of receiving them were subjected to warrantless wiretaps. Under the Huston plan, governmental investigative agencies were to spy on any American deemed to be a target of intelligence interest, and President Nixon personally approved the plan at least temporarily. At President Nixon's direction, Ehrlichman created the Plumbers to make investigations not sanctioned by law, and the Plumbers burglarized the office of Dr. Fielding to obtain data not admissable in evidence in courts of law. The White House had the telephone of Nixon's brother, Donald Nixon, tapped, and caused the FBI to make a full field investigation of Daniel Schorr, a CBS newsman, because his comments were not favorable to the administration. Finally, CREEP hired persons to infiltrate by deception the organizations of persons seeking the Democratic nomination to oppose Nixon's reelection, and surreptitiously to transmit to it information relating to their plans and purposes.

The Nixon White House habitually sought to divert attention from criticism of President Nixon by red-herring tactics which did not scruple to impugn the characters of others. When the press began to make caustic comments about President Nixon's federal income tax returns and payments in December 1973, the Nixon White House, acting through an unidentified aide, made Senator Weicker and me victims of this propensity by issuing a statement to the news media asserting that questions ought to be asked about our income tax returns. Senator Weicker and I immediately inserted copies of our 1972 federal income tax returns—the only ones we had in Washington—in the *Congressional Record*. At the time, I made this statement:

> In view of the fact that I have never made any statement whatsoever relating to the controversy raging about the President's income tax returns, I am somewhat surprised to hear this statement made. I have been preparing my own federal and state tax returns for about

50 years now. When I practiced law, I did not prepare income tax returns for clients, but I did prepare many inheritance tax returns which were filed both with State and Federal taxing authorities. And it is my proud boast that every tax return I have ever filed . . . has been accepted by the Federal and State tax authorities just as I wrote it.

This is the first time in 50 years that anyone has ever questioned the accuracy of my income tax returns. And it is done by a man who . . . has not got enough courage to identify himself. It is done in the form of attempting to drag a red herring across the trail. Mr. President, I withdraw the term "red herring," because I think this is a putrefied minnow instead of a red herring.

11

FINANCING
WATERGATE

WHEN it adopted Senate Resolution 60 without a dissenting vote, the Senate gave the Select Committee the mandate to determine by investigation and study whether any illegal acts, or improper acts, or any unethical acts had been committed by any persons in the presidential election of 1972.

In so doing, the Senate expressly empowered the Select Committee to discharge these functions: first, to inform the Congress and the American people whether any illegal, improper, or unethical acts had been committed in such election; second, to ascertain whether existing laws were sufficient to prevent or punish the repetition of such acts, if they had been committed; and, third, to recommend the enactment of new congressional legislation to effect that purpose in the event it ascertained that existing laws were insufficient to do so because of deficiencies in them or because they did not cover such acts.

The circumstance that the acts of the witness did not violate an existing law did not impair the power or the duty of the Select Committee to interrogate him in respect to them. The resolution expressly provided that in that event the committee could interrogate the witness to ascertain if his legal acts were improper or unethical, or ought to be made illegal by Congress in the public interest.

In approving Senate Resolution 60, the Senate was aware that money sometimes has a corrupting influence in politics.

Consequently it conferred on the Select Committee the specific power to investigate these things:

1. "Any transactions or circumstances relating to the source, the control, the transmission, the deposit, the storage, the concealment, the expenditure, or use of any moneys . . . collected or received for actual or pretended use in the presidential elction of 1972 . . ."

2. Whether any of these moneys "were placed in any secret fund or place of storage for use in financing any activity which was sought to be concealed from the public, and if so, what disbursement or expenditure was made of such secret fund, and the identities of any person or group of persons . . . having any control over such secret fund or the disbursement or expenditure of the same."

3. "Whether any . . . records, . . . relating to any matters . . . the Select Committee is authorized and directed to investigate . . . have been concealed, suppressed, or destroyed by any persons . . . , and if so the identities and motives of any such persons . . ."

When it exercised this specific power, the Select Committee discovered these astounding and indisputable facts:

1. The finance arm of CREEP maintained a secret fund in cash aggregating $1,777,000 altogether in safes in its Washington offices, which were controlled by its director, Stans, and its treasurer, Sloan.

2. The finance arm of CREEP disbursed $1,027,000 of this secret fund in cash to finance activities of the political arm of CREEP and purposely concealed this disbursal from the public.

3. The burglary and the bugging of the Democratic National Committee's offices in the Watergate were financed out of cash sums totaling $199,000 which Sloan took from this secret fund and delivered in installments to Liddy, the chief counsel of the finance arm of CREEP, on the instructions of Magruder, the deputy director of the political arm of CREEP.

4. The records of the finance arm of CREEP relating to the secret fund were destroyed within a few days after the burglars were caught in the offices of the Democratic National Committee in the Watergate with forty-five $100 bills which came from the secret fund in their possession.

The Select Committee called on Stans and Sloan for an explanation of these matters. Sloan told the committee freely and fully all he knew about them. At the conclusion of his testimony I observed that he had "strengthened my faith in the old adage that an honest man is the noblest work of God."

Much of the evidence given by Sloan is recounted in other contexts. I state at this point only what he told the committee concerning the secret fund, the transactions of Liddy and Barker in respect to the Mexican and Dahlberg checks, and the destruction of the records relating to the secret fund.

According to him, the secret fund had two sources. A substantial part of it was delivered to the finance arm of CREEP by Kalmbach, and represented unspent contributions remaining from Nixon's 1968 presidential campaign.

Prior to April 7, 1972, when the Federal Election Campaign Act repealed and superseded the Corrupt Practices Act, the law required public reporting of contributions and expenditures connected with a presidential election, but not contributions and expenditures related to a quest for a presidential nomination.

The varying provisions of the two acts were construed to make contributions and expenditures antedating April 7, 1972, unreportable. According to Sloan, Stans procured an avalanche of contributions for President Nixon just before April 7, 1972, by exploiting this circumstance and assuring the donors their identities and the amounts of their contributions would not be revealed. A substantial part of these pre-April 7 contributions were stored in the safes controlled by Stans and Sloan, and constituted the second source of the secret cash fund. Among them were the $112,000 portion of the proceeds of the Mexican and Dahlberg checks which Barker had remitted through Liddy to the finance arm of CREEP.

In explaining why Liddy had transmitted the Mexican and Dahlberg checks to Barker for collection, Sloan testified that Liddy, as chief legal adviser of the finance arm of CREEP, had informed Stans and him that under the law CREEP could distribute large contributions in allotments of $3,000 to different committees supporting Nixon, and thus relieve the contributors involved of liability for federal taxes on gifts of $25,000 or more. Sloan stated, in substance, that Liddy's action was simply designed to convert the checks into cash, and to enable the finance arm of CREEP to comply with this provision of law in behalf of the donors of the moneys represented by these checks.

Sloan affirmed that the secret fund totaled $1,777,000 altogether, that $750,000 of it was eventually deposited in banks, and that the other $1,027,000 was disbursed to Liddy and various others in cash.

As treasurer of the finance arm of CREEP, Sloan kept original records of cash contributions received, and cash disbursements made. The records showed the amount, the date, and the name of the recipient of each cash disbursement. These original records were destroyed by Sloan on June 23, 1972, six days after the Watergate break-in.

In explaining his action, Sloan testified that at Stans's request he had prepared a single summary of all cash transactions of the finance arm of CREEP down to April 7, 1972, and given it to Stans upon the assumption that Stans would preserve it as the permanent record of such transactions. After so doing, Sloan testified further, he destroyed the original records at the suggestion of Kalmbach, who told him he was destroying his own records. The summary he gave Stans, Sloan explained, was a compilation in aggregate form of his original records. For example, Sloan said, the summary he gave Stans listed Liddy as receiving a total of $199,000 without setting forth the dates of his receipt of the various constituent parts of the total.

As Deputy Postmaster General and director of the Bureau of the Budget under President Eisenhower and Secretary of Commerce under President Nixon, Maurice H. Stans, who possessed a brilliant intellect, rendered valuable public services to the nation. When he testified before the Select Committee, Stans asserted that he had no personal knowledge of the Watergate break-in and bugging, that he did not participate in any efforts to cover them up, and that he had no information concerning any of these events except that gleaned by him from the news media.

He also asserted, in essence, that all actions taken by the finance arm of CREEP and himself in connection with President Nixon's re-election campaign were above reproach. His demeanor in testifying indicated to me that Stans deemed it an unpardonable sin for any member of the Select Committee or its staff to doubt or question his immaculate appraisal of his conduct or that of the finance arm of CREEP.

Stans justified the action of the finance arm of CREEP in maintaining the secret fund and using nontraceable cash from it to finance hidden activities of the political arm of CREEP on the ground that no law forbade such conduct. He testified that the records relating to the secret fund were destroyed simply to preserve the confidentiality of persons who had made contributions to Nixon's presidential campaign before April 7, 1972, and because he no longer had any need for them.

No law required the finance arm of CREEP to report to any public official its receipts and disbursements of contributions antedating April 7, 1972. Stans asserted that the lack of such a reporting requirement freed the finance arm of CREEP of any obligation to keep or preserve any records of such matters, authorized it to destroy any such records as it had, and gave to persons making contributions to it before April 7, 1972, inviolable rights to have their identities and the amounts of their contributions kept secret. He further maintained that the rights of these contributors nullified any rights of the American people to know the identities and motives of those who were seeking by their contributions to influence the selection of the President of the United States.

Stans affirmed that the destruction of records of the secret fund was unrelated to Watergate, and that the fact that they were destroyed shortly after the burglars were apprehended in the offices of the Democratic National Committee was a "pure and innocent coincidence."

Stans invoked the structural setup of the Committees to Elect the President to justify his claim that neither the acts nor the omissions of the finance arm of CREEP or himself could be justly charged with any responsibility whatever for Watergate.

He asserted that the sole function of the finance arm of CREEP was to raise sufficient moneys to finance the activities of the political arm of CREEP, and that neither it nor he had any obligation or power to determine whether those activities were lawful or unlawful and did not attempt at any time to do so. He maintained that the validity of this assertion was not impaired in any way by the circumstance that he and two other members of the finance arm were members of a six-man budget committee which budgeted the expenditures of the moneys collected by the finance arm to defray the costs of the activities of the political arm. He vehemently denied that he had any obligation as director of the finance arm of CREEP to determine why Liddy, its chief legal adviser, was receiving thousands of dollars in cash from his committee's secret fund to carry out some project for Magruder, the deputy director of the political arm of CREEP, of which he was ignorant. He conceded, however, that he made no real effort to ascertain the truth in respect to this matter, notwithstanding he, Liddy, and Magruder had offices in the same building and he had ample opportunity to query them about it.

The views expressed by Stans in his testimony were incompatible with these basic convictions of mine:

—The managers of presidential campaigns exercise enormous

142

political power, and their conduct ought to be guided by ethical considerations that transcend the minimum requirements of criminal laws.

—The lack of a law prohibiting improper activities does not confer sanctity upon them. It discloses the need for the enactment of a law outlawing them.

—The people of our land have an inherent right to know the identities and motives of those who make enormous contributions to influence the selection of their President.

—Irrespective of legal requirements, those who manage the moneys of others for political purposes have an ethical obligation to the public to make and preserve accurate records of their receipts and disbursements, and this ethical obligation ought to prompt them to deposit their receipts in banks and to make their disbursements by checks.

—If they maintain secret funds and finance hidden political activities by nontraceable cash, they damage irreparably the confidence of the public in the integrity of the political process. This is true because such secret political activities become known sooner or later, and engender in the minds of the people the conviction that politicians love darkness rather than light because their deeds are evil.

—Those who solicit, receive, and disburse contributions for political purposes are obligated to their contributors and to our country to take appropriate steps to ensure that those contributions are not used to finance criminal activities.

As director of the finance arm of CREEP, Stans was obligated to direct and control its activities. As a consequence, I was unable to give intellectual assent to the proposition that he had no obligation whatever to determine why Liddy, whom he had employed to render legal services to his committee, was receiving thousands of dollars in cash from his committee's funds.

Under Senate Resolution 60, the Select Committee was commanded and empowered to seek the truth in respect to the activities of the finance arm of CREEP, and to recommend the enactment of congressional legislation which the truth relating to them made appropriate.

In a conscientious effort to assist the committee to perform its mission, I interrogated Stans with much vigor because I honestly believed that was the only way in which the committee could perform its mission. My questions sought information concerning his views, acts, and omissions in respect to the matters the committee was expressly authorized and directed to investigate.

Stans admitted he had destroyed Sloan's summary of the cash transactions of his arm of CREEP after the break-in. He dismissed as "pure and innocent coincidence" the fact that his destruction of the summary occurred after the burglars had been arrested in the Watergate.

As one who had achieved fame and fortune in private life as an accountant and investment banker, Stans must have known the value of financial records as evidence of truth. He assured the committee, however, that he had simple reasons which justified his destruction of the records of the cash transactions of his committee, notwithstanding it handled money entrusted to it by others to further President Nixon's political fortunes.

After all, he said, the law justified his action because it did not require his committee to keep any record of anything it did before April 7, 1972. Besides, he said, he kept the summary on his desk several days, and ascertained from it the names of contributors of cash and the unexpended balance of cash on hand, which were the only entries in it of interest to him. Since it was neither his "concern nor interest to know who the disbursements" of cash "had gone to," he had no further use for the summary, and destroyed it. He added that he knew he could reconstruct the information in the summary if he had any occasion for so doing.

Finally and most important, Stans declared, he destroyed the final record of all the cash transactions of his committee to ensure that the names of those who made cash contributions to it before April 7, 1972, would not be revealed. The record of a disbursement in cash does not reveal the identity of the donor of the cash disbursed. Hence, the assertion of Stans that he destroyed the summary to protect the confidentiality of donors did not seem to afford a scintilla of justification for his destruction of the records the Select Committee was seeking—the records of the cash disbursements to Liddy which financed the Watergate affair.

Consequently, I observed to Stans that his simple reasons for his destructive action were "too simple for me to understand."

Stans admitted that he temporarily loaned $50,000 out of his committee's cash to Alexander Lankler, a Maryland Republican leader, to mix temporarily with other receipts of a fund-raising dinner honoring

Vice-President Agnew. I put these questions to Stans and received these answers from him concerning this temporary loan:

> QUESTION: And they wanted to make it appear that they took in $50,000 more than they actually took in, didn't they?
> ANSWER: They wanted to make it look more successful than it apparently was.
> QUESTION: In other words, they wanted to practice a deception on the general public as to the amount of honor that was paid to the Vice President.
> ANSWER: Mr. Chairman, I am not sure this is the first time that has happened in American politics.
> QUESTION: You know, there have been murder and larceny in every generation, but that hasn't made murder meritorious or larceny legal. That was the objective, wasn't it?
> ANSWER: That was the objective, yes.

To test the assertion of Stans that he could reconstruct the contents of Sloan's summary, I asked him, in essence, if he could tell the Select Committee about the disbursement of any part of the $1,027,000 cash outlay his committee made. He confessed, in effect, that the only disbursement of which he had knowledge was $15,000 which was disbursed at the request of Clement Stone, a major contributor to Nixon campaign funds, to aid a bipartisan committee in Illinois seeking to prevent vote frauds.

Law and logic declare every sane person must be presumed to intend the natural consequences of his act. Even though his motives may have been as pure as the aspirations of the angels, Stans destroyed the last documentary evidence of cash disbursements made by his committee which Liddy or others may have used for illegal purposes. In so doing, he deprived investigators of the benefit of the evidential maxim that one scratch of a pen is better than the slippery memories of many witnesses.

Fortunately, however, the retentive memory of Sloan, the treasurer, whose trustworthiness was conceded by all, was able to recall many of the cash disbursements, including the $199,000 received by Liddy.

Magruder informed Sloan after his meeting with Mitchell in Key Biscayne that the political arm of CREEP had authorized a budget of $250,000 for work Liddy was going to do for CREEP, and told him to pay $83,000, a portion of the budgeted amount, to Liddy in one lump sum. Sloan, who had no knowledge of Liddy's mission, told Stans of Magruder's statement, expressed misgivings about paying such a substantial sum to Liddy when he had no knowledge of what Liddy was going to do with it, and asked Stans to ascertain from Mitchell whether Magruder had the authority to order him to make the payment to Liddy.

After consulting with Mitchell, Sloan testified, Stans informed him that Mitchell confirmed Magruder's authority to direct him to make the payment. In discussing with him at that time his misgivings about his ignorance of the purpose of the outlay, Sloan said Stans declared, "I do not want to know and you don't want to know."

Stans's testimony in respect to this event differed little from that of Sloan. According to Stans, he saw Mitchell and put to him Sloan's inquiry concerning Magruder's authority. Mitchell advised him, Stans said, that Sloan should pay to Liddy any amounts Magruder told him to pay, that he [Mitchell] did not know the purpose of the proposed payment to Liddy, and that if Sloan wanted to know its purpose he would "have to ask Magruder because Magruder is in charge of the campaign and he directs the spending."

Stans affirmed that he reported his conversation with Mitchell to Sloan, and made this statement to him: "I don't know what's going on in this campaign and I don't think you ought to try to know."

By way of justifying this statement, Stans told the Select Committee: "We were the cashiers, we received the money, and we paid the bills. They had the responsibility for everything they did. . . . It did not seem that it was incumbent upon us to question the propriety of any payment, whether it was to Liddy or anybody else, and we did not."

I asked Stans this question: "And you did not have enough curiosity to inquire as to what they were going to spend the money for?" Stans responded, "I did not have any time for curiosity. I had to raise $40 million and I worked at a frenzied pace during the entire period I was there." I inquired, "You did have some authority in determining the amounts of money that were to be expended, did you not?" Stans replied, "Only in the aggregate by categories and I had very little authority on that."

I put to Stans this question: "Are you telling me in effect that Mr. John Mitchell was running the show and you had very little voice in it except to raise the money he wanted to spend?" He replied, "No. I am not quite telling you that. I am telling you that in the budget committee meetings, I was not very successful in holding down the level of spending."

As CREEP was structured, Nixon campaign funds were budgeted for expenditure by a budgetary committee composed of Mitchell and two other officials of the political arm of CREEP, together with Stans and two other officials of the finance arm of CREEP. Stans disclaimed substantial knowledge of proposals made in the budgetary committee for expenditures, and asserted that his chief function as a member was to prevent excessive outlays.

This testimony prompted me to put this somewhat rhetorical question to Stans: "Can you explain to a simple-minded man like me the mental processes by which you can determine how much money ought to be spent for a particular project unless you know what the project is?"

By way of answer, Stans reiterated that the budgetary committee dealt with categories of outlays rather than specific expenditures, and added, "I was only arguing to keep the expenditures down to the limits that I thought I could raise."

Stans told the Select Committee that, shortly after the break-in, he fired Liddy because he would not answer questions of the FBI, and Sloan confided in him that Magruder had attempted in vain to persuade him to make false statements to the prosecutors and give false testimony to the grand jury substantially minimizing the amount of money the finance arm of CREEP had given Liddy.

Stans also gave the Select Committee some intriguing testimony concerning a transaction he had with President Nixon's personal attorney, Kalmbach, on June 29, 1972, twelve days after the Watergate break-in. On that day he met Kalmbach in a Washington hotel. Kalmbach told Stans he was engaged in a White House project not related to the campaign, and needed all the money he could get in cash to carry it out. In response to questions, Kalmbach advised Stans he could not tell him who asked him to get the money or why he wanted it but Stans "would have to trust him." Without more ado, Stans gave Kalmbach $75,000 in cash originally donated to the furtherance of Nixon's political fortunes. Stans admitted he subsequently learned that Kalmbach used the money for payments to the seven original Watergate defendants.

On June 23, 1972, six days after the Watergate break-in and the day on which Sloan destroyed his original records and gave the summary to Stans, the finance arm of CREEP still had a balance of $81,000 in cash in its safes. As Stans testified, Sloan "expressed some concern about it because he was going on vacation and under the tense situation that was building up he didn't want to hold the cash in his custody." As he further testified, Stans thereupon consulted Robert C. Mardian, who had followed Mitchell from the Department of Justice to CREEP, and Mardian advised him to "get the money out of the office and out of the campaign." Upon Mardian's advice, Stans said he had the $81,000 transferred from his committee to LaRue, whom he described as the right-hand man of Mitchell as political campaign director.

My efforts to elicit information from Stans were not pleasing to Senator Gurney, who uttered this protest: "I for one have not appreciated the harassment of this witness by the Chairman in the questioning that has just finished. I think this Senate Committee ought to act in fairness."

As a practitioner of the Biblical admonition "A soft answer turneth away wrath," I said, "I have asked the witness questions to find out what the truth is. . . . I am sorry that my distinguished friend from Florida does not approve of my method of examining the witness. I am an old country lawyer and I don't know the finer ways to do it. I just have to do it my way."

My father was a wise man who taught me many things of value. He taught me, for example, that no man worth his salt would refrain from doing his duty to avoid criticism. He insisted this teaching was implicit in the words of the Gospel according to Luke: "Woe unto you, when all men speak well of you."

Some of Stans's admirers in the news media and elsewhere castigated me for my interrogation of him. This did not surprise me. I knew that all men would not speak well of me if I made a real effort to discover the truth concerning Watergate-related events.

Stans received special consideration. Assistant Attorney General Petersen excused him from testifying in person before the grand jury in conformity with established procedures to spare him embarrassment. The Select Committee refrained from interrogating him and Mitchell about the Robert Vesco contribution and its aftermath to avoid prejudicing them in the future trial of the charges then pending against them in the United States District Court for the Southern District of New York.

The Select Committee also received in evidence at Stans's request letters of his attorneys and of Richard Whitney as well as affidavits of Larry A. Jobe and Joseph E. Carson, former officers of the Department of Commerce, which covered approximately twenty-four pages of the hearing record, and which merely corroborated testimony Stans had given to the committee in a televised hearing denying assertions of Magruder and an inconsequential bit of McCord's evidence.

Nevertheless Stans was displeased because the committee did not read the letters and affidavits aloud in a televised hearing. He was also displeased because the committee did not receive as evidence an argumentative communication of his attorneys, who had no personal knowledge of the contents of the communication.

The Select Committee and Congress did not share Stans's immaculate appraisal of what he and the finance arm of CREEP did in the presidential election of 1972. The committee recommended and Congress enacted laws to prohibit similar operations in the future.

Congress incorporated many of the legislative recommendations of the Select Committee in the Federal Election Campaign Act Amendments of 1974, which became law on October 25, 1974, and which have been judicially declared to be "by far the most comprehensive reform legislation ever passed by Congress concerning the election of the President, the Vice President, and members of Congress."

These amendments established the Federal Election Commission to supervise and regulate the nomination and election of these federal officers. I mention only those of their provisions that have a direct impact on activities similar to those of the finance arm of CREEP in the presidential election of 1972.

They outlaw enormous contributions by placing ceilings on contributions to candidates seeking nomination or election to the presidency, the vice-presidency, or Congress. Under them, no individual or group of individuals can contribute more than $1,000 to a single candidate in any election, and no political committee can contribute more than $5,000 to any single candidate in any election. Besides, they impose an overall limit of $25,000 on all the contributions an individual is permitted to make to all candidates for federal offices in a particular year.

They outlaw the maintaining of secret political funds and the making of secret expenditures for hidden political purposes in connection with candidates for nomination or election to any federal offices in two ways: first, they require all contributions to be deposited in banks designated by the candidate as his campaign depositories; and, second, they impose drastic record-keeping and reporting requirements on the treasurer of any political committee supporting the candidate.

Under their record-keeping requirements, the treasurer of the committee is enjoined to keep detailed and exact records disclosing these things:

—All contributions made to or for the committee.

—The identifications of every person making a contribution in excess of $10 and the date and amount of it, and the occupation and the principal place of business of every person whose contribution exceeds $100.

—All expenditures made by or on behalf of the committee.

—The identification of every person to whom any expenditure is made, the date and amount of it, and the name and address of the candidate on whose behalf such expenditure was made.

The treasurer of the political committee is also required to obtain and keep receipted bills disclosing the particulars of every expenditure exceeding $100 made by or for the committee, and of any such expenditures of lesser amounts to the same person if they total more than $100 during a calendar year.

The amendments require the reporting of all contributions exceeding $10 to the Federal Election Commission, and direct that commission to subject to public inspection the names of persons making contributions of more than $100 in any calendar year.

They outlaw the use of nontraceable cash by political committees by prohibiting cash contributions and expenditures in excess of $100.

12

BREAK-IN
AND COVER-UP

As Dean testified, the White House had an insatiable appetite for political intelligence. At an early stage of the campaign Magruder and Dean discussed with John J. Caulfield, who afterwards became an aide to Mitchell at CREEP, Caulfield's plan, which he called Sand-wedge, to provide security and political intelligence for President Nixon's reelection campaign. This plan was never approved.

Mitchell admitted to the Select Committee that as Attorney General he held two meetings with Liddy, Magruder, and Dean in his office, where Liddy presented to him plans for burglarizing and bugging the offices of the Democratic National Committee, and one meeting with Magruder and LaRue at Key Biscayne, Florida, after he had left the Department of Justice and assumed the management of the political arm of CREEP, at which Magruder presented to him a version of Liddy's plans.

Mitchell claimed he rejected the plans presented to him at the three meetings, and Magruder conceded this was true in respect to the two plans presented to Mitchell while he was still serving as Attorney General.

The testimony showed that Liddy enlisted the help of Hunt in seeking to procure the implementation of his plans for the burglarizing and bugging of the offices of the Democratic National Committee. They jointly visited Hunt's friend Colson, at the White House, and at their request Colson urged Magruder by telephone to expedite the activation of Liddy's plan. Magruder said Colson told him on this occasion "to get off the stick and get the budget approved for Liddy's plan to get information on Democratic Chairman Lawrence O'Brien."

The meeting at Key Biscayne was held on March 30, 1972, and occurred shortly after Colson's exhortation to Magruder.

According to Magruder, he prepared three documents explaining the final version of Liddy's plan in detail, gave one copy to Strachan for delivery to Haldeman so that Haldeman or Strachan "could get back to us if [they had] any questions," and gave another copy to Mitchell when he talked to him about the plan at Key Biscayne. The testimony of the three men who attended the Key Biscayne meeting differed sharply. Mitchell asserted he disapproved the Liddy plan as presented by Magruder. LaRue declared Mitchell neither approved nor disapproved the plan, but ended the conversation on the subject by saying it was "not something that will have to be decided at this meeting." Magruder affirmed, however, that Mitchell approved the plan and authorized a budget of $250,000 for its activation.

According to Magruder, he forthwith advised Sloan, treasurer of the finance arm of CREEP, of Mitchell's action, and shortly afterwards notified Sloan to pay $83,000 of the allocated funds to Liddy without delay and to pay him the remainder at his request, without giving Sloan any inkling of the nature of Liddy's project.

He also testified he gave Strachan notice of Mitchell's approval of Liddy's plan with the expectation that he would convey information of it to Haldeman, who he said actually "stood next to the President . . . in the executive branch of the government."

According to McCord and Alfred C. Baldwin, III, the latter, acting upon an arrangement between them, monitored by electronic devices from a room in the Howard Johnson Motel across the street from the Watergate from May 26, 1972, until the burglars were caught in the early morning of June 17, 1972, conversations on the phones in the offices of the Democratic National Committee intercepted by bugs McCord and the four Cubans had planted in the phones on May 28, the night of their first surreptitious entry.

After so doing, Baldwin gave McCord logs of the intercepted conversations, which numbered altogether about two hundred.

McCord testified he delivered the logs of the intercepted telephone conversations to Liddy, and Sally J. Harmony, Liddy's secretary, testified she typewrote memorandums of the logs on stationery headed "Gemstone" and returned the logs and gave the memorandums to Liddy.

Magruder testified that Liddy gave him copies of the memorandums and also copies of pictures of documents the burglars had photographed at the headquarters of the Democratic National Committee, and that he took copies of the memorandums and the pictures to Mitchell. Mitchell concluded, Magruder testified further, that there was no substance to them, and on one occasion "called Liddy . . . to his office and indicated his dissatisfaction with his work."

According to Magruder, he did not believe it wise to give Strachan copies of the Gemstone materials for delivery to Haldeman because of their sensitive nature. As a consequence, he said, he permitted Strachan to view them in his office, and Strachan concurred in his opinion and that of Mitchell that there was a "lack of substance to the documents." He could not affirm, he added, that Strachan ever gave Haldeman any information about them.

In the darkness of the early morning of June 17, 1972, Frank Wills, a night watchman at the Watergate Office Building, discovered and reported to his superiors that the garage door leading to the stairway of the building had been taped a second time so as to render its locks inoperative. As a consequence, Washington police were summoned, and within minutes Sergeant Paul W. Leeper and Officers John Bruce Barrett and Carl M. Shoffer arrived and caught McCord and the four Cubans in the offices of the Democratic National Committee wearing surgical gloves and carrying electronic and photographic equipment. The four Cubans had forty-five $100 bills in their possession, a notebook referring to Hunt, and a small check signed by Hunt in their possession.

Sometime after daybreak Liddy called Magruder in Los Angeles and informed him about the arrest of McCord and his associates. Magruder, who was on a campaign trip with Mitchell, LaRue, Mardian, and Porter, relayed what Liddy had told him to LaRue, who transmitted it to Mitchell.

At Mitchell's direction, someone in the party called Liddy and asked him to see Attorney General Kleindienst about the possibility of securing the release of McCord and the Cubans. When Liddy and a CREEP official, Powell Moore, requested him to authorize their release, Kleindienst, who had been alerted to the break-in by Assistant Attorney General Petersen, declined the request, and ordered that they be granted no special consideration.

After this, Sloan testified, Liddy came to the offices of the finance arm of CREEP before Sloan had learned about the break-in and made this statement to him: "My boys got caught last night; I made a mistake. I used somebody from here which I told them I would never do; I am afraid I'm going to lose my job."

Sloan said Liddy's statement had no meaning for him until some-time later when he read about the break-in. At that time, he asserted, he began to suspect that officials of the political arm of CREEP were deeply involved in that affair because he had given $199,000 in cash to Liddy at their instance.

After his statement to Sloan, Liddy shredded the files he had accumulated at CREEP. Shortly afterwards his secretary, at his direction, shredded her stenographic notebooks and file copies of papers mentioning him.

According to Magruder, the cover-up of Watergate was initiated at a series of meetings in Mitchell's office and apartment beginning on June 19. These meetings were attended by Mitchell, LaRue, Magruder, Mardian, and Dean. While Mitchell denied their testimony, Magruder and LaRue told the Select Committee that Magruder asked the group what he should do with his Gemstone files and Mitchell replied it might be a good idea for Magruder to have a fire in his house.

Magruder further stated it was agreed at these meetings that President Nixon's campaign for reelection would suffer damage if the truth about the burglary and bugging were revealed before the election, and a plan for hiding the truth from law enforcement officers, the press, and the public evolved.

The chief ingredient of the cover-up plan, so Magruder said, was the denial of CREEP officials that they had anything to do with the break-in and bugging of the Watergate, and to tell all interrogators that Liddy, Hunt, McCord, and the four Cubans were on a lark of their own when they perpetrated these offenses.

According to Magruder, the Gemstone files and other records of CREEP were forthwith destroyed, and the parties to the cover-up collaborated in concocting false stories to deceive and mislead the FBI agents and the prosecutors in their investigations. Magruder and Porter admitted to the Select Committee that they testified falsely before the grand jury and the petit jury in Judge Sirica's court in conformity with the cover-up story.

When he was being questioned by Senator Montoya, Magruder stated he was determined to rehabilitate himself and live a useful life, and Senator Montoya said, "I want to wish you well in your future endeavors."

As he ended his testimony, I told Magruder, "Like Senator Montoya, I have a compassionate heart," and "I recommend to you . . . the poem by Walter Malone called 'Opportunity,' " which contains "the most encouraging words ever put together by any man" and which declares " 'each night I burn the records of the day' " and " 'at sunrise every soul is born again.' "

Sloan was much troubled by the uncertainty surrounding the break-in. Shortly after its occurrence he learned the FBI wanted to interview him, and he consulted LaRue, who advised him to see Mitchell before he talked to the FBI. According to Sloan, he visited the office of Mitchell on June 21 or 22 for guidance, hoping to receive from him the assurance "that everything was all right." The only guidance Mitchell gave him, Sloan declared, was embodied in the enigma: "When the going gets tough, the tough get going."

After Mitchell's Delphic utterance, Sloan affirmed, he visited President Nixon's appointments secretary, Dwight L. Chapin, and his chief adviser on domestic affairs, John Ehrlichman, in the White House, to inform them of his "strong suspicion that the command . . . of the political side of the campaign was involved in the affair" and to suggest that "someone in the White House" should "take a look at their campaign organization."

This visit occurred on June 23, six days after the break-in. Sloan declared that Chapin admonished him "that the important thing is that the President be protected" and suggested that he take a vacation. Sloan testified that Ehrlichman said "he didn't want to know the details" because "his position personally would be to take executive privilege on this matter until after the election."

Sloan asserted that shortly thereafter Magruder and LaRue sought unsuccessfully to persuade him to inform the prosecutors and even to testify before the grand jury that he gave Liddy $40,000 instead of $199,000, and Dean and LaRue undertook to induce him to plead the Fifth Amendment rather than to reveal anything. These events, Sloan declared, impelled him to resign as CREEP treasurer July 14.

Stans, Mitchell, Magruder, and Liddy had offices in the same building. Stans consulted Liddy frequently for legal advice. Notwithstanding his opportunities for acquiring knowledge or satisfying curiosity, Stans assured the Senate Select Committee he made no effort prior to the break-in to learn from Magruder or Liddy why his committee's general counsel was receiving substantial sums of cash from his committee's treasurer to finance a project of which he was totally ignorant, or, subsequent to the break-in, to learn from Mitchell and Magruder how it happened that burglars were caught in the headquarters of the opposition political party with forty-five $100 bills that came from his committee in their possession.

Stans also assured the Select Committee that after these events he and President Nixon discussed the reelection campaign by telephone and in person, and that these events were not mentioned by either of them.

Magruder told the Select Committee that on June 24, 1972, seven days after the break-in, he attended a meeting with Mitchell and Stans, and Stans asked Mitchell, "what had happened." Instead of giving Stans any details "as to what had actually happened," Magruder affirmed, Mitchell merely stated, in substance, that the Watergate burglary was an operation of the political arm of CREEP that "had gone wrong," that "that is where" the money given by Sloan to Liddy "had gone," that Liddy was involved; and that the finance arm of CREEP would probably have to terminate Liddy's employment. According to Magruder, nothing further was said at this meeting except this: "We indicated to Mr. Stans the problem we had with the money, and would he try to work with Mr. Sloan to see if Mr. Sloan could be more cooperative about what had happened with the money, and how much there was and Mr. Stans indicated that he would."

When Stans subsequently testified before the Select Committee, he stated that he had no record and no recollection of any meeting with Mitchell on June 24, 1972, and that he was not told "what happened at Watergate . . . at any time" by Sloan, Magruder, LaRue, Ehrlichman, Haldeman, or Mitchell.

Mitchell served as Nixon's Attorney General from January 1969 until March 1972, when he resigned to accept formally the post of campaign director of the political arm of CREEP. He relinquished that post two weeks after Watergate "to spend more time with his family," and was succeeded by Clark MacGregor, a distinguished former congressman from Minnesota.

After it was announced that Mitchell was to testify before the Select Committee, his talkative wife, Martha, telephoned Helen Thomas, a journalist, and told her, "I don't like Vice President Agnew, but, by

God, I think he's better than Nixon." She added that she was urging her husband to tell everything he knew about White House connections with Watergate, regardless of whom it affected, and that President Nixon should resign.

When Mitchell testified before the Select Committee, I asked him if he remembered a colloquy we had had on January 14, 1969, when he appeared before the Senate Judiciary Committee, which was then considering his nomination for the post of Attorney General. He replied. "I remember it very well, Senator." I then read to him this account of the colloquy:

> SENATOR ERVIN: Mr. Mitchell, until comparatively recent years it has been customary for Presidents to appoint the Postmaster General his chief political adviser and agitator. Unfortunately, during recent years this role has been largely taken away from the Postmaster General, and given to and exercised by the Attorney General. To my mind there is something incompatible with marrying the function of the chief political adviser and chief agitator with that of prosecutor of crimes against the government. Now, I would just like to know whether you think that the primary function and objective of the Attorney General should be giving political advice or doing political agitating before congressional committees or enforcing Federal law and acting as an adviser to the President and his cabinet in legal matters rather than political.
>
> MR. MITCHELL: Senator, I would hope that my activities in a political nature and of a political nature have ended with the campaign. I might say that this was my first entry into a political campaign, and I trust it will be my last. From the termination of the campaign and henceforth my duties and functions will be related to the Justice Department, and as the legal and not the political adviser of the President.
>
> SENATOR ERVIN: Thank you, sir. I commend your answer.

I then stated, "I am very sorry that you didn't carry out the purpose you announced on that occasion."

Mitchell replied, "Mr. Chairman, that would have been my fondest wish. Unfortunately, it is very, very difficult to turn down a request by the President of the United States."

When he appeared before the Select Committee, Mitchell denied he had approved the Watergate project, or authorized any expenditure to finance it, or had participated in any way in the destruction of records of CREEP, or in the payment of money to any of the seven original Watergate defendants after the break-in. He asserted that the break-in and the bugging were a complete surprise to him, and his meetings with Magruder, LaRue, Dean, and Mardian after the break-in were held to discuss what had happened and not to formulate any cover-up.

Mitchell further declared he had no knowledge of the relevant facts until June 21 or 22, 1972, when LaRue and Mardian, who had talked to Liddy, gave him a briefing on Watergate and "the White House horrors." According to Mitchell's terminology, "the White House horrors" were the burglarizing of the office of Ellsberg's psychiatrist by Liddy and Hunt; the removal from Washington by Liddy of Dita Beard, the lobbyist allegedly involved in efforts to end antitrust proceedings against the International Telephone and Telegraph Company; the falsifying of State Department cables by Hunt to indicate that the late President Kennedy was implicated in the murder of the late South Vietnamese President Ngo Dinh Diem; and the alleged scheme of Colson to have the Brookings Institute fire-bombed.

After the break-in, Mitchell testified, a general consensus arose that "the best thing to do was to keep the lid on," and that he, Dean, Haldeman, and Ehrlichman were primarily concerned that information concerning "the White House horrors" should not reach the prosecutors. When asked if Haldeman and Ehrlichman had participated actively in a cover-up of Watergate, Mitchell merely replied, "I would say they had a very active concern, just as I had."

Mitchell declared he never told President Nixon the facts he had learned about Watergate and "the White House horrors" before the election because he wished to "keep the lid on through the election," and believed President Nixon would have had to choose between becoming involved in the cover-up or making disclosures which might have damaged his reelection chances had he been told. He added he did not tell President Nixon the facts after the election because knowledge of them would have affected his presidency.

When he asserted that President Nixon did not ask him anything about Watergate, I observed that "if the cat hadn't [had] any more curiosity than that it would still be enjoying its nine lives, all of them."

Mitchell confessed to the committee that he knew that others were hiding the facts and that Magruder told him he was going to commit perjury before the grand jury "rather than to reveal the truth."

I thereupon put this question to Mitchell: "Am I doing you an injustice to ask you whether or not you preferred for Magruder to commit perjury rather than to reveal the truth?" Mitchell replied, "The preference, obviously, was that the matter not be disclosed."

Gordon Strachan assured the committee he knew nothing whatever concerning the Watergate affair until the burglars were apprehended, and denied the truth of all Magruder's testimony indicating the contrary.

He asserted that his sole function as Haldeman's liaison with CREEP was to report the activities of CREEP about which he acquired information. After his meeting with Mitchell and LaRue in Key Biscayne, Magruder called him by phone and reported briefly on about thirty major campaign decisions made at that meeting. In enumerating them, Strachan declared, Magruder described one of them as follows: "A sophisticated political intelligence-gathering system has been approved with a budget of 300." Strachan added, "Unfortunately he neither gave me, nor did I ask for any further details about the subject."

Strachan testified that in early April 1972 he prepared one of his regular "political matters" memos for Haldeman. This memo, he said, was eight or ten pages long with more than a dozen tabs or attachments. It contained this short paragraph: "Magruder reports that 1701 [CREEP] now has a sophisticated political intelligence gathering system with a budget of 300. A sample of the type of information they are developing is attached at tab H." At tab H, he said, he enclosed a political intelligence report entitled "Sedan Chair II," which he had received from CREEP and which contained political intelligence relating to Senator Humphrey's Pennsylvania organization. Strachan added that Haldeman returned the memo to him with a check mark beside the entry relating to the political-intelligence-gathering plan, indicating Haldeman had read it.

According to Strachan, he furnished Haldeman with what he called a "talking paper" specifying the sophisticated political-intelligence-gathering plan and other items that Haldeman was to discuss with Mitchell at a meeting they held on April 4, 1972.

After the meeting, Haldeman returned the talking paper to him, Strachan asserted, under circumstances indicating that Haldeman and Mitchell had discussed the plan, and Strachan placed it and the "political matters" memo embodying the reference to the plan and the political report entitled "Sedan Chair II" in the political files.

Sometime later in April, Strachan declared, "Mr. Haldeman called me into his office . . . and told me to contact Mr. Liddy and tell him to transfer whatever capability he had from Muskie to McGovern with particular interest in discovering what the connection between McGovern and Senator Kennedy was."

Pursuant to this direction, Strachan said, he called Liddy to his office in the basement of the White House and transmitted Haldeman's instruction to him.

Senator Muskie withdrew from the presidential race on April 27, 1972. On May 15 McCord visited McGovern's headquarters to plant a bug in the office of Frank Mankiewicz, his campaign director, but did not succeed in his purpose for lack of time. On the nights of May 27 and 28 attempts to make surreptitious entries into McGovern's head-quarters failed because they were occupied.

On June 19, two days after the break-in, Strachan said, he pulled out the file relating to the sophisticated political-intelligence-gathering plan Haldeman had discussed with Mitchell on April 4 because he "had pretty strong suspicions . . . the break-in at the Democratic National Committee headquarters was related to this plan."

On the following morning, Strachan said, he showed the file to Haldeman, who said, "Well, make sure our files are clean." Interpreting this remark to be an instruction from Haldeman to do so, Strachan continued, he shredded the memo relating to the intelligence plan, the report entitled "Sedan Chair II," the talking paper, some memos relating to Segretti, a memo relating to Haldeman's instruction to him to tell Liddy to transfer his capability from Muskie to McGovern, and other specified items. A few days later, Strachan continued, he reported his action to Haldeman and assured him he "had in fact made our files clean."

When he appeared before the Select Committee, Haldeman testified he had absolutely no recollection of seeing the "political matters" memo relating to the sophisticated political-intelligence-gathering plan, or the talking paper relating to it, or the report entitled "Sedan Chair II." He asserted further he did not recall telling Strachan to contact Liddy and tell him to transfer his capability from Muskie to McGovern, with special emphasis on the relationship to Senator Kennedy, or giving Strachan any instructions to destroy any materials, or receiving any report from Strachan that he had done so or that he had made the files clean.

13

JOHN DEAN, DEVASTATING WITNESS

THE most impressive and convincing witness to appear before the Select Committee was John Dean. The cause of truth was well served when Dean retained Charles N. Shaffer and Robert C. McCandless as his attorneys. They knew that lawyers cannot serve clients most advantageously unless clients reveal to them the absolute truth as they recall it in respect to all relevant matters. They adjured Dean to prepare a written statement setting forth the truth concerning everything he knew about Watergate, including all incidents derogatory to himself. The result was a 246-page statement. They also adjured Dean to tell the committee the truth as he recalled it when he testified.

Dean had testified in executive session before the staff of the Select Committee on June 16 and confessed a sin additional to his Watergate misdeeds. In May 1972 a substantial amount of Nixon campaign funds had been delivered to Colson to pay for newspaper advertisements ostensibly emanating from citizens who appreciated Nixon's conduct of the Vietnam war. When $14,000 of these funds were returned unspent, they were entrusted to Dean for safekeeping.

Dean used $4,850 of this money without authority for honeymoon and personal expenses, and evidenced its use by depositing his personal check with the remaining funds. He was compelled to leave the White

House before redeeming this check. After that event he replaced the $4,850, and on the advice of his attorneys put the entire fund in a trustee account for transfer to those entitled to it.

Dean's appearance before the Select Committee was originally scheduled for June 18. At the request of the Democratic and Republican leaders of the Senate, who did not want the hearings to be held while Soviet Communist Party leader Leonid I. Brezhnev was visiting Washington, the Select Committee recessed its hearings for a week, and thus postponed Dean's appearance to June 25.

During this week what Dean had told the staff about his unauthorized use of the $4,850 and some other events was leaked to the press, and politicians and segments of the press protective of the White House used his admission of the unauthorized use of the money in a virulent effort to discredit him as a witness prior to his appearance before the committee.

About the same time J. Fred Buzhardt, special counsel to the White House, drafted and sent to the committee a memorandum charging that Dean and "his patron," Mitchell, were chiefly responsible for planning and covering up Watergate, and that Dean was "the principal author of the political and constitutional crisis that Watergate now epitomizes."

Buzhardt informed the committee that his memorandum did not express the official view of the White House, and that he submitted it for use merely as a basis for cross-examining Dean. Senator Inouye used it for this purpose when he interrogated Dean.

Dean spent the entire day on June 25 reading his 246-page statement to the committee. After so doing, he laid his statement aside, and exhibited a remarkably retentive memory throughout four days of oral testimony.

During these four days he was subjected to searching questioning by the chief counsel, the minority counsel, and the seven members of the committee. Some of the questioning was hostile and even downright insulting. Despite this, Dean kept his composure and testified calmly, positively, unexcitedly, and convincingly, and left the witness stand after his ordeal with his testimony unshaken.

Dean frustrated the efforts to discredit him by confessing at the beginning of his testimony to the committee, a jammed Caucus Room, and a television audience of millions that he had obstructed justice and encouraged the commission of perjury in his efforts to cover up the truth about Watergate, and that he had made an unauthorized use of the $4,850. After so doing, he described the roles he said others had played in the Watergate affair.

Dean testified as follows:

Although he bore the high-sounding title of counsel to the President, he was in reality merely a messenger who obeyed the instructions of Haldeman and Ehrlichman, and virtually everything he did to abet the cover-up of the Watergate was directed or approved by one of them.

On January 27 and February 4, 1972, at Magruder's request, he met with Magruder, Liddy, and Attorney General Mitchell in the latter's office in the Department of Justice, and Liddy presented to Mitchell his plans for spying on the officials of the Democratic National Committee, which Mitchell rejected. He reported to Haldeman what happened in detail. He had no information about the meeting Magruder, Mitchell, and LaRue held at Key Biscayne on March 30, 1972, until after the break-in.

When he reached San Francisco on his return from a trip to the Far East, he learned for the first time of the break-in, and returned to his office on the morning of June 19, two days after Watergate.

As a result of a phone call from Ehrlichman, he interviewed Liddy, who informed him that the men caught in the Watergate were his men, that Magruder "had pushed him" into burglarizing the office of the Democratic National Committee to replace a malfunctioning bug planted there during a prior burglary, that he used McCord because Magruder had cut his budget "so badly," that Magruder had obtained intercepted phone calls between the first and second break-ins, and that one of the Cubans had a check signed by Hunt because the Cubans were Hunt's friends. Liddy assured him "he was a soldier and would never talk."

He arranged to meet with Ehrlichman during the midafternoon of June 19. Before this meeting occurred, Strachan came to his office, and informed him Haldeman had instructed him to go through all of Haldeman's files over the weekend and remove and destroy damaging materials. Pursuant to this instruction, Strachan told him he had made the files completely clean. Strachan told him the materials destroyed included memorandums from CREEP, documents relating to wiretap information from the Democratic National Committee, notes of meetings with Haldeman, and a document which reflected that Haldeman had instructed Magruder to transfer his intelligence gathering from Senator Muskie to Senator McGovern.

He met with Ehrlichman in the latter's office in the midafternoon and reported to him in full his conversation with Liddy. He also told Ehrlichman about his January 27 and February 4 meeting with Mitchell, Magruder, and Liddy. Ehrlichman stated he wanted to meet later with Colson, and wanted him to be present.

Later that afternoon he attended a second meeting with Ehrlichman and Colson in Ehrlichman's office. At Ehrlichman's direction, he telephoned Liddy and told him "to have Hunt get out of the country." After so doing, he had misgivings about having done this. Colson shared his misgivings, and Ehrlichman agreed. At Ehrlichman's direction, he called Liddy again to retract his instructions to Hunt, and Liddy informed him he had already passed on the message and it might be too late to retract. Colson and Ehrlichman agreed it was imperative that the contents be removed from Hunt's safe in the Executive Office Building and that he take custody of them.

After departing from Ehrlichman's office, he met with Mitchell, Mardian, and Magruder, who informed him they had been discussing matters before he arrived. He had no recollection of what was said after he arrived other than "discussions of how to handle the matter from a public relations standpoint."

On June 20, three days after the break-in, he assumed custody of the contents of Hunt's safe, which included a pistol, a briefcase containing electronic equipment, and many documents. Outside of Hunt's personal papers, the documents consisted of many classified State Department cables relating to the early years of the Vietnam war, and these politically sensitive documents: numerous memorandums to Colson regarding Hunt's rather critical assessment of Krogh's handling of the White House Plumbers; a psychological study of Ellsberg made by someone who did not know him personally; a bogus cable (i.e., various cables spliced together into one cable) regarding the involvement of persons in the Kennedy administration in the fall of the Diem regime in Vietnam; a memorandum regarding some discussion about the bogus cable between Colson and William Lambert, a *Life* magazine writer; and some materials relating to an investigation Hunt had conducted for Colson concerning the tragedy at Chappaquiddick.

Pursuant to directions previously given him, he reported to Ehrlichman concerning the contents of Hunt's safe, and Ehrlichman ordered him to shred all of the politically sensitive documents and to "deep-six" the briefcase, i.e., toss it into the Potomac River. When he suggested to Ehrlichman that he do this himself, Ehrlichman replied, "No, thank you." After reflecting upon the matter, he decided the materials should be handled in another way.

He decided to give all the contents of Hunt's safe other than the politically sensitive documents to FBI agents, and the politically sensitive documents, which he put into two envelopes, to acting FBI Director Gray. By so doing, he could say, if ever questioned about the matter, all the contents of Hunt's safe had been delivered to the FBI. Immediately prior to June 28, everything except the sensitive documents were delivered to FBI agents. He informed Ehrlichman of this fact, and, at Ehrlichman's direction, brought the two envelopes containing the politically sensitive documents to Ehrlichman's office, where they were delivered to Gray. Ehrlichman described the documents "as politically sensitive, but not related to Watergate." They advised Gray that the politically sensitive documents "must never be leaked or made public." During the ensuing January, Gray told him he had destroyed the documents, and that he must "hang tight" on disclosing Gray's receipt of them.

With the prior approval of Ehrlichman, he and his assistant, Fred F. Fielding, prepared White House aides and employees for testifying before the FBI by discussing with them their areas of knowledge and the questions they would probably be asked, and he attended the questioning by the FBI of Chapin, Colson, Ehrlichman, Strachan, Young, and other crucial witnesss.

He attended a meeting in Mitchell's office on June 23 or 24 at which Mardian "raised the proposition that the CIA could take care of this entire matter if they wished in that they had funds and covert procedures for distributing funds." At Mitchell's suggestion, he spoke to Ehrlichman about the possibility of the White House contacting the CIA for assistance, and Ehrlichman, who thought it an idea worth exploring, instructed him to contact General Vernon A. Walters, the deputy director of the CIA, on two occasions. General Walters advised him that he believed it would be "a terrible mistake" for the CIA to get involved, and that it would not do so unless the President gave it a direct order to that effect. He reported his conversation with General Walters to Haldeman and Ehrlichman, and the proposal was dropped.

He had conversations on a regular basis with Gray regarding the status of the FBI investigation. Mardian, Mitchell, Haldeman, and Ehrlichman urged him to seek access to FBI reports setting forth the data they were collecting about Watergate. When he contacted him,

Gray said he would furnish FBI reports to him upon his assurance "that this information was being reported to the President and that was the principal purpose of the request." Although he was not reporting directly to the President, he gave Gray this assurance. He believed he was justified in so doing because he reported what he did and discovered to Haldeman and Ehrlichman, who had "daily discussions with the President," and assumed they were transmitting the information he gave them to the President. He began receiving FBI reports after July 21, permitted Mardian and the attorneys for CREEP, Paul L. O'Brien and Kenneth W. Parkinson, to read them constantly and extended the opportunity of doing so to Richard A. Moore while he was preparing a report on the Segretti matter for Ehrlichman.

On June 28 he attended a meeting with Mitchell and LaRue, and possibly Mardian, in Mitchell's office, and advised them that there could be no CIA assistance. A discussion ensued concerning "the need for support money in exchange for silence from the men in jail, and if the CIA would not do it they would have to find money somewhere else." LaRue said Stans had only $70,000 or $80,000. At Mitchell's instance, he conveyed to Haldeman and Ehrlichman Mitchell's request that they approve the use of Kalmbach to raise the necessary money, and Haldeman and Ehrlichman authorized him to contact Kalmbach for this purpose. He met with Kalmbach in Washington on June 29, and the payment of hush money began.

From June 21 through June 30 he had frequent discussions with Haldeman and Ehrlichman in which he reported to them information they had requested of him and information he had received from others. In these discussions they talked about Mitchell and Magruder's scheme to stop grand jury indictments from going any further than Liddy by having Magruder tell a fabricated story, i.e., that he did not know what Liddy was doing. They discussed it and "no one was sure it would hold up." In reply to a question from Haldeman, he said he did not think Magruder would stand up if he was indicted. After Mitchell had resigned and been succeeded by MacGregor, they learned that Porter would corroborate Magruder's fabricated story. After learning that the success of the strategy of containing Watergate, i.e., stopping the indictments with Liddy, depended on Magruder's testimony, Haldeman and Ehrlichman asked him frequently "how Magruder was doing in relationship to the FBI and grand jury investigation." He did not hear Magruder's story "in full detail until just before his grand jury appearance in mid-August, 1972, when" Magruder asked him if he "would be a devil's advocate and question him before he went before the grand jury." He did so. After this session with Magruder, he was told by Higby that Magruder "had been to see him, to tell Haldeman he was ready."

After Magruder had testified before the grand jury, he contacted Petersen at Haldeman's request to ascertain how Magruder had done before the grand jury, and Petersen advised him that Magruder "had made it through by the skin of his teeth." He informed Haldeman, Mitchell, and Magruder what Petersen had said, and Haldeman "was very pleased because this meant that the investigation would not go beyond Liddy."

In September 1972 the prosecutors subpoenaed Magruder's diary, which reflected the meetings attended by Magruder, Liddy, Mitchell, and him in Mitchell's office in the Department of Justice in January and February. At Mitchell's request, he met with Mitchell and Magruder to discuss how Magruder "should handle this matter before the grand jury." At his suggestion, Magruder said he would testify they held those meetings to discuss election laws. He later learned Magruder had testified before the grand jury that one meeting had been canceled and the other had been held to introduce Liddy to Mitchell and discuss election laws.

Either he or his assistant, Fielding, prepared members of the White House staff for their appearances before the grand jury by discussing with each of them in advance the questions he was likely to be asked and the areas it was not necessary for him to "get into." At his request, Colson, Krogh, Young, Chapin, and Strachan, and, at Ehrlichman's demand, Stans were excused by Petersen from going before the grand jury for interrogation, notwithstanding the grand jurors had specifically asked that Stans appear before them. Their testimony was taken by the prosecutors in the Justice Department for reading to the grand jury.

Before August 29, 1972, the White House, speaking through Ziegler, repeatedly assured the press and the public that the President would not get involved in the Watergate investigation, that no inquiry was being made by the White House into the matter, that the FBI and other authorities were pursuing the investigation, and that the President would not be receiving any special reports on the matter because that would be inappropriate. Notwithstanding these public announcements, President Nixon suddenly announced at a press conference at San Clemente on August 29 that John Dean had investigated Watergate and made a report which cleared everybody then employed at the White House or in the administration from any complicity in the Watergate affair. He was astonished to hear the President's statement on TV for the first time because it was false. He had never made any such report to anybody. As phrased by him, he said, "Had I been consulted in advance by the President, I would have strongly opposed the issuing of such a statement for several reasons, which I would have told the President." Although he believed that nobody employed at the White House on August 29 had any advance knowledge that there was going to be a break-in of the Democratic National Committee on June 17, he was disabled by his knowledge and suspicions to say unequivocally what President Nixon said his nonexistent report declared. He had attended the January and February meetings at which Liddy had presented his plans; Magruder had indicated to him after the break-in "that there had been White House pressure to get the plan moving"; he had "never been able to determine whether Haldeman had advance knowledge or not"; he "was aware Gordon Strachan had . . . daily liaison with . . . Magruder and had carried information relating to wire-tapped conversations into the White House and later destroyed incriminating documents at Haldeman's direction"; and he suspected "Colson was far more knowledgeable than he protested."

On September 15, 1972, the grand jury returned indictments against Liddy, Hunt, McCord, and the four Cubans, and adjourned. The strategy of containing Watergate had succeeded. Although he had had virtually no personal contact with President Nixon up to that time, he was summoned to the President's Oval Office, where he found President Nixon and Haldeman. They were "in very good spirits," and his reception was "very warm and cordial." What President Nixon said convinced him the President was involved in the cover-up of the Watergate break-in. The President told him that Haldeman had kept him posted on his handling of the Watergate case, that he (the President) appreciated "the good and difficult job he had done," and that he (the President) was pleased "the case had stopped with Liddy." He told the President that all he "had been able to do was to contain the case and assist in keeping it out of the White House," that "there was a long way to go before this matter would end," and that he "certainly could make no assurances that the day would not come when this matter would start to unravel." The President "said that he certainly hoped that the case would not come to trial before the election." During the ensuing conversation, they discussed efforts to prevent the holding of the proposed Patman hearings, criticized the press for trying to make

Watergate a major issue, declared they would use the Internal Revenue Service after the election to attack their enemies, and talked about the President's post-election plans to replace people in all the agencies who were "not on their team." In discussing the proposed Patman hearings, the President observed that they "did not need the hearings before the election."

He had virtually no other personal contact with President Nixon until February 27, 1973, when the President summoned him to the Oval Office and instructed him to report directly to him concerning all Watergate-related matters.

During his five days before it, Dean told the Senate Select Committee many other things. Dean testified in detail concerning what happened in the secret meetings he had with President Nixon individually and with President Nixon, Haldeman, Ehrlichman, and Mitchell during the period beginning on February 27 and ending on April 17, 1973. What he said in respect to them conforms to what has been previously stated. His remarkable memory was in error in these insignificant respects: first, he thought some of the things that happened on March 21 occurred on March 13; and, second, he thought he met Kalmbach at the Mayflower Hotel instead of the Mayflower Coffee Shop in the Statler-Hilton Hotel the day the "hush money" program was initiated.

He positively contradicted the public statements made by President Nixon on April 17, May 22, and 30, and other times in which the President claimed that he had no knowledge of the cover-up of Watergate before March 21, that he initiated a search for the truth on that day, and that he condemned "any attempts to cover-up in this case, no matter who is involved."

On the contrary, Dean asserted, President Nixon was aware of the cover-up operations as early as September 15, 1972; he (President Nixon) initiated no search on March 21 because by then he knew the full implications of Watergate; and his efforts after March 21 were directed to saving himself, Haldeman and Ehrlichman from exposure rather than discovering or revealing the truth.

I put to Dean the somewhat rhetorical question whether he knew anything President Nixon did between the break-in and the day he was testifying, i.e., June 28, 1973, to perform his constitutional duty "to take care that the laws be faithfully executed." Dean asked to be excused from answering.

Dean recounted in detail what the Nixon White House did to block

the Patman hearing. According to Dean, Ehrlichman expressly authorized Colson to promise Hunt presidential clemency for silence early in
January 1973, and at the same time Mitchell and Paul L. O'Brien, an
attorney for CREEP, eagerly sought information from him concerning
his efforts to have Caulfield induce McCord to agree to join Liddy,
Hunt, and the four Cubans in remaining silent.

Dean also informed the committee in detail as to what happened in
February 1973, when he met with Haldeman, Ehrlichman, and Moore
at La Costa to devise plans for stymieing the Select Committee's investigation of Watergate, and fortified his testimony on this point by
presenting a written memorandum from Haldeman to him dated
February 10, 1973, which was admitted in evidence as an exhibit. The
contents of this memorandum justified Dean's description of it as
specific instructions from Haldeman to him "on perpetuating the
Watergate tactics or the cover-up by a counteroffensive against the
forthcoming Senate hearings."

Dean's testimony revealed the fear of the White House in general
and Ehrlichman and Krogh in particular that the Fielding burglary
might be revealed. The CIA had loaned Hunt a camera before the
burglary; Hunt had taken pictures of Liddy standing before the office
building in Beverly Hills in which Dr. Fielding had his offices; Hunt
had returned the camera with the undeveloped negatives of these
pictures in it; the CIA had found the negatives in the camera and
developed them; and the resulting pictures clearly portrayed Liddy
standing before the office building and signs indicating where Dr.
Fielding and another physician were to park their automobiles.
Although it was not otherwise aware of the significance of the pictures,
the CIA knew Liddy and Hunt were under indictment for Watergate-
related offenses and their trial was scheduled to begin within a few
weeks. For this reason, the CIA gave the pictures to the Department of
Justice, which made no effort to ascertain when and where the pictures
were taken.

Dean said he did not believe the Justice Department "knew what
the pictures were all about but that any investigator worth his salt
would probably track down the incident as a result of the pictures."
According to Dean, Ehrlichman must have shared this view because, at
his urging, Dean sought to persuade the CIA to retrieve them from the
Department of Justice and "get them back to the CIA where they might
be withheld from the committee investigators." The CIA, Dean added,
had been "unwilling to do so."

On March 28 or 29, 1973, Dean said he and Krogh discussed the possibility that the Select Committee might "stumble into the Ellsberg burglary," and during the course of their conversation Krogh declared he had received his orders for the burglary right out of the Oval Office and did not believe Ehrlichman was aware of the incident until shortly after it happened.

Dean's testimony shocked the nation, and Senator Baker and I observed that the President ought to respond to it. While Senator Baker suggested that the committee ought to seek information from the President in "whatever manner can be arranged," I stated that the committee should have direct presidential testimony because "you can't cross-examine a written statement."

When former Attorney General Kleindienst, Assistant Attorney General Petersen, and former Acting FBI Director Gray testified before the Select Committee, their attention was directed to this portion of President Nixon's televised speech on May 30, 1973: "As a result, on March 21, I personally assumed the responsibility for coordinating intensive new inquiries into the matter, and I personally ordered those conducting the investigations to get all the facts and to report them directly to me right here in this office."

Kleindienst, Petersen, and Gray declared that President Nixon never gave them any such order.

14

WHITE HOUSE ACTIVITIES AND IGNORANCE

O N June 20, three days after the break-in, Ehrlichman notified Gray that Dean "would be handling an inquiry into Watergate for the White House" and that he should deal directly with Dean in the investigation. Two days later Gray informed Dean the FBI had discovered that the Mexican and Dahlberg checks had been deposited in Barker's account in a Miami bank; that the Mexican checks prompted him to call Richard M. Helms, director of the CIA, who assured him there was no CIA involvement; and that the FBI was going to make appropriate inquiries in Mexico and elsewhere to trace the checks.

Dean carried the information he received from Gray on June 22, 1972, directly to the White House. Exactly what the White House knew about the Mexican and Dahlberg checks at that particular time was not revealed until August 5, 1974, when President Nixon released the tapes of June 23, 1972. It is certain, however, that the White House was highly desirous of stopping further investigation of the checks by the FBI.

On the following day, June 23, Haldeman and Ehrlichman summoned Helms and General Vernon A. Walters, deputy director of the CIA, to the White House. In response to a question, Helms said he told Haldeman the CIA was not involved in the Watergate break-in. According to Helms and Walters, Haldeman stated "the pursuit of the FBI investigation in Mexico might uncover some CIA activities or assets," and directed General Walters to tell Gray to "restrain" or "taper off" the FBI probe in Mexico.

According to Walters and Gray, Walters visited Gray the same day and told him the White House wanted the FBI to "taper off" its probe in Mexico because CIA activities in Mexico might be revealed if the FBI pursued it.

Within the next few days, Walters declared, he ascertained CIA operations would not be interfered with if the FBI made a full Watergate investigation in Mexico, and so advised Gray and Dean. Notwithstanding this information, Dean kept contacting Gray and Walters, and insisting that the CIA was involved in Watergate and should provide bail and pay salaries for Liddy, Hunt, McCord, and the four Cubans. He also maintained that the FBI would expose a covert CIA operation if it continued its investigation of the Mexican and Dahlberg checks.

According to Gray, the FBI slowed its investigation of the Mexican and Dahlberg checks until July 6. On that day Walters assured Gray in writing that the CIA was not involved in any way, and Gray phoned President Nixon and told him he and Walters "feel that people on your staff are trying to mortally wound you by using the CIA and FBI and by confusing the question of CIA interest in, or not in, people the FBI wishes to interview." President Nixon merely told Gray, Gray related, "to continue to conduct your aggressive investigation."

In reply to questions by Senator Talmadge, Gray testified he believed the warning he gave President Nixon on July 6, 1972, was adequate to put him on notice that members of the White House staff were engaged in an improper use of the CIA and FBI, that he was prepared to name Ehrlichman and Dean as the offending persons if the President had asked him the questions he had anticipated being asked, and that the President asked him no questions whatsoever.

Ehrlichman and Haldeman testified that they were actuated by considerations of national security when they met with Helms and Walters on June 23. According to Ehrlichman, Haldeman explained on that occasion "that the meeting was held at the President's request . . . because of the President's concern . . . that CIA activities were involved in the Watergate" or "some totally unrelated CIA activity might be exposed by the investigation of the Watergate."

Inasmuch as the FBI investigation of the Mexican checks was calculated to reveal and did, in fact, reveal that Nixon campaign funds were used to finance the Watergate break-in, the attempt to suppress the investigation was calculated to protect the political security of President Nixon rather than the national security of the United States.

While it withheld from the CIA knowledge of the existence of the Plumbers, the Nixon White House did not scruple to obtain CIA assistance for the White House Plumbers in their extra-legal activities.

Evidence received by the Select Committee indicated that President Nixon abominated Ellsberg for allegedly leaking the Pentagon Papers to the press; that Colson, who was reputed to be the White House's "hatchet man" and to have ready access to President Nixon, notwithstanding Haldeman's "Berlin Wall," was desirous of obtaining a psychological profile on Ellsberg to use in discrediting him; and that Young, who had direct supervision of the Plumbers, induced the CIA to have its specialists prepare and furnish to the Plumbers two psychological profiles on Ellsberg which proved unsatisfactory for Colson's purposes.

General Robert E. Cushman, a former deputy director of the CIA, testified that on July 7, 1971, Ehrlichman called him by telephone and said "that Howard Hunt had been hired as a consultant to the White House on security matters, that he would be coming to see me, and could I lend him a hand."

When he came, General Cushman said Hunt declared "he had been charged with a highly sensitive mission by the White House which involved an interview of a person whose ideology he was not certain of, and . . . he felt he had to disguise himself to conduct this interview, and he requested that the Agency provide him with the materials to establish that alias and to mask his appearance or change it so that he would not be identifiable to the person he was interviewing."

As a result of this and subsequent requests from Hunt, the CIA furnished Hunt and Liddy with fake identification papers, and Hunt with a wig and a voice-altering device, a tape recorder, and a clandestine camera enclosed in a tobacco pouch. As Hunt's requests mounted, Cushman said, the CIA notified Ehrlichman the agency would deny any further requests from him.

Senator Baker made this query famous during the hearings: "What did the President know, and when did he know it?"

Although he was unwilling to answer Senator Baker's question on oath before the committee and subject himself to interrogation concerning it, President Nixon repeatedly assured the press and the people in televised speeches and news conferences that he received no believable information whatever concerning the origin of the Watergate burglary and bugging or any efforts to cover them up at any time during the nine months between June 17, 1972, and March 21, 1973.

Experience has demonstrated the impossibility of enforcing intelligent and logical rules of evidence in congressional hearings. Consequently, witnesses are permitted to express in such hearings their opinions concerning something of which they are necessarily ignorant, i.e., the contents of other men's minds.

Mitchell, Stans, Moore, Ehrlichman, and Haldeman were, therefore, permitted to express opinions to the effect that they believed President Nixon was just as ignorant about Watergate and its cover-up as he professed to be. Ehrlichman and Haldeman additionally explained the reasons for President Nixon's ignorance.

According to their testimony, Dean had the responsibility for discovering and relaying to them the truth about all Watergate-related matters, and they had the responsibility of telling President Nixon, who was completely engrossed in other things, what Dean told them about Watergate. Inasmuch as he was derelict in the performance of this duty, they averred, Dean left them in a state of ignorance about Watergate, and they necessarily left President Nixon in a state of ignorance about that affair. They asserted, in effect, that although he was in regular communication with them in respect to matters of their concern, Dean gave them virtually no information about Watergate beyond the assurance that no persons then employed in the White House were implicated in any way in it.

The most intriguing exponent of President Nixon's ignorance was Richard A. Moore, special counsel to the President, who exhibited much charm, intelligence, and theatrical ability. As he testified, I concluded the stage had suffered a tragic loss when he chose the career of a lawyer rather than that of an actor.

Although he was a vigorous man eighteen years my junior, Moore gave the television audience the impression he was a man of great antiquity tottering on the brink of eternity. As a consequence, scores of irate persons called my senatorial office to protest what they deemed to be the merciless interrogation to which he was subjected by committee counsel Terry F. Lenzner.

Moore testified he believed "that the President knew nothing about the critical facts relating to Watergate at any time between the 17th day of June, 1972, and the 21st day of March, 1973."

I undertook to challenge gently the probative value of one man's opinion concerning the contents of the mind of another man by putting this question to Moore: "Do you not agree with me that of all the inhabitants of this earth the one best qualified to testify as to the knowledge the President had concerning the Watergate affair or anything else at any time between the 17th day of June, 1972, and the 21st day of March, 1973, is President Nixon?" Moore replied, "I could agree to that."

In interrogating Moore, I undertook to elicit some light on his testimony that there had been no sign or clue which should have led the President to discover the truth about Watergate before March 21, 1973, and on the assertions of Ehrlichman and Haldeman that Dean was responsible for their ignorance and that of the President concerning Watergate.

He conceded that during the two months after the burglary at the Watergate was discovered, the newspapers, television, and radio contained many statements concerning the Watergate matter. He also conceded that it could be safely assumed that the President, Haldeman, Ehrlichman, and other presidential aides read the newspapers, and that he did not know of anything John Dean did to keep them "from reading the newspapers and watching television and listening to the radio."

Holding photostatic copies of articles from the *Washington Post* in my hand, I drew from Moore admissions that the *Post* published these statements concerning Watergate within two months after the discovery of the break-in:

One of the five burglars arrested in the Watergate was McCord, the security officer of CREEP, the organization entrusted by President Nixon with his campaign for reelection.

McCord had bugged the Democratic National Committee offices in the Watergate and had furnished data obtained by the bugging to persons employed at CREEP.

Checks representing $114,000 of contributions to President Nixon had been deposited in the account of Barker, one of the Watergate burglars, in a Miami bank, and the proceeds of the checks had been withdrawn by Barker in cash, largely in new $100 bills.

Forty-five new $100 bills had been found in the possession of Barker and three of the other Watergate burglars at the time of their arrest.

Liddy, the chief legal adviser to CREEP, and Hunt, a White House consultant, were arrested for complicity in the burglary a few days after the burglary.

The $100 bills found in the possession of four of the burglars at the time of their arrest were part of $199,000 that Sloan, the treasurer of CREEP, delivered in cash to Liddy prior to the burglary on the order of Magruder, the deputy director of CREEP.

Sloan had delivered the $199,000 to Liddy with misgivings after being advised by Stans, President Nixon's chief fund-raiser and director of the finance arm of CREEP, that Mitchell, the director of the political arm of CREEP, had informed him that Magruder had authority to order Sloan to make the payment.

When I asked Moore if these circumstances ought not to have convinced the President and his aides that something was rotten in CREEP and moved them to take action, Moore said, in effect, that their immediate inaction was justified because the FBI was investigating, and their subsequent inaction was justified because the Department of Justice had advised them that nobody was involved in Watergate except the seven original defendants.

More than four hundred years before President Nixon and his most intimate advisers professed their ignorance of Watergate and the ensuing efforts to cover it up, John Heywood recorded this ancient proverb: "Who is so deafe, or so blynde as is hee/ That wilfully will nother here nor see?"

15

HUSH MONEY

KALMBACH assured the Select Committee when he appeared before it that he had no prior knowledge of the Watergate break-in, had not participated in any efforts to cover up that incident, and had not engaged in any act of campaign sabotage.

He testified that Dean sent him this message by long-distance telephone on June 28, eleven days after the break-in: "We would like to have you raise funds for the legal defense of these defendants and for the support of their families," and asked him to come to Washington without delay to discuss doing so. Pursuant to this request, Kalmbach affirmed, he met Dean in Washington the next morning.

When he asked Dean "whether or not it would not be perhaps preferable to have a public committee formed to raise funds for these people and for these purposes," Kalmbach asserted, Dean replied, "There was no time for this" and it was essential to keep the activity secret because it would be misinterpreted if it became known. When he agreed to accept the assignment, Kalmbach declared, Dean told him LaRue would give him directions "as to specific amounts and specific individuals" and Anthony T. Ulasewicz would be an appropriate person "to act as the distributor for the funds."

Although he believed it absolutely legal for him to raise, and

Ulasewicz to distribute, funds for the legal defense of the seven original Watergate defendants and the support of their families, Kalmbach said he became concerned as the days went by about Dean's authority to give him the assignment as well as with the clandestine character of the undertaking. For this reason, Kalmbach testified, he visited Ehrlichman on July 26, and this colloquy ensued:

Kalmbach: "John, I am looking right into your eyes. I know Jeanne and your family, you know Barbara and my family. You know that my family and my reputation mean everything to me, and it is just absolutely necessary, John, that you tell me, first, that John Dean has the authority to direct me in this assignment, that it is a proper assignment, and that I am to go forward on it."

Ehrlichman: "Herb, John Dean does have the authority, it is proper, and you are to go forward."

Ehrlichman explained, Kalmbach said, that the secrecy was necessary because "getting these funds to these people for this purpose could get into the press and be misinterpreted." Ehrlichman added, Kalmbach said, that if this happened, "they would have our heads in their laps."

Kalmbach affirmed that, in effect, he construed Ehrlichman's remarks to indicate that publicity of the undertaking "would jeopardize the campaign."

Kalmbach testified additionally as follows:

1. He raised approximately $220,000 all in cash, for distribution in proportions specified by LaRue among the Watergate defendants. He got the bulk of this money from Stans, who gave him $75,100 on June 29; from LaRue, who gave him $40,000 about July 19; and from Thomas V. Jones, a Nixon friend and contributor, who gave him $75,000 in early August. The money he received from Stans and LaRue represented Nixon campaign funds, and the money contributed by Jones constituted his personal funds. He assured Stans and Jones he needed the money for a special White House project, but did not disclose to them what specific use was to be made of it.

2. He delivered approximately $190,000 of the money in cash to Ulasewicz, who distributed it in surreptitious ways to the Watergate defendants. To ensure the secrecy of what they did, he and Ulasewicz communicated with each other only in person or by public pay phones, used assumed names, referred to others by fictitious names, and used code words to disguise the substance of their communications.

3. As articles highly critical of the Watergate affair multiplied in the press, he lost confidence in Ehrlichman's assurance that what he was

doing was proper, and he and Ulasewicz notified Dean and LaRue they would no longer carry out the assignment. To this end, he met Dean and LaRue in Dean's office in the Executive Office Building, gave them an accounting of his activities, burned the records of his receipts and disbursements in their presence, made arrangements to have Ulasewicz deliver to LaRue the undistributed balance of the money approximating $30,000, and withdrew from the assignment.

Ulasewicz was a jovial person who added a comic touch to a depressing investigation. He described in his droll way how he traveled about with large sums of cash in paper bags, and made undetected deliveries of $25,000 to Bittman, $8,000 to Liddy, $154,500 to Hunt's wife, and approximately $30,000 to LaRue. According to his testimony, Ulasewicz effected the delivery to Bittman by placing the money on the ledge of a telephone booth in Bittman's office building and notifying Bittman by telephone of its location, and the deliveries to Liddy, Hunt's wife, and LaRue by depositing the money in lockers in the National Airport in Washington and notifying them by telephone of the locations of nearby telephone booths to which he scotch-taped the keys to the lockers. He made certain the intended recipients got the money by standing by until they appeared and obtained it. Ulasewicz stated that Hunt's wife, in turn, distributed the money she received among the defendants.

Ulasewicz also told the Select Committee he had been employed by the White House at times to investigate the drinking, sexual, and social activities, and the domestic problems of political opponents of the Nixon administration.

Senator Weicker put to him this question: "It's fair to say that you dealt in dirt, isn't it?" Ulasewicz replied, "Allegations of it, yes."

Ulasewicz said he told Kalmbach "something here is not kosher," and they withdrew from the assignment.

After the withdrawal of Kalmbach and Ulasewicz, the task of transmitting money to the Watergate defendants was assumed by LaRue, a Mississippian of standing and wealth, who was a confidant of Mitchell and an active official of CREEP.

LaRue informed the Select Committee he had reached the decision in April 1973 to testify truly concerning his knowledge of Watergate. On the evening of June 19, two days after the break-in, he said, he met with Mitchell, Magruder, Mardian, and Dean in Mitchell's Washington apartment, and they discussed the break-in. In the course of their discussion, he added, Magruder asked for advice as to what disposition he should make of some sensitive files based on electronic surveillance, and Mitchell said it "might be a good idea if Mr. Magruder had a fire." Two days later, he stated, Mardian and Liddy met with him in his Washington apartment, and Liddy told them that he and Hunt had set up the Watergate operation and "had recruited the five people that had been caught in the Democratic National Committee" offices. Liddy also told them, LaRue said, about participating in the burglary of the office of Dr. Fielding, and an unsuccessful attempt to burglarize the campaign offices of Senator McGovern. Liddy assured them, LaRue declared, that he would never disclose what he knew about these things to law enforcement officers.

LaRue informed the committee that during the ensuing weeks he met almost daily with Mitchell, Mardian, Magruder, and Dean, and that they agreed to do everything they could to keep the connection between Watergate and CREEP a secret. As a result, he declared, Magruder's cover-up story evolved, and he knew in advance that Magruder was going to commit perjury to divert attention from the truth.

LaRue also admitted he was apprehensive that some of the Watergate defendants might "spill the beans" and so he joined other persons connected with CREEP in an effort to finance them pending their trials.

From about the last of September 1972 through March 1973, LaRue testified he disbursed cash from campaign funds aggregating $230,000 for the benefit of the Watergate defendants. Of this total, he said, he gave $210,000 to Hunt's lawyer, Bittman, who divided it among the various defendants and their lawyers.

LaRue testified that a substantial part of the disbursements he made were from an unspent portion of $350,000 in cash which CREEP originally allocated to the White House for polling operations and the White House afterwards returned to CREEP through the agency of Haldeman's aide, Strachan.

According to LaRue, he made all of the disbursements on the order of Dean except the last amounting to $75,000, which he made to Bittman on the evening of March 21, 1973, on the authority of Mitchell.

Near the end of LaRue's testimony, I asked him this question: "Well, don't you agree, in the light of hindsight, that it was not very appropriate to use money contributed to elect the President to keep burglars silent?" He replied, "I will agree with that, Senator; yes, sir."

I then made this comment:

> I can't resist the temptation to philosophize just a little bit about Watergate. The evidence thus far introduced or presented before this committee tends to show that men upon whom fortune had smiled benevolently and who possessed great financial power, great political power, and great governmental power, undertook to nullify the laws of man and the laws of God for the purpose of gaining what history will call a very temporary political advantage.
>
> The evidence also indicates that the efforts to nullify the laws of man might have succeeded if it had not been for a courageous Federal Judge, Judge Sirica, and a very untiring set of investigative reporters. But you come from a state like the State of Mississippi, where they have great faith in the fact that the laws of God are embodied in the King James version of the Bible, and I think that those who participated in this effort to nullify the laws of God overlooked one of the laws of God which is set forth in the seventh verse of the sixth chapter of Galatians: "Be not deceived. God is not mocked; for whatsoever a man soweth, that shall he also reap."

When they appeared before the Select Committee, Ehrlichman and Haldeman denied the payments made by Kalmbach and LaRue for the benefit of the Watergate defendants were hush money to buy their silence. On the contrary, they asserted, the payments constituted, in effect, benevolent gifts motivated solely by the immaculate purpose of providing the Watergate defendants with family support and legal representation during their trials.

While Ehrlichman was testifying to this effect, I put to him these questions and received from him these answers:

> QUESTION: Mr. Ehrlichman, do I understand that you are testifying that the Committee to Re-Elect the President and those associated with them constituted an eleemosynary institution that gave $450,000 to some burglars and their lawyers merely because they were sorry for them?
> ANSWER: I am afraid I am not your best witness on that, Mr. Chairman. I do not know what their motives were. I think those will appear in the course of the proceeding.
> QUESTION: You stated this was a defense fund just like that given to Angela Davis and Daniel Ellsberg, did you not?
> ANSWER: I stated that was my understanding of it.
> QUESTION: Well, Daniel Ellsberg and the Angela Davis defense funds were raised in public meetings and the newspapers carried news items about them, did they not?
> ANSWER: I am not sure that we know who the donors to those funds

were. I dare say there are many people in this country who contributed to those funds who would not want it known.

QUESTION: But do you not think most of the people contributed their funds because they believed in the causes they stood for?

ANSWER: I assume that.

QUESTION: Well, certainly, the Committee To Re-Elect the President and the White House aides, like yourself, did not believe in the cause of burglars or wiretappers, did you?

ANSWER: No.

QUESTION: I have always thought that if a political committee enacted the role of an eleemosynary institution, it would, like the Pharisee, brag about it on all opportunities. Do you agree with me that a Doubting Thomas might think that this money was routed in this clandestine way, not only to keep it secret, but also to keep these people who were receiving the money secret?

ANSWER: No. I don't agree with that because I don't know that.

I put these questions to Haldeman and received these answers from him:

QUESTION: Can you justify in the light of the information you have the use of politically raised funds to pay or defray the defense costs of persons charged with burglarizing and bugging the Democratic National headquarters in the Watergate?

ANSWER: On my own I can't make that justification. I don't know what basis the justification or reasoning was on the part of those who did make that decision.

QUESTION: Unfortunately I was not born yesterday and I have observed political organizations a long time, and I have never yet seen a political organization which was an eleemosynary institution. But assuming that the Committees To Re-Elect the President were eleemosynary institutions, can you tell this committee why it was when they picked out the objects of their eleemosynary concern that they didn't select anybody except seven men who were accused of complicity in burglarizing and bugging the headquarters of the opposition political party?

ANSWER: Mr. Chairman, as I have said, I can't speak to the reasons or factors in the decisions that were played by other people.

At the time he gave Kalmbach the assignment to raise money for the seven original Watergate defendants, Dean testified, he told him the money was to be given to them for their silence. His most dramatic and damning testimony on this aspect of Watergate and, indeed, on President Nixon's involvement in the cover-up operations was based on what transpired in three secret meetings held on March 21, 1973. In the first meeting the President met with Dean alone; in the second meeting, he met with Dean and Haldeman; and in the third meeting he met with Dean, Haldeman, and Ehrlichman.

Dean testified that before the meetings he had concluded the cover-up ought to be terminated, and he sought the first meeting with the President to urge him to put an end to it.

At the outset of the meeting, Dean affirmed, he told President Nixon there was a cancer growing on his presidency and the cancer might destroy his presidency unless it was promptly excised. In elaboration of this thesis, he asserted, he informed the President how officers of CREEP and White House aides had covered up Watergate since June 17, 1972, by paying "hush money," perjury, and other means, and advised him that the maintenance of the cover-up would become more difficult in the days ahead. He specifically told the President, he related, that even then Hunt was threatening to expose the seamy things he had done for Ehrlichman while he was with the White House Plumbers if he was not paid $72,000 for living expenses and $50,000 for attorney fees before he appeared before Judge Sirica for sentencing on March 23; that the convicted Watergate defendants would probably make blackmail demands for their continued silence after Judge Sirica sent them to jail; and that "these people are going to cost a million dollars over the next two years."

Dean asserted that instead of ending the cover-up, as he had hoped, President Nixon explored means for continuing it, and mentioned use of presidential clemency as a possible means of accomplishing that objective. After being advised by Dean that consideration of politics and public relations made it "impossible for the President to extend clemency to Hunt or the others," Dean said, the President rejected the possible use of clemency by saying, "No, it's wrong, that's for sure."

According to Dean, President Nixon then turned to "hush money" as a means for continuing the cover-up. To this end, Dean said, the President made statements to him in the first secret meeting and to him and Haldeman in the second secret meeting authorizing and urging an immediate payment to Hunt to buy time and his continued silence, and declaring he was able to raise and willing to spend an additional million dollars to satisfy demands for money the convicted Watergate defendants might make after their imprisonment. Haldeman approved the President's decision as announced in the second meeting, Dean said, by saying, in essence, "We've got to turn off" exposure "at whatever . . . cost it takes." During the third meeting, Dean asserted, President Nixon and Haldeman agreed the payment to Hunt would solve the immediate problem. Shortly after the third meeting adjourned, LaRue delivered his final payment of $75,000 to Hunt's lawyer, Bittman.

Haldeman appeared before the Senate Select Committee as a witness on July 30. As the testimony he gave at that time indicated, President Nixon realized the injurious nature of Dean's evidence as to what happened in the secret meetings on March 21, and Haldeman, obviously acting at President Nixon's request, charged that Dean lied when he said the President sanctioned the payment of "hush money."

Before Haldeman testified, however, the Select Committee made a devastating discovery which ultimately drove President Nixon from the White House.

16

DISCOVERY
OF THE
NIXON TAPES

FRIDAY, July 13, 1973, was an unlucky day for Richard M. Nixon. On that day the staff of the Select Committee discovered the existence of President Nixon's secret tapes. In a very real sense the discovery was fortuitous. When the Senate established its Select Committee to investigate the Watergate, the cover-up was holding firm, and evidence throwing light on the truth of that event was largely unavailable.

In its search for truth, the committee collected the names of persons who were not suspected of any complicity in Watergate but were reasonably believed to possess information that might have some relevancy to that affair. In this way the committee acquired the name of Alexander P. Butterfield, a retired Air Force officer, who had served as an assistant to the President from 1969 until 1973, when he became administrator of the Federal Aviation Administration.

In describing his secret meeting with President Nixon on April 15, Dean told the Select Committee "the President almost from the outset began asking me a number of leading questions, which made me think the conversation was being taped and that a record was being made to protect himself."

On the late afternoon of Friday, July 13, 1973, Butterfield was interrogated by two of the most useful members of the committee staff,

Scott Armstrong, an investigator, and Donald G. Sanders, deputy minority counsel, who were seeking to ascertain what he knew that was relevant to the matters being investigated.

Some days before, White House counsel J. Fred Buzhardt had supplied the committee with summaries of Nixon-Dean conversations with the request that they be used in cross-examining Dean.

While he was interrogating Butterfield, Armstrong exhibited to him Buzhardt's summaries. They excited in Sanders' mind the thought that they were too specific to be based on mere recollections. Prompted by this thought, Sanders called Butterfield's attention to Dean's testimony about his April 15 meeting with President Nixon, and asked him this question: "Do you know of any basis for the implications in Dean's testimony that conversations in the President's office are recorded?"

Butterfield replied, "I was hoping you fellows wouldn't ask me that." Butterfield thereupon disclosed that President Nixon had had taping devices installed in the Oval Office, his office in the Executive Office Building, and the Cabinet Room in 1971, and that they were still in operation when he went to the Federal Aviation Administration on March 14, 1973.

It is rather ironic that the Nixon-Dean conversation of April 15, which triggered the revelation, was not recorded because the devices in the Oval Office had run out of tape on that occasion.

It was impossible to overmagnify the importance of Butterfield's revelation. As a consequence, the committee replaced the first witness, Kalmbach, scheduled for Monday, July 16, 1973, with Butterfield. He told the committee and a startled nation that President Nixon's offices in the White House and the Executive Office Building had been bugged and the telephones in them had been tapped with voice-activated eavesdropping devices since the spring of 1971, and that presumably tapes of all conversations between President Nixon and others occurring in those offices or by means of those phones since that time were in the possession of the White House.

Butterfield testified that the President had had the eavesdropping devices installed for historical purposes and that during his tenure in the White House nobody knew of their existence except the President, Haldeman, Higby, some secret service personnel, and himself.

By the letter of its counsel, Buzhardt, the White House confirmed the existence of the eavesdropping devices, and undertook to justify President Nixon's use of them by asserting that the Johnson administration had indulged in a similar practice.

Butterfield's testimony made indisputable the fact that the White House had in its possession taped records of conversations between President Nixon and John Dean which would provide a conclusive answer to the question troubling the nation: Did John Dean lie or tell the truth when he swore President Nixon was aware of efforts to cover up the Watergate burglary, and was to some extent a party to them?

Some intriguing questions concerning the tapes have arisen. Why did President Nixon tape what others said to him without their knowledge? Was he bugging for history? Did he distrust those with whom he conversed? There are no conclusive answers to these questions.

With his penchant for red herrings, President Nixon suggested that former President Johnson had advised him to eavesdrop electronically, and was therefore responsible for what he did.

Why did President Nixon not destroy the tapes after Butterfield made their existence known? There is an answer to this question. President Nixon constantly invoked the constitutional doctrine of separation of governmental powers to justify arbitrary executive action. He obviously believed that this constitutional doctrine separated the occupant of the presidency from all accountability to Congress, the courts, and other earthly authorities. Hence, he was convinced that no one would ever hear his tapes without his consent.

17

EHRLICHMAN
AND HALDEMAN
AS WITNESSES

THE chief protagonists of the Nixon White House in the hearings were Ehrlichman and Haldeman. Ehrlichman, who began his testimony on July 24, testified five days. He was followed by Haldeman, who testified three days.

They were well represented by the same attorneys, John J. Wilson, a veteran of the Washington bar, and his able associate, Frank H. Strickler. There was no conflict in their testimony; but the demeanors they exhibited in giving it were drastically different. Ehrlichman displayed an arrogant contempt for the committee, and was repeatedly embroiled in stormy controversies with Dash, Talmadge, Inouye, Weicker, and me. Haldeman testified with composure and politeness.

Both Ehrlichman and Haldeman testified they had no personal knowledge of the Watergate burglary and bugging, and did not participate in any way in any subsequent cover-up efforts. On the contrary, they affirmed that they and President Nixon had no inkling of any cover-up efforts until Dean talked to the President on March 21. Ehrlichman asserted additionally that President Nixon did not learn the complete truth about the break-in and ensuing cover-up efforts until April 14, when he completed an inquiry he made after March 30 at the President's direction.

As has already been stated, Ehrlichman and Haldeman attributed their ignorance and that of President Nixon to Dean's failure to keep them informed concerning Watergate-related events, and defended the payments of moneys to the original Watergate defendants and their attorneys as humanitarian efforts to ensure the defendants fair trials.

Ehrlichman was vitriolic in his references to Dean, and prolific in his denials of adverse testimony. Although he admitted that Sloan visited him in July 1972, he asserted he never ascertained what Sloan wanted to tell him, and he merely advised Sloan to get a lawyer. While he conceded that Kalmbach visited him on July 26, he denied that Kalmbach asked him anything about his money-raising activities or that he expressed to Kalmbach any opinion concerning them.

On April 19, 1973, Ehrlichman had a telephone conversation with Kalmbach which he taped without Kalmbach's knowledge. The conversation occurred an hour before Kalmbach was to be interviewed by the prosecutors and a day before he was to testify before the grand jury concerning the payments to the Watergate defendants and their attorneys. The transcript of this telephone conversation, which was received in evidence at the hearings, corroborated Kalmbach and contradicted Ehrlichman in respect to their conversation of July 26, 1972.

In addition, the transcript showed that Ehrlichman told Kalmbach that Dean was trying to obtain immunity from the prosecutors by implicating Haldeman and him, and asked Kalmbach, in effect, to emphasize these things to the prosecutors: first, that the objective of the payments was humanitarian, and, therefore, legal; and, second, that Dean masterminded the payments.

The transcript also disclosed that Ehrlichman warned Kalmbach that when he appeared before the grand jury on the following day, he would be asked whom "you've spoken [to] about your testimony," and that after giving Kalmbach this warning, Ehrlichman made this statement to him: "I would appreciate it if you would say you've talked to me in California because at that time I was investigating this thing for the President."

The transcript indicates that Kalmbach construed this statement as a request from Ehrlichman for him to testify their conversation had occurred at a prior time in California rather than the day before his appearance before the grand jury in Washington.

On being questioned about his telephone conversation with Kalmbach, Ehrlichman asserted he was not seeking to induce Kalmbach to commit perjury before the grand jury, but was simply undertaking to remind Kalmbach that they had previously talked in California about his prospective testimony before the grand jury.

Mardian, who denied the testimony of Dean, Mitchell, and Magruder implicating him in the cover-up, had preceded Ehrlichman before the committee. Mardian testified that in June or July 1971, William Sullivan, an FBI official who was not overly fond of J. Edgar Hoover, informed him he held logs covering the wiretapping by the FBI of seventeen government employees and newsmen suspected of leaking or receiving leaks of information from the National Security Council, and he was apprehensive that Hoover might use them "to maintain his position as Director" of the FBI.

Deeming this a matter of urgency, Mardian said, he flew to San Clemente and relayed to President Nixon what Sullivan had told him. According to Mardian, President Nixon instructed him to obtain the logs from Sullivan and deliver them to Ehrlichman, and he forthwith carried the presidential instruction into effect. The objective of so doing, Mardian intimated, was to make the logs inaccessible to Hoover.

On being questioned, Ehrlichman admitted receiving the logs from Mardian and keeping them in his filing cabinets, where they still were when he left the White House. He asserted, however, he did not ascertain their contents until about the time of the dismissal of the prosecution against Ellsberg.

Ehrlichman admitted talking to United States District Judge W. Matthew Byrne, Jr., the presiding judge in the Ellsberg case, on two occasions while the trial was in progress, about the possibility of his accepting appointment as FBI director. He conceded he acted on the order of President Nixon, but maintained his conduct was not improper or unethical because it was not designed to influence the judge's judicial action in the case.

Ehrlichman denied that he had ordered Dean to "deep-six" Hunt's briefcase, or to shred the sensitive documents taken from Hunt's safe; or had ordered Gray to destroy the sensitive documents; or had authorized Colson to extend an offer of clemency to Hunt; or had sought CIA aid in the cover-up. He asserted that Haldeman had Dean contact the CIA merely to ascertain whether there was basis for the President's fear that the FBI investigation in Mexico might expose CIA activities; that the sensitive documents taken from Hunt's safe were given to Gray simply to prevent their contents from being leaked to the press; and that he did not have any recollection of ever asking General Cushman to extend any CIA assistance to Hunt.

Gray, who testified after Ehrlichman, had this to say about the documents taken from Hunt's safe:

> Mr. Dean then told me that those files contained copies of sensitive and classified papers of a political nature that Hunt had been working on. . . . I distinctly recall Mr. Dean saying that these files were "political dynamite," and "clearly should not see the light of day." It is true that neither Mr. Ehrlichman nor Mr. Dean expressly instructed me to destroy the files. But there was, and is no doubt in my mind that destruction was intended. . . . I burned them during Christmas week. . . . But immediately before putting them in the fire I opened one of the files. It contained what appeared to be copies of "top secret" State Department cablegrams. I read the first cable. I do not recall the exact language but the text of the cable implicated officials of the Kennedy administration in the assassination of President Diem of South Vietnam.

When Gray had the fire at his home in Stonington, Connecticut, in December 1972, he burned the tangible evidence of a seamy thing Hunt had done for Colson. Hunt made this plain when he was a witness before the committee. Colson denied the committee his testimony on this and other matters by hiding behind the Fifth Amendment. On that occasion, at least, his discretion was greater than his valor. But his action in so doing left an intriguing question unanswered: Did Colson discuss the seamy thing with anybody else in the White House?

When it began to plan President Nixon's reelection campaign, the Nixon White House suspected that Senator Edward M. Kennedy might be nominated by the Democratic Party to oppose him. So it hired Hunt and Ulasewicz to dig up data or dirt about Chappaquiddick.

Colson had a more abstruse brainchild. He believed, Hunt testified, that Senator Ted Kennedy in particular and the Democratic Party in general would be discredited in the coming election, particularly in the eyes of Catholic voters, if it could be demonstrated "that a Catholic United States administration had in fact conspired in the assassination of a Catholic chief of state of another country."

As a consequence, Hunt affirmed, he was given "access to State Department cables covering the period of the Diem assassination," and studied them in the hope they would afford "documentation that the Kennedy administration was implicitly, if not explicitly, responsible for the assassination of Diem and his brother-in-law."

After studying the cables, Hunt asserted, he reported to Colson "that there was no hard evidence such as a cable emanating from the White House or a reply coming from the Saigon Embassy" establishing what they had been hoping to demonstrate. On receiving this information, Hunt related, Colson suggested Hunt "might be able to improve upon the record" by creating or fabricating "cables that could substitute" for the documentation they had been hoping to find. Hunt swore that he "did in fact fabricate cables for the purpose of indicating the relationship of the Kennedy administration and the assassination of Diem," and that he showed the fabricated cables to Colson, who was desirous of getting them published, and who put him in touch with William Lambert of *Life* magazine with this end in view.

According to Hunt, he had "warned Mr. Colson previously that the [fabricated] cables were not technically capable of withstanding professional scrutiny." For this reason, Hunt stated, they were willing "to permit Mr. Lambert to hand-copy the texts of the fabricated cables," but were unwilling to allow him to remove them "for photocopying purposes." Hunt added Lambert did not use them.

Hunt has an odd justification for his and Colson's efforts to prostitute history and defame a dead President. He surmised there had once been a real cablegram in State Department files revealing what Colson wished to demonstrate and some culprit had "abstracted" it.

President Nixon was infuriated by Daniel Ellsberg's release of the Pentagon Papers to the press. He suspected Ellsberg had supplied the Soviets with a copy of them.

Ellsberg always denied doing so, and maintained that there was nothing in the portions of the Pentagon Papers he released which could endanger our national security interests. Secretary of Defense Melvin Laird is said to have informed President Nixon that 98 percent of the materials in the Pentagon Papers could be declassified without endangering any security interest of the United States. The Supreme Court, by a 6–3 decision, refused to enjoin publication of the Pentagon Papers by *The New York Times* and the *Washington Post* because the Department of Justice had failed to prove their publication would endanger national security.

Despite all this, President Nixon ordered Ehrlichman to set up within the White House the secret group called the Plumbers to "stop security leaks and to investigate other sensitive security matters." Ehrlichman testified, in substance, that President Nixon took this action because he did not believe the FBI would obtain the information the White House was seeking about Ellsberg and others.

Although Ehrlichman had general supervision of the Plumbers, David Young and Egil Krogh were actively in charge of their operations as co-chairmen. Liddy and Hunt were assigned to the task of assisting them, and the group was completely organized by July 24, 1971. While he was not formally connected with them, Colson took an active interest in their activities.

On June 28 Ellsberg was indicted in the United States District Court in California on two criminal counts based on his possession and release of the Pentagon Papers. Notwithstanding, Colson and Hunt persuaded the Plumbers to adopt a plan to destroy Ellsberg's "public image and credibility." To this end, they undertook to assemble all available derogatory information about him.

Ellsberg had received psychiatric treatment from Dr. Lewis Fielding. At the request of the White House the CIA had prepared psychological profiles on Ellsberg which proved insufficient for Colson's purpose to destroy his public image and credibility. The Plumbers were anxious to obtain access to Dr. Fielding's files relating to Ellsberg's mental or emotional state because they hoped the files would enable the CIA to prepare a psychological profile more to Colson's liking.

Inasmuch as they were convinced that the FBI was not going to obtain from Dr. Fielding the information they desired, Krogh and Young addressed this recommendation to Ehrlichman on August 11, 1972: "We would recommend that a covert operation be undertaken to examine all the medical files still held by Ellsberg's psychoanalyst covering the 2-year period in which he was undergoing analysis." Ehrlichman admitted he approved this recommendation by initialing it at the appropriate place and adding these words: "If done under your assurance that it is not traceable."

Ehrlichman maintained vigorously, however, that he did not thereby sanction the burglarizing of Dr. Fielding's office. In approving "a covert operation," he said, he merely intended that investigators seeking Dr. Fielding's files relating to Ellsberg "would not identify themselves as investigators of the White House or anything of this kind, and that their identities would not be known to the people they were interrogating."

He assumed, he declared, that the investigators would obtain the highly confidential psychiatric records relating to Ellsberg from nurses or nurses' aides.

Young and Krogh construed his approval of their recommendation, however, to authorize them to assign Liddy and Hunt to the task of burglarizing Dr. Fielding's office in a quest for his files on Ellsberg. Acting through Bernard L. Barker, Eugenio R. Martinez, and Felipe De Diego, their hired accomplices of Cuban ancestry, they did that on the night of September 3–4, 1971. The surreptitious entry failed to reveal the files on Ellsberg, which Dr. Fielding subsequently stated he had withdrawn for safekeeping.

Since he had not authorized or anticipated any break-in, Ehrlichman asserted, he was greatly shocked when Young and Krogh informed him of the Fielding break-in.

While disclaiming any responsibility for the action of Liddy and Hunt, Ehrlichman insisted that the President has the inherent power under the Constitution to authorize burglaries, such as the Fielding break-in, whenever he decides in his unreviewable discretion that such action protects the national security. He quoted President Nixon as having declared in March 1973 that this particular break-in "was an important, vital national security, well within the constitutional function of the President."

Ehrlichman made this assertion on July 24, his first day on the witness stand. By so doing, he provoked the stormiest of his controversies with Dash, Talmadge, Inouye, Weicker, and me.

Ehrlichman and his attorneys invoked the Act of Congress embodied in 18 U.S.C. 2511 to support his contention. I pointed out that, subject to enumerated exceptions, this statute merely makes interceptions of specified wire and oral communications crimes; that the exceptions in the statute relating to the President confer no statutory powers on him; and that the statute has no possible application to surreptitious entries unrelated to interceptions of the specified communications.

Ehrlichman and his attorneys countered with the assertion that by enacting one of the statutory exceptions in 18 U.S.C. 2511 Congress had recognized the inherent constitutional power of the President to authorize surreptitious entries, such as the Fielding break-in. This exception is in these words: "Nothing in this chapter or in section 605 of the Communications Act of 1934 . . . shall limit the constitutional power of the President to take such measures as he deems necessary . . . to protect national security information against foreign intelligence activities."

I said, "Foreign intelligence activities had nothing to do with the opinion of Ellsberg's psychiatrist about his intellectual or emotional or psychological state."

Ehrlichman asked, "How do you know that, Mr. Chairman?"

I replied, "Because I understand the English language. It is my mother tongue."

Attorney Wilson and I thereupon exchanged these comments:

> WILSON: The CIA must have thought that it had some foreign relationship because they have done an ineffective profile on Ellsberg.
> ERVIN: Well, the CIA had no business doing that because the law prohibits them from having anything to do with internal security.
> WILSON: Sir, you would not consider that foreign intelligence activity is—
> ERVIN: No, it was a domestic intelligence activity. These people were from the Plumbers, from the White House, doing this.
> WILSON: We had a man passing secrets to the Soviet government.
> ERVIN: Well, Ellsberg's psychiatrist wasn't doing that.

The evidence received by the committee made the relevant facts plain. The Plumbers were White House vigilantes possessing no statutory authority whatever. They committed a forcible, surreptitious, and warrantless entry of a psychiatrist's office to seize legally confidential psychiatric records relating to his patient. Under the law, those records could not have been admitted in evidence in any court in America without the consent of the patient unless the presiding judge ruled their admission was essential to the doing of justice in a pending case. The Plumbers were not seeking the records for use as evidence in court or to protect national security. They were seeking them solely because they hoped to use them "to destroy the image and credibility" of the patient, who was awaiting trial on criminal charges.

In making and possessing his records of Ellsberg's psychiatric state, Dr. Fielding was not engaged in "foreign intelligence activities"; and in seeking to obtain those records by a forcible, surreptitious, and warrantless entry, the Plumbers were not protecting "national security information against foreign intelligence activities," even if they acted with the approval of President Nixon. They were, I maintained, committing a rank burglary in violation of the Fourth Amendment.

The Constitution, I asserted, did not confer upon the President the arbitrary power to suspend any of its provisions. On the contrary, I said, it gave him no powers except those expressly stated and those necessarily implied from them. The Constitution was written that way, I declared, to restrain the President from tyranny.

Attorney Wilson had represented one of the steel companies in the famous steel-seizure case, where the Supreme Court held that President Truman had no inherent constitutional power to seize the steel mills during the Korean War. In calling attention to this case, I noted: "I think that is authority that if the President has no inherent power to seize steel mills in time of war to carry on the war, he has no inherent power to steal a document from a psychiatrist's office in time of peace."

When the hearings were resumed on July 25, Mr. Wilson and the committee renewed the discussion of the previous day.

Attorney Wilson made an eloquent argument in support of Ehrlichman's contention. In the course of it, he told an anecdote about a country lawyer.

After he finished his argument, I said, "Mr. Wilson, I have enjoyed your argument. I have long known you to be one of the nation's truly great lawyers. I am a country lawyer myself, and sometimes I get emphatic in the statement of my views because I have never been able to straddle fences very well."

Senator Baker observed, "The Chairman is fond of pointing out from time to time that he is just a country lawyer. He omits to say he graduated from Harvard Law School with honors."

I responded, "I would like to say a word in my own defense on that point. I had a friend introduce me to a North Carolina audience. He said he understood that I was a graduate of the Harvard Law School, but added, 'Thank God, nobody would ever suspect it.'"

Senator Talmadge's questioning of Ehrlichman on July 25 was especially penetrating. He asked him, in effect, if the inherent constitutional power of the President to authorize covert break-ins extended to murder, robbery, and other crimes. Ehrlichman confessed he did not know where to draw the line.

In reply to Talmadge's questions, Ehrlichman testified he had no knowledge that President Nixon expressly authorized the Fielding break-in and he had read President Nixon's subsequent statement denying it. He added:

> On the 24th of July [1971] I sat in a meeting where the President gave Mr. Krogh his charter, his instructions. I must say that the President put it to Mr. Krogh very strong that he wanted Mr. Krogh and the people in the unit to take such steps as were necessary, and I can recall in that conversation specific reference to the use of polygraphs and summary procedure for the discharging of Federal employees who might have been involved in this episode.

Talmadge and Ehrlichman indulged in this colloquy:

> TALMADGE: Do you remember when we were in law school we studied a famous principle of law that came from England, and also is well known in this country, that no matter how humble a man's cottage is, that even the King of England cannot enter without his consent.
> EHRLICHMAN: I am afraid that has been considerably eroded over the years, has it not?
> TALMADGE: Down in my country we still think it is a pretty legitimate principle of law.

This colloquy prompted me to make these observations:

> But I do want to take this occasion to amplify the legal discussion and I want to mention a little of the Bible, a little of history, and a little of law.
> The concept embodied in the phrase every man's home is his castle represents the realization of one of the most ancient and universal hungers of the human heart. One of the prophets described the mountain of the Lord as being a place where every man might dwell under his own vine and fig tree with none to make him afraid.
> And then this morning, Senator Talmadge talked about one of the greatest statements ever made by any statesman, William Pitt the Elder. Before this country revolted against the King of England he said this: "The poorest man in his cottage may bid defiance to all the forces of the crown. It may be frail, its roof may shake, the wind may blow through it, the storm may enter, the rain may enter, but the King of England cannot enter. All his force dares not cross the threshold of the ruined tenement."
> And yet we are told here today, and yesterday, that what the King of England can't do, the President of the United States can.
> The greatest decision that the Supreme Court of the United States has ever handed down in my opinion is that of *Ex Parte Milligan* which is reported in 4 Wallace 2, and the things I want to mention appear on page 121 of that opinion.
> In that case President Lincoln, or rather some of his supporters, raised a claim that since the Civil War was in progress that the military forces in Indiana had a right to try for treason, a man whom they called a Copperhead in those days because he was sympathetic toward the South. He was a civilian who had no connection with the military forces. So they set up a military commission and tried this man, a civilian, in a military court, and sentenced him to death.
> One of the greatest lawyers this nation ever produced, Jeremiah Black, brought the battle to the Supreme Court and he told in his argument, which is one of the greatest arguments of all time, how the Constitution of the United States came into being. He said that the people who drafted and ratified that Constitution were deter-

mined that not one drop of the blood which had been shed throughout the ages to wrest power from arbitrary authority should be lost. So they went through all of the great documents of the English law from Magna Carta on down, and whatever they found there they incorporated in the Constitution to preserve the liberties of the people.

Now although the Constitution gave a civilian the right to trial in civilian courts, and the right to be indicted by a grand jury before he could be put on trial and then a right to be tried before a petit jury, the Government argued that the President had the inherent power to suspend those constitutional principles because of the great emergency which existed at that time when the country was torn apart in the civil strife.

The Supreme Court of the United States rejected the argument that the President had any inherent power to ignore or suspend any of the guarantees of the Constitution, and Judge David Davis said, in effect: "The good and wise men who drafted and ratified the Constitution foresaw that troublous times would arise, when rulers and people would become restive under restraint and seek by sharp and decisive measures to accomplish ends deemed just and proper, and that the principles of Constitutional liberty would be put in peril unless established by irrepealable law."

Then he proceeded to say: "And for these reasons, these good and wise men drafted and ratified the Constitution as a law for rulers and people alike, at all times and under all circumstances."

Then he laid down this great statement: "No doctrine involving more pernicious consequences was ever invented by the wit of man than that any of its provisions can be suspended during any of the great exigencies of government."

And notwithstanding that we have it argued here in this year of our Lord 1973 that the President of the United States has a right to suspend the Fourth Amendment and to have burglary committed just because he claims, or somebody acting for him claims, that the records of a psychiatrist about the emotional and mental state of his patient, Ellsberg, had some relation to national security.

Now, President Nixon himself defined the national security in one of his directives as including only two things: national defense, and relations with foreign countries. How in the world opinions of a psychiatrist about the mental state or the emotional state or the psychological state of his patient, even if his patient was Ellsberg, could have any relation to national defense or relations to a foreign country is something which eludes the imagination of this country lawyer.

Much of Haldeman's testimony has already been stated. Its thrust was that President Nixon and he were ignorant of the truth respecting

Watergate and without information of any cover-up efforts prior to March 21, 1973. He attributed their ignorance to their engrossment in presidential duties, and to Dean. Dean misled them, he affirmed, by assuring him that nobody in the White House was implicated in Watergate, and by failing to inform him of any Watergate-related incidents to the contrary.

In absolving himself from complicity, Haldeman gave innocent explanations of some events, denied any recollection of other events, and rejected as false testimony implicating him in the cover-up.

He admitted he approved Chapin's hiring of Segretti to harass candidates for the Democratic presidential nomination, but asserted he did so with the understanding that Segretti would not perpetrate any illegal or unethical political tricks upon them. He insisted that payments of money to Watergate defendants and their lawyers constituted humanitarian endeavors. While he conceded he instructed Strachan to return to CREEP the unspent part of the $350,000 allocated by it to the White House, he insisted he did so simply because the White House had no need for the money and he was without information that CREEP intended to use it for payments to the defendants.

Haldeman declared he had no recollection of ever receiving any memorandum or talking paper from Strachan notifying him that Mitchell had approved Magruder's project for a sophisticated intelligence-gathering plan.

He stated he had no information from any source of the existence of the plan, and had never discussed it with Mitchell or received any data based on the wiretapping of phone conversations in the Democratic National Committee.

Haldeman denied the testimony of Magruder, Dean, and Strachan tending to show he had information about Watergate and its cover-up before March 21, 1973, or that he encouraged the cover-up by deed or word. He asserted that information subsequently received by him indicated that Mitchell, Magruder, and Dean were responsible for Watergate and the ensuing cover-up operations.

On the basis of his recollection and his interpretation of the secret tape covering their meeting which President Nixon had temporarily entrusted to him just before he was scheduled to testify before the committee, Haldeman rejected as false Dean's testimony that President Nixon was aware of the cover-up as early as September 15, 1972. He insisted that President Nixon was pleased that no one in the White

House was named in the indictments returned that day and commended Dean merely because he believed proper acts on his part had contributed to that result.

Some inferences seem inescapable. Sometime in April President Nixon became apprehensive that Dean might testify before the committee and give testimony of a devastating character concerning the three secret meetings of March 21. At that time he entrusted his secret tapes covering these meetings to Haldeman, who was then his chief of staff, and had Haldeman make a report to him concerning their contents.

The testimony Dean gave the committee in respect to these secret meetings shocked the nation, and made it imperative for the White House to attempt to counteract it.

Haldeman was available to contradict what Dean said about the second meeting, and Haldeman and Ehrlichman were available to contradict what he said about the third meeting. But the only human being on earth who could claim he had personal information contradictory of what Dean said about the first secret meeting was President Nixon, and he was unwilling to testify on oath before the committee and thus subject his testimony to the best test of truth—cross-examination.

The White House and Haldeman collaborated on a plan to solve this quandary. While he was unwilling to give the committee or the special prosecutor access to any of his tapes, the President entrusted to Haldeman, now a private citizen, the tapes of March 21, and Haldeman constructed an addendum to his general statement on Watergate in which he placed an interpretation on the tapes covering all three of the secret meetings of March 21 contradictory of Dean's testimony incriminatory of President Nixon.

The addendum was adroitly phrased. It did not contradict Dean's testimony in substance except to the extent that it incriminated President Nixon. It stated the tapes disclosed that President Nixon was trying to bring out Dean's views rather than to express his own purposes, and that instead of approving the final payment to Hunt, President Nixon was merely exploring what Dean thought should be done in respect to his demand.

The most crucial specific difference between the addendum and Dean's testimony related to the anticipated blackmail demand of the Watergate defendants for as much as $1 million. The addendum admitted the President stated, as Dean had testified, that he would be able to raise the money without difficulty, but precluded such action by adding "that would be wrong."

When his reading of his general statement on the Watergate reached its mention of the March 21 meetings, Haldeman paused and said:

> I was not present for the first hour of the meeting, but I did listen to the tape of the entire meeting—including that portion before I came in. While I am free to testify to everything which I can recall happening during the time I was present, the President has directed that I not testify as to any facts which I learned solely by listening to the tapes of the meeting. My counsel will present a letter in this respect, and I shall obey the decision of the committee as to its ruling thereon. Depending on that decision, I shall issue an appropriate addendum to this statement concerning the March 21 meeting.

At this point Attorney Wilson presented to the committee a letter signed by Buzhardt, the White House special counsel. The letter stated, in substance, that President Nixon had instructed Haldeman to decline to testify as to facts about meetings or portions of meetings he did not attend "which he learned solely by listening to a tape recording of such meeting" and "that the President, in so instructing Mr. Haldeman, is doing so pursuant to the constitutional doctrine of separation of powers."

After consultation with the other members of the committee, I made this statement:

> I have read Mr. Buzhardt's letter giving his view of executive privilege and have taken the position all the time . . . that the matters which this committee is authorized by Senate Resolution No. 60 to investigate are not covered by executive privilege of any kind. Furthermore, I think if Mr. Haldeman has been authorized by the White House to hear tapes, even though he was not present when the tapes were made, that he is authorized to testify about them. I am sorry in a way this is not a court of law where you can rule, but the best evidence of what these tapes say is the tapes themselves, and as a member of the committee I continually pray that the Good Lord will give the White House guidance to let this committee hear the tapes.
>
> But as far as I am concerned I overrule the claim of executive privilege interposed in the last paragraph of Mr. Buzhardt's letter. . . .
>
> I am constrained, however, to observe that it is a strange thing that Mr. Haldeman can hear the tapes, but this committee cannot hear them. And I hope that they will eventually be made available to the

committee because we have heard a lot of complaints about hearsay testimony and this is hearsay, but if Mr. Haldeman is permitted to hear the tapes, it looks like the representatives of the American people in the Congress ought to be allowed to hear them. So you have got a ruling, and you may proceed.

Haldeman thereupon proceeded to read his addendum.

The White House's objection to Haldeman's testifying about his interpretation of the tape covering the first meeting of March 21 was clearly a subterfuge to evade the charge the President was waiving his claim of executive privilege in respect to the tapes. If it had been upheld, the specious objection would have thwarted the objective the President had in view when he entrusted the tapes to Haldeman.

Recognizing the shadowboxing for what it was, I observed, "This is what I would call a powderpuff objection. If they had really meant the objection to be sustained, they would have been right here raising Cain about it themselves."

I elicited the admission from Haldeman that the contents of his addendum had been communicated to the White House before his appearance before the committee.

Attorney Wilson interjected this inquiry: "What is wrong with that, Mr. Chairman?"

I replied, "I am not saying anything is wrong. It just shows there has been a little of what we call in North Carolina 'connegling together.'"

The Nixon-Haldeman "connegling" backfired. The courts eventually upheld the special prosecutor's subpoena for the tapes covering the secret meetings of March 21, and he submitted them to the grand and petit jurors. They found that the testimony of Dean rather than that of Haldeman harmonized with the tapes. As a result, Haldeman was indicted and convicted of perjury as a recompense for preparing and presenting the addendum to the Select Committee.

18

NIXON'S PROFESSIONS AND PERFORMANCES

HONESTY is the best policy in politics as well as in other affairs. The failure to respect this simple truth destroyed the Nixon presidency.

The Watergate break-in was no "third-rate burglary." It was an extraordinary political event.

As soon as the break-in became known, honesty demanded that President Nixon forthwith put to Mitchell, the director of the political arm of CREEP, and Stans, the director of its finance arm, these questions: How did it happen that burglars were caught in the head-quarters of the opposition political party in the darkness of night with my campaign funds in their possession? How did it happen that the burglars were led by McCord, the security officer of CREEP? How did it happen that this bizarre operation was masterminded by Liddy, the general counsel of CREEP, and Hunt, a White House consultant with an office in the Executive Office Building?

According to Mitchell and Stans, President Nixon did not ask them any of these questions. Indeed, they said, he did not say a mumbling word to them on the subject of Watergate.

During the investigation various people made substantially this statement to me: "If it should discover facts implicating President Nixon in any way, the committee must suppress those facts for the country's sake. It would be disastrous if it were revealed that the President was involved."

My response to them was invariably this: "The Committee will follow the truth wherever it leads. The committee will do this because it is right and because it is impossible to establish a sound administration, or a good government, or an enduring nation on the suppression of truth."

Truth is the most potent force in the universe. President Nixon's political fortunes would have been enhanced and not diminished if he had acted forthrightly at the outset in respect to Watergate. President Calvin Coolidge triumphed in 1924 because he faced Teapot Dome with Yankee candor and courage.

President Nixon's professions and performances in respect to the Watergate investigations were discordant. He professed a desire for the truth to be revealed, and did everything he could to prevent that from happening.

By televised speeches, televised news conferences, and statements through his press secretary, President Nixon assured the American people at all times that he had no information of any efforts to cover up Watergate before March 21, 1973, and that he had not countenanced or participated in any cover-up operations at any time.

From June 25 through June 29 Dean testified under oath and the peril of prosecution for perjury that President Nixon was aware of cover-up operations as early as September 15, 1972, and, after that time, had actually encouraged and participated in them.

Dean's testimony engendered a belief in the minds of those of us who were members of the committee that common sense, forthrightness, his own interests, and the interests of America required President Nixon to establish, if he could, by his own testimony and any documentary evidence controlled by him, the truth of the assertion he made from afar, i.e., that Dean was a liar when he implicated him.

Even apart from this, we believed it was President Nixon's duty to the country to make available to us any documents he controlled which would shed light on the serious matters we had been commanded by the unanimous vote of the Senate to investigate.

After Dean testified, Senator Baker, Senator Weicker, and I emphasized that it was critically important for the committee to get a presidential response in some form to Dean's testimony charging the President with involvement in cover-up operations.

What we said must have prompted the July 6 letter that President

Nixon addressed to me as chairman of the Committee. By this letter, the President stated that he would not testify before the committee or permit it access to his presidential papers, which he defined as any "papers prepared or received by former members of my staff," and that his decision was based on his "obligation to preserve intact the powers and prerogatives of the Presidency, and not upon any desire to withhold information relevant" to the committee's inquiry.

To justify his decision, the letter said: "Formulation of sound public policy requires that the President and his personal staff be able to communicate among themselves in complete candor, and that their tentative judgments, their explanation of alternatives, and their frank comments on issues and personalities at home and abroad remain confidential." To bolster this assertion, President Nixon forwarded to the committee the letter President Truman, after he had retired, wrote to Chairman Harold H. Velde, of the House Un-American Activities Committee, on November 12, 1953, in which he refused to submit himself to interrogation by that committee in respect to the official decisions he had made while serving as President.

By his letter, the President further stated he had already cooperated with the committee in genuine, extensive, and extraordinary ways by permitting present and former White House staff members to testify unrestrictedly before the committee and by waiving attorney-client privilege in respect to his former counsel, Dean.

In closing, the letter stated that the White House staff would "continue to cooperate fully with the Committee in furnishing information relevant to its investigation except in those instances" where the President "determined that meeting the Committee's demands would violate" the President's constitutional responsibility to defend the office of the presidency against encroachment by other branches.

President Nixon claimed credit he did not merit that White House aides were testifying before the committee without pleading executive privilege and that he had waived the attorney-client privilege in respect to Dean. He belatedly consented to these things only after I, in my capacity as chairman, had repeatedly informed the White House that the committee would ask the Senate to have its sergeant at arms arrest and bring before it for appropriate action any present or former White House aide who refused to appear and testify in obedience to a subpoena; that the committee denied that executive privilege covered criminal and political activities; and that the committee knew that the attorney-client privilege was not designed to prevent the disclosure of illegal cover-up plans or operations in which client and lawyer participated.

Inasmuch as the President declared in his letter that he would not permit the committee to have access to presidential papers, the President's pledge that the White House staff would "continue to cooperate fully" with the committee in the future was devoid of substance.

President Nixon's letter of July 6 is clearly susceptible of the interpretation that it was a cleverly contrived public relations effort to mislead Americans into believing he was cooperating with the committee, and to deceive them as to the real issue joined between him and the committee. Unlike the House Un-American Activities Committee, the Senate Select Committee was not seeking any information concerning confidential communications made within the executive branch to enable the President to perform his official duties in a lawful manner. On the contrary, it was seeking evidence to ascertain whether presidential aides had committed improper, unethical, and illegal acts in the presidential election of 1972, and affording President Nixon an opportunity to refute—under circumstances lending some credibility to what he said—Dean's allegations that he had been a knowing participant in cover-up operations.

The committee was conducting a constitutionally authorized investigation. In its last analysis, President Nixon's claim that, as President, he was exempt from the obligation to testify and furnish evidence resting on all other human beings within the borders of our land was based on the strange proposition that an exercise of its constitutional powers by the Senate would impair for all time the constitutional powers of the President. The Constitution is not a self-destructive instrument, and does not speak with a forked tongue. There was not a scintilla of sound reason in President Nixon's assertion that "the powers and prerogatives of the Presidency" would be irreparably injured if he appeared before the committee and told it the truth.

After President Nixon's letter of July 6 became public, I expressed the opinion that the committee had the power to subpoena him to testify, but did not favor its doing so. I added that if he withheld evidence from the committee and the American people, he would subject himself to the "unfavorable inference" which arises against anyone who refuses to furnish to an investigatory body evidence he possesses. Senator Talmadge propounded a question which increasing numbers of Americans were beginning to ask: "If he has nothing to hide, why does he refuse to appear?"

Contemporary writings possess a higher probative value than the slippery memories of witnesses. Hence, the Select Committee requested the White House to furnish it contemporary documents relevant to the matters it was authorized to investigate.

During early days the White House honored requests for inconsequential papers but delayed action interminably on requests for papers of significance. As the result of this obstructive tactic, substantial unanswered requests of the committee for documentary evidence were pending at the White House at the time President Nixon announced by his letter of July 6 that he would thereafter deny the committee access to the documents it was seeking, i.e., papers prepared or received by his former aides.

Being desirous of avoiding an open break with President Nixon and obtaining documentary evidence necessary to enable it to elicit from his former aides to the maximum extent the truth about Watergate, the committee met in executive session on July 12, and unanimously adopted a resolution containing two sections.

The first section declared that the committee maintained it was entitled to have access to every document in the possession of the White House which was relevant to prove or disprove any of the matters the committee was authorized by Senate Resolution 60 to investigate; and the second section authorized the chairman to meet with the President to ascertain whether there was any reasonable possibility of working out any reconciliation between the position of the committee and that announced by the President in his letter of July 6, 1973, which would permit the committee to gain access to documents necessary to empower it to make the inquiry authorized by Senate Resolution 60.

A copy of the resolution was forthwith sent by hand to President Nixon. As chairman of the committee, I sent a letter to him with it. By my letter, I informed the President his action of July 6 posed "the very great possibility of a fundamental constitutional confrontation between Congress and the Presidency," and requested an opportunity for representatives of the committee and its staff to meet with him and his staff to try to find ways to avoid such a confrontation.

Other members of the committee urged me to telephone President

Nixon and seek to make arrangements with him for convening the requested meeting without delay.

After allowing sufficient time for the hand-carried copy of the resolution and my letter to reach the White House, I telephoned President Nixon, and had an exceedingly brief conversation with him. Everything said by us in it is summarized in these words:

I expressed the hope we could meet soon and devise methods to avoid the threatened confrontation. President Nixon, who appeared to be emotionally distraught, exclaimed that the committee was "out to get him." I said, "Mr. President, we are not out to get anything except the truth." The President then told me he was sick, his physician had diagnosed his sickness as viral pneumonia, and he was going to Bethesda Naval Hospital as soon as a few tasks were completed. I wished him a speedy recovery, and he said he would meet with me to discuss the problem after his release from the hospital.

President Nixon's promise raised our hope for an amicable end to the impasse. We believed a meeting could develop a plan whereby representatives of the committee and representatives of the White House could select and make available to the committee the limited number of documents it was seeking.

Our hope was soon dashed. White House aides told the press that the President would not alter his position, and that his offer to meet with me was a mere courtesy. What they said was soon confirmed by President Nixon in person. When he returned from Bethesda Naval Hospital on June 20, he made a speech to White House aides and employees in the Rose Garden in which he said, "Let others wallow in Watergate. We're going to do our job."

He then advised me by letter he was willing to meet with me, but he did not believe that anything would be accomplished by our meeting. His attitude convinced me this was so, and the meeting was never held.

While President Nixon was a patient at Bethesda, Butterfield revealed the existence of the tapes. The committee and the Special Prosecutor forthwith requested him to make available to them tapes covering specified conversations or days. The initial request of the committee was modest. It asked President Nixon for five tapes covering the conversations he had with Dean on September 15, 1972, February 28, 1973, and March 13 and 21, 1973. At the same time the committee specifically asked the President for the documents mentioned in a letter I had written to Leonard Garment on June 21.

If President Nixon had been forthcoming with the tapes, investigations of Watergate could have been concluded with dispatch. He was not forthcoming. As a consequence, he condemned the nation to "wallowing in Watergate" an additional year. President Nixon flatly refused to make any of his tapes available to either the committee or the Special Prosecutor, and his refusal to permit the committee to have access to the tapes requested by it was embodied in a letter dated July 23, addressed to me as chairman. The letter was as follows:

> I have considered your request that I permit the Committee to have access to tapes of my private conversations with a number of my closest aides. I have concluded that the principles stated in my letter to you of July 6th preclude me from complying with that request, and I shall not do so. Indeed the special nature of tape recordings of private conversations is such that these principles apply with even greater force to tapes of private Presidential conversations than to Presidential papers.
>
> If release of the tapes would settle the central questions at issue in the Watergate inquiries, then their disclosure might serve a substantial public interest that would have to be weighed very heavily against the negatives of disclosure.
>
> The fact is that the tapes would not finally settle the central issues before your Committee. Before their existence became publicly known, I personally listened to a number of them. The tapes are entirely consistent with what I know to be the truth and what I have stated to be the truth. However, as in any verbatim recording of informal conversations, they contain comments that persons with different perspectives and motivations would inevitably interpret in different ways. Furthermore, there are inseparably interspersed in them a great many very frank and very private comments, on a wide range of issues and individuals, wholly extraneous to the Committee's inquiry. Even more important, the tapes could be accurately understood or interpreted only by reference to an enormous number of other documents and tapes, so that to open them at all would begin an endless process of disclosure and explanation of private Presidential records totally unrelated to Watergate, and highly confidential in nature. They are the clearest possible example of why Presidential documents must be kept confidential.
>
> Accordingly, the tapes, which have been under my sole personal control, will remain so. None has been transcribed or made public and none will be.
>
> On May 22nd I described my knowledge of the Watergate matter and its aftermath in categorical and unambiguous terms that I know to be true. In my letter of July 6th, I informed you that at an appropriate time during the hearings I intend to address publicly the subjects you are considering. I still intend to do so and in a way that

preserves the Constitutional principle of separation of powers, and thus serves the interests not just of the Congress or of the President, but of the people.

Upon receipt of President Nixon's letter, the committee met in executive session and unanimously directed me as its chairman to issue subpoenas duces tecum commanding the President to make available to the committee the tapes previously requested and certain documents.

When the committee met in open session in the Senate Caucus Room on the afternoon of July 23, I read President Nixon's letter and made these impromptu comments:

> This is a rather remarkable letter about the tapes. If you will notice, the President says he has heard the tapes or some of them, and they sustain his position. But he says he's not going to let anybody else hear them for fear they might draw a different conclusion.
>
> In other words, the President says that they are susceptible of two different interpretations, one favorable to his aides and one not favorable to his aides.
>
> I deeply regret this action. I have very different ideas of separation of powers from those expressed by the President. If such a thing as "executive privilege" is created by the doctrine of separation of powers, it has these attributes. First, if it exists at all, it only exists in connection with official duties.
>
> Second, under no circumstances can it be invoked on either alleged illegal activities or political campaign activities.
>
> I am certain that the doctrine of separation of powers does not impose upon any President either the duty or the power to undertake to separate a congressional committee from access to the truth concerning alleged criminal activities.
>
> I was in hopes that the President would accede to the request of this Committee for these tapes and these papers. I love my country. I venerate the office of the President, and I have the best wishes for the success of the present incumbent of that office, because he is the only President this country has at this time.
>
> A President not only has constitutional powers which require him to take care that the laws be faithfully executed, and I think it's his duty under those circumstances to produce information which would either tend to prove or disprove that criminal activities have occurred. But beyond that, the President of the United States, by reason of the fact that he holds the highest office in the gift of the American people, owes an obligation to furnish a high standard of moral leadership to this Nation and his constitutional duties, in my opinion, and undoubtedly his duty of affording moral leadership to the country, place upon him some obligation under these circumstances.

We have evidence here that during the time the President was running for reelection to the highest office in the gift of the people of this Nation, that some of his campaign funds were found in the possession of burglars in the headquarters of the opposition political party. And I think that high moral leadership demands that the President make available to this committee any information in the form of tapes or records which will shed some light on that crucial question: How did it happen that burglars were caught in the headquarters of the opposition party with the President's campaign funds in their pockets and in their hotel bedrooms at the time? And I don't think the people of the United States are interested so much in abstruse arguments about the separation of powers or executive privilege as they are in finding the answer to that question.

I deeply regret that this situation has arisen, because I think that the Watergate tragedy is the greatest tragedy this country has ever suffered. I used to think that the Civil War was our country's greatest tragedy, but I do remember that there were some redeeming features in the Civil War in that there was some spirit of sacrifice and heroism displayed on both sides. I see no redeeming features in Watergate.

After I concluded my comments, Senator Baker made this statement, which merits a commendatory preservation:

It is difficult for me to express my disappointment that we have arrived at a place where at least the leading edge of a confrontation on the question of separation of powers between the Congress and the White House is before us. You have pointed out that this committee has authorized by unanimous vote the issuance of a subpoena *duces tecum* for certain documents and certain portions of the so-called Butterfield tapes relevant to the inquiry of this committee. As my colleagues on the committee know, I have tried as hard as possible to find a way around this confrontation. I have suggested several alternative possibilities. Even now, I don't despair that no way can be found to reconcile the differences in the conflict that impends between the Congress and the executive department. But I concur with my colleagues on the committee in the evaluation that there was no practical course of action except to authorize the action which has been described. I voted for it and I support it.

I think the material sought by the subpoena *duces tecum* or, more accurately, by the subpoenas *duces tecum*, are essential, if not vital, to the full, thorough inquiry mandated and required of this committee.

I shall refrain from expressing my evaluation of the entire situation—that is, the totality of the testimony and the inferences to be drawn from it—until we have heard all of the information, all of the witnesses, all of the testimony, and examined all of the documents that are made available to us. On February 28, 1974, or prior thereto, if the committee files its report at an earlier date, I will express my conclusions, but not before.

It is my fervent hope, however, that when we finally get to the business of writing a report, that we have available all relevant information and that we can in fact write a definitive statement on Watergate—without trying to indict or punish anyone and certainly without trying to persecute anyone or to protect anyone.

The committee has been criticized from time to time for its absence of rules of evidence, of the right of confrontation, of cross-examination by counsel, and a number of other legal concepts. We do not have defendants, either, and we are not trying to create defendants. We are trying to find facts, to establish circumstances, to divine the causes, and to ascertain the relationships that make up in toto the so-called Watergate affair. I am unhappy that it is necessary for us to come to the brink of a constitutional confrontation. Although that is a hackneyed phrase, it is accurate—a constitutional confrontation between the Congress and the White House—a confrontation that has never been resolved in its totality by the courts. It involves a principle and a doctrine that has never been fully elaborated and spelled out. We must fully discharge our obligation as a committee.

I have no criticism of any person. I will not sit in judgment of any person or the conduct of any person until all of the evidence is taken. But I can do no less than try to gain all of the information necessary to support later conclusions.

While these events were occurring an amusing incident took place.

As soon as it discovered the existence of the tapes, the committee subpoenaed Alfred C. Wong, the secret service agent supposedly in charge of them, to appear before Senator Baker and me in an executive session on the following day, July 17, for interrogation. When he appeared, Wong was accompanied by the general counsel of the Department of the Treasury, which has jurisdiction of the secret service, and the general counsel handed the committee a letter dated the previous day which President Nixon had written to Secretary of the Treasury George P. Schultz. By this letter, the President directed that no officer or agent of the secret service should give to the committee any "testimony concerning matters observed or learned while performing protective functions for the President or their duties at the White House."

Pursuant to the letter, Wong declined to testify on the grounds of executive privilege, and the committee decided it would serve no good purpose to engage in any controversy with the administration on this subject.

Two days later I received a telephone call from a man who professed to be Secretary Shultz and to be relaying to me a message from President Nixon. I immediately informed the committee in open session of what the caller told me. In so doing, I said: "I am pleased to announce that Secretary Shultz has called me and advised me that the President has decided to make available to the committee tapes of conversations which may have been with witnesses before the committee and which are relevant to the matters which the committee is authorized to investigate. Secretary Shultz has further advised me that the President will meet with me in my capacity as the Chairman of the Committee at a convenient time next week, and arrange procedures by which these tapes can be made available to the committee. I am very much gratified by this information. I think the information will enable the committee to expedite its investigation, and I think it was a very wise decision on the part of the President."

Soon afterwards White House attorney Garment telephoned committee counsel that Secretary Shultz had stated he had had no such conversation with me. After verifying this information, I made this report with amusement to the committee in open session:

It appears a hoax has been perpetrated . . . upon the Chairman of the Committee. . . . (I have just) had a conversation with the man who . . . assured me he was the real Secretary Shultz (Laughter), and he informed me that he had had no conversation with me today, (and) that whoever did it was somebody else. . . . So it is just an awful thing for a very trusting soul like me to find that there are human beings, if you can call them such, who would perpetrate a hoax like this. . . . So notwithstanding the fact that my trust in humanity has been grossly abused by someone . . . and notwithstanding the fact that some people think the telephone is an instrument of the devil anyway (laughter), I am going to assume that the information which counsel received at one end of a telephone line from somebody at the other end was indeed information conveyed to them by White House Counsel, and that the recent information is correct. . . . And I trust that nobody in the future will attempt to deceive and mislead a trusting and unsuspicious individual like the Chairman of this committee in any such fashion. (Laughter) . . . The Counsel suggests we have had some talk about dirty tricks. I think it is the unanimous opinion of this committee that this is a right dirty trick. (Laughter)

The committee and its members were harassed by events more somber than this prank. The committee was surreptitiously advised on several occasions that bombs had been planted in the Senate Caucus Room, where hearings were held. I received many furtive threats that I was going to be assassinated, and while I never discussed the matter with my colleagues, I am satisfied they had a similar experience.

The Capitol Hill police, which was the recipient of many of the furtive threats against me, offered to furnish me a plain-clothes bodyguard to accompany me wherever I went. While I accepted the service of a police officer to aid me in making my way through the immense crowd which jammed the hallway leading to the Senate Caucus Room, I declined the service of a bodyguard on other occasions. In so doing, I told the Capitol Hill police I had long since decided I was not immortal, and did not believe a legion of bodyguards could protect me against the pot shot of a crackpot.

The unkindliest threat of all reached me at our apartment a few minutes before my wife and I left to attend a reception which some friends were giving us on our fiftieth wedding anniversary. The threat was that I would be assassinated if I dared to attend the reception.

Incidents of this nature were not entirely without humor. About this time I went to Cincinnati, and delivered the commencement address at the University of Cincinnati. On my return to my suite in a local motel, I found two Cincinnati police officers awaiting me. They advised me their chief had received a furtive call announcing my impending assassination, and had ordered them to spend the night in my suite to protect me until I left Cincinnati. One of them displayed true Irish wit by saying, "I don't know how much the Chief is concerned about the possibility of your assassination. But I am absolutely convinced he doesn't want it to happen in Cincinnati."

Pursuant to the direction of the committee, I issued two subpoenas duces tecum directing the President to furnish the committee the tapes and documents it was seeking. On the date of their issuance, July 23, the subpoenas were delivered to White House counsel by Rufus Edmisten and Terry Lenzner.

Two days later President Nixon informed the committee by letter that he would not obey the subpoenas because the tapes and documents covered by them could not "be made public consistent with the confidentiality essential to the functioning of the office of the President."

In closing his letter, the President said, "To the extent that I have custody of other documents or information relevant to the work of the Select Committee and that can properly be made public, I will be glad to make these available in response to specific requests."

The closing statement was obviously a public relations gimmick designed to mislead people into believing President Nixon was willing to aid the committee in its search for the truth about Watergate. He had already made plain to the committee his determination not to furnish it with any of the documents which it was seeking or which were relevant to its inquiry, i.e., documents prepared or received by his former aides.

President Nixon's letter was delivered to the committee on July 26 while it was conducting public hearings. Inasmuch as its efforts to secure President Nixon's cooperation had proved unavailing, the committee forthwith interrupted the taking of testimony and voted in open session to go to court and seek a judgment requiring President Nixon to surrender to it the requested documents and tapes.

By a nationwide televised speech and a supplementary statement on August 15, and news conferences on August 22 and September 5, 1973, President Nixon undertook to reply to the testimony received by the committee tending to implicate him in the cover-up of Watergate. In so doing, he merely rehashed his former claims that he had not participated in Watergate or its cover-up, that after learning of the cover-up efforts of others in March he sought to ascertain and expose the truth, and that the constitutional doctrine of the separation of powers obligated him to withhold documents and tapes from the committee and the special prosecutor.

On October 3, 1973, I made a speech in the Senate on the constitutional and pragmatic aspects of the confrontation between the committee and President Nixon. I had prepared the speech with painstaking care and called it "Confrontation at the Watergate." At its outset, I revealed my state of mind in this fashion:

> Let me make one thing clear. Nothing I say should be construed to intimate any opinion on my part on a question which disturbs many Americans at this moment, that is, whether the President was personally implicated in any stage of the Watergate affair or its alleged coverup.
>
> My experience of 15 years in judicial offices precludes me from forming or entertaining any opinion on this point at this time. This is true because my experience as a judge has inculcated in me these abiding convictions: First, the most sacred and solemn task devolving upon any human being is that of judging aright the conduct of one of his fellow travelers to the tomb; and, second, anyone cast

in this role does a grave disservice to truth and justice if he finalizes his judgment respecting another's conduct before he has received and weighed all the evidence relating to it which is available to him.

I am acting upon the presumption that the President is morally and legally blameless in respect to any stage of the Watergate affair, and will continue to do so unless competent and credible evidence received by the select committee compels me ultimately to reach a contrary conclusion.

The validity of my assertion to this effect is not impaired by the fact that I may have interrogated with vigor some of the witnesses who have testified before the select committee. Long experience as a trial lawyer has taught me that vigorous interrogation is oftentimes the only way in which truth can be extracted from an evasive or reluctant witness, or a witness who professes a high degree of forgetfulness.

After this, I explained the constitutional power of the Senate to conduct investigations of matters of national concern through committees for legislative purposes; pointed out that the Senate had unanimously created the Senate Select Committee to investigate the Watergate affair in the exercise of its constitutional power; summarized the damning testimony the committee had thus far received concerning the origin of the Watergate burglary and subsequent efforts to cover it up; and charged that President Nixon was obstructing the committee's investigation by withholding from it documents and five tapes controlled by him which contained "highly important evidence tending to show what happened in connection with the Watergate affair, who participated in the ensuing coverup operations, and who was without legal or moral responsibility."

I then discussed how President Nixon had refused to accord the committee access to the documents and tapes voluntarily, and defied subpoenas duces tecum calling for their production, and the committee had been compelled to institute a suit against him in the United States District Court for the District of Columbia in a final effort to obtain access to them. I added, "Fortunately there has been no prior necessity for a suit of this nature, and I will make no prediction in respect to its outcome."

I charged that President Nixon was acting arbitrarily in withholding the documents and tapes from the committee, and in so doing, was violating the Constitution he had taken an oath to support. On this aspect of the matter, I explained in detail my views of the true scope of executive privilege.

In so doing, I emphasized the absurdity of President Nixon's claim that the Constitution impliedly empowered the President to conceal the truth about criminal activities while expressly commanding him to take care that the laws be faithfully executed.

I then proceeded to argue that the excuse President Nixon gave for obstructing the committee's investigation distorted the separation-of-powers principle and ignored reality. In elaborating this argument, I declared:

> The President undertakes to justify his refusal to make available to the select committee evidence it needs to perform its constitutional function by asserting, in substance, that the doctrine of the separation of the powers of Government confers upon him an absolute power to withhold the tapes and memorandums from the committee and that he would seriously impair his capacity and that of his successors to discharge the duties of the Presidency if he should make the specified tapes and memorandums available to the committee.
>
> I submit the President's position is, in reality, incompatible with the doctrine of the separation of powers of Government. This is so because the select committee is exercising the constitutional power of the Senate to conduct the investigation, and the doctrine of the separation of the powers of Government requires the President to recognize this and to refrain from obstructing the committee.
>
> But even if the President is vested with the autocratic power he claims and is exempt from the obligation resting upon all other Americans to produce evidence relevant to a congressional investigation, the Constitution assuredly does not obligate him to hinder the search for truth or forbid him voluntarily to make the tapes and memorandums available to the committee.
>
> His predecessors in the Presidency—Thomas Jefferson, Abraham Lincoln, Ulysses S. Grant, and Theodore Roosevelt—did not construe the Constitution to require them to hide the truth from grand juries, courts, and congressional committees.
>
> When Chief Justice John Marshall as circuit justice was presiding at the trial of Aaron Burr for treason in Richmond, Va., in 1807, counsel for Aaron Burr applied to him for a subpoena duces tecum requiring Thomas Jefferson, the President of the United States, to make available for use as evidence a letter written to him by a military adviser, Gen. James Wilkinson, and certain official papers. When he granted the application, Chief Justice Marshall observed that it is the character of the testimony sought and not the character of the person possessing it which determines whether a subpoena will issue.
>
> Jefferson made the letter and other papers available to the court in obedience to the subpoena, and in addition offered to testify by deposition in respect to any other information desired.

During the Civil War one congressional committee investigated the publication by The New York Tribune of a speech prepared by Abraham Lincoln before the speech was delivered or released, and another congressional committee investigated a rumor that Mrs. Lincoln was disloyal to the Union. On both of these occasions Abraham Lincoln, President of the United States, voluntarily appeared and testified before these congressional committees in respect to the matters under investigation.

President Ulysses S. Grant voluntarily testified by deposition when one of his former aides was being tried in court upon a criminal charge, and several years after he had left the Presidency Theodore Roosevelt demanded and was accorded the opportunity to testify before a congressional committee, which was investigating the manner in which campaign contributions were obtained for his benefit when he was running for reelection against Alton B. Parker.

The Constitution did not collapse, the powers of the Presidency were not impaired, and the heavens did not fall when Thomas Jefferson, Abraham Lincoln, Ulysses S. Grant and Theodore Roosevelt voluntarily cooperated with courts and congressional committees, in their search for truth, and such dire consequences would not ensue if President Nixon should voluntarily make the five specified tapes and the memoranda available to the Select Committee.

To be sure President Nixon invokes as a precedent for his refusal to make the tapes and memorandums available the action of President Truman in declining to appear in person and testify before the Un-American Activities Committee of the House concerning the manner in which he had performed his constitutional and legal duties during his Presidency.

Former President Truman's action does not afford any support for President Nixon's position.

The select committee does not seek to require President Nixon to furnish to it testimony concerning his official acts. It is merely asking him to make available to it documentary evidence relating to illegal and unethical and political activities—matters not covered by executive privilege.

I deeply deplore President Nixon's action. It obstructs the select committee in the performance of its constitutional task, and, in addition, is calculated to induce multitudes of people to believe that he withholds the tapes and memorandums because their contents are adverse to him.

19

BATTLE FOR
THE TAPES

PRESIDENT Nixon's refusal to produce tapes and obey subpoenas for them prompted the Select Committee and the Special Prosecutor to institute civil proceedings against him in the United States District Court for the District of Columbia.

The committee sued for the five tapes it was seeking, and Special Prosecutor Cox undertook by a show-cause order to secure designated tapes which the grand jury investigating the Watergate affair had subpoenaed.

The President assigned to Professor Charles A. Wright, of Texas University Law School, who had been his part-time legal consultant in the past, primary responsibility for arguing these cases on his behalf.

Prior to the filing of the committee's suit, Senator Baker and I suggested on the CBS program *Face the Nation* that, as a basis for ending the confrontation, President Nixon allow us to listen privately to the five tapes the committee was seeking and report their contents to our colleagues. This conciliatory suggestion died aborning.

Cecil Emerson, who served for a time on the White House legal staff during Watergate days, afterwards intimated that President Nixon was "probably the most unique client in the world" because he insisted in dictating his own legal strategy. Be this as it may, the arguments that

Wright made in presenting his cause to the courts in the committee and Cox cases harmonized with the claims of President Nixon that the occupant of the presidency was not answerable to Congress or the courts in any way during his tenure in office, and could not even be prosecuted for the most heinous crime until he had been impeached by a majority vote of the House of Representatives and convicted and removed from office by a two-thirds vote of the Senate for "treason, bribery, or other high crimes and misdemeanors."

The committee failed to obtain access to the tapes it was seeking in the suit it brought against President Nixon. On October 17 Judge Sirica adjudged that the District Court had no jurisdiction of the committee's suit because Congress had not enacted any statute authorizing a suit of that nature against the President.

The committee had not entirely ruled out the possibility of a decision to that effect. Before instituting the suit, the committee had met in executive session with its legal staff and two of the nation's foremost constitutional scholars, Philip B. Kurland, of the University of Chicago Law School, and Alexander Bickel, of Yale Law School, and canvassed the jurisdictional question.

Kurland and Bickel had expressed grave misgivings on the subject. I was inclined to share their misgivings. The legal staff of the committee had done much research on the question, however, and was convinced that the suit could be successfully maintained. Besides, members of the committee were aware that notwithstanding the unanimous vote for Senate Resolution 60, there was a hard-core group of Senators who did not really favor the Watergate investigation, and feared they might oppose interminably any proposal expressly conferring on the committee the power to sue. For these reasons, I swallowed my misgivings, and joined the other members of the committee in authorizing the suit.

The committee noted an appeal to Judge Sirica's ruling. While the appeal was pending in the United States Court of Appeals for the District of Columbia Circuit, Senators Baker, Talmadge, Inouye, Montoya, Gurney, Weicker, and I introduced a bill, which became law without President Nixon's signature on December 17, 1973. By its enactment, Congress conferred upon the United States District Court for the District of Columbia in express terms jurisdiction of the committee's suit for the five tapes it was seeking, and declared, in effect, that the committee in suing the President for them was acting with valid legislative purposes and seeking information vital to the fulfillment of its legitimate legislative functions.

The Court of Appeals thereupon remanded the committee's case to Judge Sirica for reconsideration in the light of the newly enacted law.

Because of the press of other Watergate matters, Judge Sirica transferred the suit to Judge Gerhard Gesell, who entered final judgment on February 8, 1974, refusing to enforce the committee's subpoenas. The committee forthwith appealed Judge Gesell's ruling to the United States Court of Appeals. Notwithstanding time was of the essence, the Court of Appeals delayed its ruling on the appeal until May 23, 1974, when it affirmed Judge Gesell's ruling.

When their opinions are reduced to simple terms, Judge Gesell denied the committee the tapes because he concluded its use of them would not serve the public interest; and the Court of Appeals upheld his ruling because it concluded the committee did not need them to complete the task assigned to it by its parent body.

I submit that under our Constitution the power of a constitutionally created Senate committee to receive evidence relevant to an investigation it is conducting for legislative purposes is not dependent upon its satisfying the federal judiciary that its use of the evidence will serve the public interest or that it needs the evidence to perform its assigned task. These are matters for the determination of senators and not for judges.

It was impossible, however, for the committee to obtain a Supreme Court review of the judgment of the Court of Appeals. The power of the committee to conduct further investigation of the Watergate affair was scheduled to expire on June 30, 1974, and the committee itself was to cease to exist three calendar months later. The committee recognized that the question of its right to have access to the tapes it sought would become moot long before it could obtain a Supreme Court review of the ruling of the Court of Appeals, and for this reason did not indulge in the futility of asking the Supreme Court to review it.

The evidence received by the committee, as well as the diligence of Henry Ruth and his other assistants, enabled Special Prosecutor Cox to select with accuracy Nixon tapes relevant to the investigation the Watergate grand jury was conducting.

The Nixon White House strenuously resisted Cox's case for the nine tapes the grand jury had subpoenaed. When they confronted each other in their historic argument before Judge Sirica, Wright asserted that as long as a President is in office he has an absolute and unreviewable power to withhold evidence from grand juries and other public investigative bodies, and Cox maintained that the public has the right to demand evidence from all men, including the President. Cox added this citation from Justice Robert H. Jackson: "Men have discovered no technique for long preserving free government except that the executive be under the law."

On August 29 Judge Sirica entered an order which happily was without precedent in America's past. He commanded President Nixon "to produce forthwith for the court's examination *in camera*" the nine tapes subpoenaed by the grand jury. The order was designed to enable the court to examine the tapes in private, preserve the confidentiality of such portions of the tapes as might properly be covered by executive privilege, and make available to the grand jury such portions of the tapes, if any, as might indicate criminal conduct in the Watergate affair or any efforts to cover it up.

During and since the trying days of the investigation President Nixon has had a propensity for insinuating that Democrats who took official positions adverse to him in respect to the Watergate affair did so simply because they were "political animals" or "partisan vipers." Inasmuch as Judge Sirica was a Republican in politics who had been appointed to his judicial post by President Eisenhower, President Nixon could not lay that flattering unction to his soul on this occasion. Judge Sirica was an upright judge who did not permit his fidelity to duty and his love for America to be dimmed by such extraneous matters as political considerations.

President Nixon appealed Judge Sirica's unprecedented order to the United States Court of Appeals for the District of Columbia Circuit. In the hope of ending the constitutional confrontation, the Court of Appeals recommended that Cox and Wright make an out-of-court compromise to settle the controversy about the tapes.

The indomitable Cox and the adamant White House could not compromise, and the Court of Appeals was compelled to pass on the validity of Judge Sirica's order.

In presenting President Nixon's appeal to the Court of Appeals, the President's counsel argued that Judge Sirica's order threatened "the continued existence of the Presidency as a functioning institution." On October 12, 1973, the Court of Appeals rendered a 5–2 decision which repudiated this argument, affirmed Judge Sirica's order, and remanded the case to Judge Sirica to enable him to receive the subpoenaed tapes and implement his order. The Court of Appeals delayed the operation of its ruling until October 19 to afford President Nixon an opportunity to determine whether he wanted to appeal it to the Supreme Court.

President Nixon was apparently unwilling to trust his own attorneys with knowledge of his tapes and their contents. When they argued the special prosecutor's case in his behalf, they based their argument on the assumption that the nine subpoenaed tapes existed. Afterwards they discovered that the telephone conversation of the President and Mitchell on June 20, 1972, and the personal conversation of the President and Dean on April 15, 1973, had not been taped.

On November 14, 1973, they made an astounding discovery in respect to the tape of June 20, 1972. This tape originally recorded a conversation of President Nixon and Haldeman concerning Watergate which occurred three days after the burglars were caught in their act of burglary and which lasted eighteen minutes and fifteen seconds.

They discovered that the eighteen-minute and 15-second conversation had been expunged from the tapes by some unidentified being whom General Haig may have rightly described as "a sinister force." Evidence received by Judge Sirica relating to this gap on the tape indicated that the President's first recorded remarks about Watergate had been deliberately expunged, and that this event had occurred at a time when nobody except presidential aide Stephen Bull, presidential secretary Rose Mary Woods, and President Nixon had access to the tape.

Exactly what the President and Haldeman said on this occasion has not been revealed. A brief contemporary memorandum of their conversation made by Haldeman states, in essence, that the President gave instructions to Haldeman "to take certain actions of a public relations character which related to the Watergate incident."

Special Prosecutor Cox and his associate based the grand jury subpoenas for nine presidential tapes upon inferences drawn largely from the testimony of Dean before the Select Committee that the contents of the tapes were relevant to the grand jury's investigation. They did not know what was recorded on the tapes. But President Nixon did. He knew that his own words imprinted by his own voice upon the existing and unmutilated subpoenaed tapes conclusively refuted the positive assurances he had been giving to the American people in televised speeches and televised news conferences and through the agency of his press secretary since August 1972, that he was innocent of involvement in the cover-up of Watergate.

Although the contents of the subpoenaed tapes are stated in detail elsewhere, their highlights are set forth at this point to make understandable the peril the judgment of the Court of Appeals posed for President Nixon.

The tape of September 15, 1972, recorded a secret meeting of President Nixon, Haldeman, and Dean shortly after the grand jury indicted the seven original Watergate defendants in which President Nixon, in essence, commended Dean for his work in restricting the indictments to the seven, and made statements corroborative of Dean's testimony to the committee that the President was aware of the cover-up operations and approved them as early as that day.

The tape of March 13, 1973, recorded a secret meeting of President Nixon and Dean in which the President voiced his concern about Haldeman's vulnerability in the Watergate affair, and Dean optimistically assured the President that Mitchell and Magruder would "contain" Watergate and stop criminal charges with the original seven defendants by asserting that Liddy and Hunt were engaged in a lark of their own when they burglarized Watergate. The tape also reflected President Nixon's penchant for red herrings. He and Dean toyed with the idea of using William C. Sullivan's dissatisfaction with J. Edgar Hoover's regime at FBI as a means of distracting attention from Watergate.

The subpoenaed tapes of March 21, 1973, covered the first two of the three secret meetings President Nixon held on the subject of Watergate with his aides on that day.

The tape of the first of the three meetings covered the conversation of President Nixon and Dean. Dean told the President that a cancer was growing on his Presidency, and that he ought to clear out the cancer by ending the cover-up. By way of elaboration of his theme, Dean detailed the origin of the break-in and the bugging, the ensuing cover-up operations, and the complicity of officials of CREEP and White House aides in these events. He also informed the President that the cover-up was becoming increasingly difficult to maintain, and cited on this point Hunt's demand for more money before his sentencing date, and the likelihood it would require $1 million to keep the Watergate defendants silent after Judge Sirica sent them to jail.

According to the tape of the first meeting, President Nixon decided that the cover-up was to be continued, and he discussed with Dean the possibility of continuing it by giving clemency to the Watergate defendants. After rejecting clemency as a political impossibility, President

Nixon sanctioned the payment of hush money as a method of continuing the cover-up. In so doing, he expressly approved an immediate payment to Hunt to buy his continued silence, and stated he was able to raise and was willing to pay $1 million to keep the seven Watergate defendants silent.

The tape of the second of the three secret meetings on March 21, which covered the conversation of President Nixon, Haldeman, and Dean, was in large measure a rehash of the first meeting. President Nixon expressly approved the immediate payment of hush money to Hunt, and sanctioned the future payment of hush money to the Watergate defendants by saying: "It is going to require approximately a million dollars to take care of the jackasses that are in jail. Let me tell you it's no problem. We could get the money. Mitchell could provide the way to deliver it."

Haldeman agreed it was necessary to continue the cover-up, regardless of its cost.

President Nixon, Haldeman, and Dean discussed the possibility that presidential aides might be compelled to testify. Haldeman was concerned about the peril of perjury, and President Nixon told him and Dean, in substance, that they could conceal the truth without danger of a conviction for perjury by asserting they had forgotten things they remembered.

President Nixon expressed apprehension that Colson had promised Hunt presidential clemency for his silence.

The tape of March 22 recorded a meeting of President Nixon, Mitchell, Haldeman, Ehrlichman, and Dean. Mitchell and Haldeman emphasized that President Nixon was creating an unfavorable image for the White House in the eyes of the public by asserting he intended to invoke an inflexible executive privilege and bar all former and existing members of the White House staff from testifying before the committee. They urged that all members of the staff, except Dean, the President's counsel, be allowed to go before the committee "under controlled circumstances." After much discussion, it was agreed that Attorney General Kleindienst and Dean should meet with Senator Baker and me, to seek to negotiate with us an arrangement whereby all the President's aides, except Dean, would be permitted to testify before the committee in secret sessions in the absence of press, television, and radio. President Nixon stated he preferred to handle the matter that way, but if that could not be arranged he declared, "I want you all to stonewall it, let them plead the Fifth Amendment, cover-up or anything if it'll save it—save the plan." The participants in the meeting also agreed that Dean should prepare a written report to the President exonerating everybody in the White House from complicity in the Watergate affair. The President concluded the meeting by declaring, "The purpose of this scenario is to clear the Presidency."

20

THE
SATURDAY-NIGHT
MASSACRE

THE judgment of the Court of Appeals affirming Judge Sirica's order presented to President Nixon a choice among four alternatives. He could deliver the existing subpoenaed tapes to Judge Sirica in obedience to the judgment, or he could appeal the judgment and risk its affirmance by the Supreme Court, or he could flatly refuse to obey the judgment, or he could destroy the existing subpoenaed tapes and thus disable himself to comply with the judgment.

Each alternative posed potential political disaster for President Nixon, who desperately sought ways during the week beginning Monday, October 15, to circumvent the dilemma presented to him by the judgment.

Apart from the external incidents of the visit which Senator Baker and I made to the White House at President Nixon's unexpected invitation on the late afternoon of Friday, October 19, I was totally ignorant at the time of everything the Nixon White House planned and did in respect to Watergate during the first five days of that week. Consequently, I had no inkling of what Haig, Wright, and Buzhardt had done at his undoubted command to aid President Nixon to escape his impending dilemma.

I have reconstructed these events on the basis of information afterwards acquired by me from contemporary letters and news conferences of participants in them and other credible data. To make the bare facts relating to these events readily understandable, I have fleshed them out by attributing to President Nixon motives and objectives the bare facts compel one to infer he contemporaneously entertained.

President Nixon rightly realized that the courage, legal acumen, and tenacity of Archibald Cox, whom he privately called "a partisan viper," had placed him in peril. He was desirous of getting rid of Cox as Special Prosecutor, abolishing the office of Special Prosecutor, and returning the investigation and prosecution of Watergate-related crimes to the Department of Justice, whose top officials held office at his pleasure.

He was willing to stop short of these objectives, however, if he could induce Cox to surrender the fruits of his victories before Judge Sirica and in the Court of Appeals, and disable himself to make any further attempts to obtain by judicial process tapes, notes, or memoranda of presidential conversations. His ultimate objective was to shield himself from the truth as revealed by his own words.

To this end, President Nixon devised an ingenious scheme, which envisaged the possibility of these successive steps:

1. Cox was to be offered the option initially of accepting a proposal, which was designed to nullify his victories in the courts and disable him to make any further attempts to obtain access by judicial process to presidential conversations.

2. If he rejected the proposal, Cox was to be barred as Special Prosecutor from seeking any tapes or documents revealing any presidential conversations relating to Watergate.

3. If he defied efforts to bar him from so doing, Cox was to be fired as Special Prosecutor under circumstances picturing him as an incorrigible and unreasonable fellow "out to get" an innocent President, who was merely endeavoring to spare the country the agony of unnecessary litigation between the Special Prosecutor and the White House.

As the first step, the Nixon White House made this proposal to Cox:

1. President Nixon would personally prepare summaries of everything the subpoenaed tapes contained relating to Watergate and deliver the summaries and the subpoenaed tapes to Senator John C. Stennis, "a very distinguished man, highly respected by all elements in American life for his integrity, his fairness, and his patriotism."

2. Senator Stennis would listen to the subpoenaed tapes, satisfy himself by so doing that President Nixon's summaries included everything on them relating to Watergate, and would submit the summaries

as verified by him to the District Court for the use of the grand jury and for any purpose for which they were needed.

3. The Special Prosecutor and counsel for the President would join in urging the court to accept the summaries as verified by Senator Stennis in lieu of the subpoenaed tapes themselves "as a full and accurate record of all pertinent portions of the tapes for all purposes for which access to those tapes might thereafter be sought by or on behalf of any person having standing to obtain such access."

4. The Special Prosecutor would "make no further attempts by judicial process to obtain tapes, notes, or memoranda of Presidential conversations."

If he had agreed to this proposal, Cox would not only have surrendered the victories he had won in the courts, but he would also have disabled himself to investigate or prosecute effectively Watergate-related crimes. Indeed, he would have made it certain that all persons whose guilt could only be established by words appearing on the subpoenaed tapes went unwhipped by justice.

This was true because trials of criminal cases in the courts are controlled by rules of evidence which are established by law and which cannot be altered by agreements designed to satisfy the desires of men, no matter who they may be.

What President Nixon or Senator Stennis might say the subpoenaed tapes revealed would be hearsay, which could not have been admitted in evidence over the objection of any person charged with a Watergate-related crime. Besides, President Nixon and Special Prosecutor Cox did not have the legal power to barter away the right of any person having standing to obtain access to the subpoenaed tapes to invoke the best-evidence rule and demand the production of the tapes themselves.

Inasmuch as Cox's acceptance of the Nixon White House proposal would have had such a disastrous impact upon his ability to investigate and prosecute Watergate-related crimes, these questions inevitably arise: How could President Nixon have expected Cox to agree to the proposal? Why did President Nixon's attorneys, who were reputable men educated in law, acquiesce in the proposal to Cox?

The categorical answer to the first question is that President Nixon never expected Cox to accept the proposal. On the contrary, he intended to use Cox's rejection of it as a means of disabling Cox to act effectively as Special Prosecutor, or by resignation or discharge to drive him from the office of Special Prosecutor.

There is no categorical answer to the second question. The answer to it may be found in one or the other of three varying explanations. The first explanation is that President Nixon was a domineering litigant who dictated his own strategy and required his attorneys to acquiesce to it. The second explanation harmonizes with Wright's argument in the courts that the President is not constitutionally subject to any judicial order while he is unimpeached and unremoved from office. Hence, Wright and Buzhardt acquiesced in the proposal because it was calculated in their view to frustrate a judgment inconsistent with the Constitution. The third explanation is understandable in the light of the fact that Haig, Wright, and Buzhardt were not permitted by President Nixon to hear the subpoenaed tapes before the Saturday-night massacre.

Instead of allowing them to listen to the tapes, President Nixon assured them he was not involved in any aspect of Watergate, and that the subpoenaed tapes would prove that. They believed what President Nixon said, and acquiesced in the proposal because they were convinced its acceptance would give Cox all the information available, i.e., that the tapes would not reveal any incriminating matters.

At various times between Monday, October 15, and Thursday, October 18, Haig, Wright, and Buzhardt sought to persuade Cox to accept the proposal. Although he could not in good conscience approve banning Cox from future attempts to obtain data from the White House, Attorney General Elliot L. Richardson also discussed the proposal with Cox at President Nixon's request. In so doing, he hoped to find an acceptable compromise.

By the late afternoon of October 18, Cox had convinced the President's emissaries that he could not conscientiously accept the proposal, and they reported that fact to the President.

On the following day, October 19, President Nixon sent this letter to Attorney General Richardson:

> You are aware of the actions I am taking today to bring to an end the controversy over the so-called Watergate tapes and that I have reluctantly agreed to a limited breach of Presidential confidentiality in order that our country may be spared the agony of further indecision and litigation about those tapes at a time when we are confronted with other issues of much greater moment to the country and the world.
>
> As a part of these actions, I am instructing you to direct Special Prosecutor Archibald Cox of the Watergate Special Prosecution Force that he is to make no further attempts by judicial process to obtain

tapes, notes, or memoranda of Presidential conversations. I regret the
necessity of intruding, to this very limited extent, on the independence that I promised you with regard to Watergate when I
announced your appointment. This would not have been necessary if
the Special Prosecutor had agreed to the very reasonable proposal you
made to him this week. . . .

By way of reply, Attorney General Richardson informed President
Nixon that the peremptory direction to him was incompatible with the
promise of independence that with the President's assent he had made
to Cox as Special Prosecutor, and he would welcome an opportunity to
discuss the matter further with him.

President Nixon ignored Richardson's reply. He had determined
that Cox should be fired. According to his scheme, however, the firing
of Cox as Special Prosecutor had to be delayed until the President had
issued a statement offering his proposal to Cox publicly and Cox had
rejected it publicly and failed to resign. President Nixon was convinced
that by this means he could make it appear that Cox had arbitrarily
rejected a very reasonable proposal, and thus win public support for his
firing.

When he afterwards issued his statement, President Nixon adroitly
assured the American people that his proposal to Cox had the approval
of Senator Stennis, Senator Baker, and me. To enable the reader to
judge the validity of this assurance, it is necessary to detail prior contacts
the Nixon White House had with Stennis, Baker, and me.

The account of Senator Stennis's contact is based on his statements
to me and a press interview of him which appeared in the *Washington
Post* on December 5, 1973.

On or about October 15, Haig and Buzhardt visited Senator Stennis
at his senatorial office. At their request he agreed that if his so doing
was approved by Senator Baker and me, he would accept from the
White House temporary custody of the tapes the Senate Select Committee was seeking, listen to them, prepare two sets of verbatim
transcripts of all the contents of the tapes relating to the Watergate
affair, and give one set of transcripts to the committee and the other to
the White House.

Senator Stennis was not asked to prepare any transcripts or verify any
summaries of the tapes for delivery to Judge Sirica. If a request of this
nature had been made of him, he declared, he would have refused to
accede to it. In his judgment as a former judge, he said, preparing
transcripts or verifying summaries for the court would have been im-

proper. Besides, "he suspected such a move would not have been accepted by the court."

The White House never delivered any tapes to Senator Stennis.

On Friday, October 19, I was at the airport in New Orleans about to take a plane to Charlotte, North Carolina. I received a long-distance telephone call from Fred Buzhardt saying that the President wanted to see Senator Baker, who had been summoned from Chicago, and me that afternoon.

At Buzhardt's suggestion, I took a Delta plane to Washington, and was met at the Friendship Airport by a presidential automobile which took me to the White House, where I arrived late in the afternoon. On my arrival I found Senator Baker, General Haig, Charles A. Wright, and Fred Buzhardt awaiting me in a room near the Oval Office.

Haig, Wright, and Buzhardt informed Senator Baker and me that Judge Sirica's order requiring President Nixon to deliver to him the tapes sought by Special Prosecutor Cox would become effective at midnight unless the President appealed the judgment of the Court of Appeals to the Supreme Court, and that the White House was hoping it could reach a satisfactory agreement with Cox concerning those tapes before that time.

Both Baker and I advised them that the committee had nothing to do with the Special Prosecutor's investigation, but that it was conducting its investigation under different constitutional principles and laws. Nothing further was said to Baker and me about Cox or his investigation. We were not told and did not know that President Nixon had previously made a proposal to Cox concerning the tapes he was seeking, that Cox had rejected it, and that President Nixon was on the brink of firing Cox as Special Prosecutor.

After a short time, Baker and I were ushered into the Oval Office, where we had a conversation with the President. I do not recall the exact words in which the conversation was couched, but I do recollect most vividly the substance of it.

President Nixon opened the conversation by affirming he wished to put an amicable end to his controversy with the committee over the five tapes sought by the committee, which covered meetings in which he and Dean had discussed the Watergate affair. He asserted he was unwilling to entrust the tapes themselves to the committee because the data on them relating to Watergate was intermixed with data referring to other things, such as matters affecting national security, federal appointments, and legislation.

President Nixon declared that after much thought he had devised a plan by which he could supply the committee with the data relating to Watergate and at the same time prevent the exposure of the other data. He said he would be willing to entrust the tapes sought by the committee to Senator Stennis, a man of unimpeachable integrity and an expert in national security affairs, and let him listen to them and furnish the committee with a transcript of everything they revealed about Watergate with all other data excised. He added he had not talked to Senator Stennis personally about the matter, but one of his aides had, and that Senator Stennis had told his aide that he was a "Senate man" and would perform this task only if it was satisfactory to Senator Baker and me.

Senator Baker and I advised President Nixon that we were only two members of the seven-man committee, and were without authority to make any agreement for the committee on this subject. We assured him, however, that we would call a special meeting of the committee and submit his proposal to it as soon as possible and inform him of its decision without delay.

I stated, however, that the public might question the authenticity of the tapes; and for that reason I would not agree as a member of the committee to the proposal unless it was understood that in the event the committee had any doubt as to the authenticity of the tapes after receiving the transcripts, Senator Stennis, at the instance of the committee, could have the aid of electronic experts to assist him in determining their authenticity. The President said he had no objection to such an understanding because "the tapes had not been doctored."

Before we left the White House, the President asked Senator Baker and me not to make any statements about our meeting with him until the White House had issued a statement concerning it. We agreed to this request.

After this, I left the White House and traveled on a military plane from Andrews Air Force Base to the commercial airport at Hickory, North Carolina, about twenty miles from my home in Morganton.

Senator Baker and I complied with President Nixon's request to visit him at the White House because we believed a decent respect for the institution of the presidency required us to do so.

My immediate reaction to our meeting with President Nixon was prompted by events which preceded the meeting and thoughts which the President's offer to the Committee engendered in my mind.

John Dean's testimony before the committee implicated President Nixon in covering up the Watergate affair. The committee believed the five tapes it sought would afford conclusive evidence of the truth or falsity of this testimony, and enable it to make a final decision in respect to this aspect of Watergate.

Only two days before the meeting Judge Sirica had dismissed the committee's suit for the five tapes for want of jurisdiction, and thereby dashed all hope of the committee of obtaining access to the tapes of President Nixon's conversations with Dean at any time in the foreseeable future.

At that time one could speculate that the President withheld the tapes the committee sought to protect himself, or to protect Haldeman and Ehrlichman, or to protect the institution of the presidency. President Nixon had consistently claimed he was innocent of all complicity in the Watergate affair, and the tapes would so disclose; and I had steadfastly maintained that he owed the committee, the country, and himself the duty of producing any tapes or other evidence controlled by him which would shed light on the subject.

Unlike the Special Prosecutor, the committee was not bound by the rules of evidence which govern the trials of criminal cases in the courts, and transcripts of the portions of the tapes relating to Watergate were receivable by it.

I had no inkling at the time that President Nixon was not acting in good faith in offering to supply the committee through the agency of Senator Stennis with transcripts of the portions of the tapes it sought. As a consequence, I gave him the benefit of all doubts and indulged the assumption that he was at long last offering to do an intelligent thing that he should have done many months earlier.

Upon returning home from Washington in the early evening of Friday, October 19, my wife informed me that I had received scores of long-distance calls from representatives of various media of communications throughout the nation. In order to keep my promise to the President to refrain from making any statement about the meeting until the White House had done so, and to avoid receiving phone calls throughout the night, I operated a mechanism that I had had installed on my phone in August 1973. This mechanism prevented my phone from ringing during the night and permitted me to enjoy undisturbed sleep. I kept this mechanism on all night. Although I heard a meager television report at eleven o'clock about the meeting in the Oval Office, it gave no details and was insufficient to acquaint me with the tenor of any statement which the White House may have made during the evening of October 19.

On the evening of Friday, October 19, President Nixon issued a statement to the American people announcing his decision not to appeal the judgment of the Court of Appeals to the Supreme Court and what he called his compromise plan for furnishing summaries of their contents rather than the subpoenaed tapes themselves to Judge Sirica.

Along with protestations inserted in it for public relations purposes, President Nixon's statement declared:

The Watergate issue had taken on overtones of a partisan political contest, raising the possibility of a constitutional confrontation in the cases involving the tapes, and tempting other nations to misread America's unity and resolve to meet challenges from abroad. The President had decided to take decisive action to avoid these things.

Although he was confident the Supreme Court would reverse the decision of the Court of Appeals, the President had concluded it was not in the national interest to leave the matter unresolved for the period that might be required for a review by the highest court.

Throughout the week Attorney General Richardson, at the President's insistence, had been offering Special Prosecutor Cox what the Attorney General considered a reasonable proposal for compromise, which would avoid the necessity for Supreme Court review. The proposal complied with the spirit of the decision of the Court of Appeals, offered the Special Prosecutor the information he claimed he needed for the grand jury, maintained the principle of an independent executive branch, and "would also have resolved any lingering thought that the President himself might have been involved in a Watergate cover-up."

The proposal specified that the President would personally prepare summaries of the contents of the subpoenaed tapes insofar as they related to Watergate, and deliver the summaries and the subpoenaed tapes themselves to Senator Stennis, who would listen to the tapes, verify by so doing that the summaries included everything on the tapes relating to Watergate, and submit the summaries as thus verified by him to Judge Sirica in lieu of the tapes themselves. The proposal required "that there would be no further attempt by the Special Prosecutor to subpoena still more tapes or other Presidential papers of a similar nature."

The President was pleased to be able to say that Chairman Sam

Ervin and Vice-Chairman Howard Baker of the committee had agreed to the "procedure" and that at their request, and the President's, Senator John Stennis had consented to listen to every requested tape and verify that the summaries prepared by the President were full and accurate.

The President was willing to let Senator Stennis hear the tapes, but was not willing to submit them to Judge Sirica for inspection in private. To allow the tapes to be heard by one district judge would create a precedent that would be available to four hundred district judges and a precedent that Presidents would be required to submit to judicial demands that override Presidential determinations on requirements for confidentiality.

Although the special prosecutor had rejected the proposal, the President had instructed his counsel not to seek Supreme Court review of the decision of the Court of Appeals. Nevertheless, the President would make available to Judge Sirica, and also to the committee, statements of the Watergate-related portions of the tapes prepared and authenticated in the manner described.

Although he had not wished to intrude upon the independence of the Special Prosecutor, the President felt it necessary to direct him, as an employee of the executive branch, to make no further attempts by judicial process to obtain tapes, notes, or memoranda of Presidential conversations.

The verified summaries furnished the court would fully satisfy any legitimate need of the Special Prosecutor and enable him to obtain indictments against those who may have committed any crimes.

What the President has done today would spare America the anguish of further indecision and litigation about Watergate, and conform to his constitutional duty to see that the laws of the nation are faithfully executed.

Although he presented his statement to the American people as verity, it was irreconcilable with truth in these respects:

—Senator Stennis had not consented to verify any summaries of any tapes for Judge Sirica.

—Senator Baker and I, who were ignorant of it, had not approved the President's proposal to Cox.

—Senator Baker and I had not agreed to accept in behalf of the committee anybody's summaries of the tapes it was seeking.

—Attorney General Richardson deemed the provision of the proposal forbidding Cox to make further efforts by judicial process to obtain tapes, notes, or memorandums of presidential conversations repugnant to the promise of independence that he had given to Cox with the President's assent at the time of Cox's appointment as special prosecutor.

—Summaries of the Watergate-related portions of the tapes sought by him would not "fully satisfy any legitimate need of the Special Prosecutor." On the contrary, acceptance of the proposal by Cox would have disabled Cox to investigate and prosecute Watergate-related crimes effectively, and would have precluded him altogether from seeking the truth as revealed by the President's own words on the tapes.

On Saturday morning, October 20, I phoned chief counsel Dash from my home in Morganton to arrange a speedy meeting of the committee to consider President Nixon's proposal to Baker and me, and learned from him for the first time what the President had done after I left the White House. I was astounded by the President's assertion that Baker and I had agreed to accept his summary of the tapes as authenticated by Senator Stennis, and that we had approved his proposal to Cox of which we knew nothing.

Nevertheless, I decided to act on the assumption that President Nixon had made his proposal to Baker and me in good faith. As a consequence, I called a meeting of the committee for Thursday, October 25, the first day on which all members could be present, to pass on the President's proposal.

After so doing, I called Senator Stennis by long-distance phone, and he detailed to me his conversation with Haig and Buzhardt.

During that afternoon Cox held a televised press conference. After disclaiming he was looking for a confrontation with the President or was "out to get him," Cox declared he could not accept the President's proposal or obey his instructions because they were inconsistent with the pledges of Attorney General Richardson guaranteeing him independence as Special Prosecutor, and because to do so would violate his own pledge to the Senate and the country to invoke judicial process to challenge exaggerated claims of executive privilege.

Since the summaries would not be receivable in evidence in court, Cox asserted that his acceptance of the proposal and instructions would deprive him of admissible evidence in prosecuting wrongdoers who abused high government office and enable them to go free.

Cox announced that the President was refusing to comply with the order of the court, and that it was his "duty as the Special Prosecutor, as an officer of the court, and as the representative of the grand jury, to bring to the court's attention" such noncompliance.

In closing, Cox said he had no intention of resigning as Special Prosecutor, and, under the agreement between the administration and the Senate, nobody could fire him except the Attorney General.

After Cox's press conference, President Nixon ordered Richardson to fire Cox. Believing such action incompatible with his pledges that Cox would have independence as Special Prosecutor and not be subject to discharge except for extraordinary improprieties, Richardson refused to do so and resigned as Attorney General. After his resignation, General Haig, acting on President Nixon's orders, directed Deputy Attorney General William D. Ruckelshaus, who had succeeded to the Attorney General's powers, to fire Cox. Ruckelshaus told Haig he could not do it, and that he was sending his resignation to the White House. Without waiting for the resignation to reach him, Nixon fired Ruckelshaus for disobeying the President's orders. Thereupon, Solicitor General Robert H. Bork, as third in the line of command at the Department of Justice, obeyed the President's orders and fired Cox.

White House press secretary Ziegler thereupon called an 8:25 P.M. news conference, and shocked the news media and the nation by announcing that Richardson had resigned, that Ruckelshaus and Cox had been fired, that the President had abolished the office of Special Prosecutor, and returned the Watergate-related investigation to the Department of Justice, and that the offices of the Watergate Special Prosecution Force had been sealed by guards to prevent the removal of files.

Meanwhile, I had driven to Asheville, North Carolina, to attend the Vance-Aycock Dinner, an annual fund-raising event of the Democratic Party. Immediately after my arrival at the hotel at which the dinner was held, I received a long-distance inquiry from Fred Buzhardt, who asked me to inform him what I understood to be the President's proposal to Senator Baker and me. I told him I understood the President proposed to entrust the tapes the committee sought to Senator Stennis, and to let Senator Stennis listen to the tapes and give the committee verbatim transcripts of exactly what the tapes had to say about the Watergate affair. Fred informed me that was in accordance with his understanding and terminated our conversation.

During the Vance-Aycock Dinner, I received information of the Saturday-Night Massacre.

On Sunday, October 21, Mary B. McBryde, one of my secretaries, drove my wife and myself by automobile from Morganton to Homestead, Virginia, where I was scheduled to speak to a business organization the next evening.

After our arrival at Homestead, I received many long-distance phone calls. One of them was from Fred Buzhardt. The others were from representatives of the news media. To my surprise, Fred repeated to me the same question he had asked me the night before. The ensuing conversation between him and me was identical with that we had had on that occasion.

Since I had decided to act on the assumption that the President's proposal to Baker and me had been made in good faith, I made no formal statement about the White House meeting, and contented myself with stating to newsmen individually in response to their inquiries exactly what had happened in the meeting and that I had called a special meeting of the committee to consider the President's proposal.

Because of the divergence between my understanding and the President's statement, I decided to ask him for a written clarification of his proposal. To this end, I dictated a telegram to Eileen Anderson, one of my secretaries, by long-distance, and instructed her to forward it to President Nixon at once. This telegram was as follows:

> October 23, 1973
> The President
> The White House
> Washington, D.C.
>
> The Senate Select Committee on Presidential Campaign Activities is going to meet Thursday morning to consider the proposal which the White House made orally to Senator Howard Baker and me last Friday afternoon. Since statements by the news media indicate that there may be some confusion about the nature and scope of the proposal and since it is essential that the Select Committee have the exact terms of the proposal before it at its meeting, I hereby respectfully request the White House to furnish me before the meeting of the Committee a statement of its understanding of the proposal. My understanding of the proposal is as follows: First, that the tape recordings requested by the Committee would be delivered to the temporary custody of Senator Stennis; second, that Senator Stennis would hear the tape recordings and separate the portions of the tapes relating to the Watergate affair from all other portions of the tapes; and third, that after so doing Senator Stennis would prepare and furnish to the Select Committee a verbatim copy of the exact words as recorded on the tapes which are relevant to the matters which the

Committee is authorized by Senate Resolution No. 60 to investigate. Senator Stennis will also identify for the committee the items on the tapes which he determines not to be relevant to the matters which the Committee is authorized to investigate. Moreover, it is my understanding that at the request of the Committee Senator Stennis would attempt to ascertain with the aid of experts the authenticity of the tapes. I trust that the understanding of the White House in respect to the proposal coincides with mine because I would be unwilling to urge the Committee to accept anyone's paraphrase or summary of what he thinks the tapes say. This is so because it is the duty of the Committee to interpret for itself exactly what the words on the tapes say.

(Signed) Sam J. Ervin, Jr., Chairman
Senate Select Committee on
Presidential Campaign Activities

I first reduced my recollection of this event to writing in 1976. At that time I had no copy of the telegram to reinforce my memory, and was under the impression that the telegram was dictated and sent on Monday morning, October 22. With my memory refreshed by a copy of it, I am now satisfied I dictated the telegram on the morning of Tuesday, October 23, just before leaving Homestead for Morganton, North Carolina.

I never received any formal reply from President Nixon. Shortly after my telegram reached him, the White House announced that the President's proposal to Senator Baker and me had been withdrawn.

In retrospect, I cannot escape the conclusion that President Nixon never had any intention of surrendering the tapes sought by the committee to Senator Stennis in accordance with the proposal he made to us, and that he had his aides consult with Senator Stennis and summon Senator Baker and me to the White House simply to lend color to his statement and win public approval for the firing of Cox.

The specious character of the statement supports this conclusion. The subsequent revelation of the contents of the tapes the committee was seeking compels it. If he had been entrusted with these tapes, Senator Stennis would have heard words imprinted upon them by President Nixon's own voice which demonstrated his involvement in the Watergate cover-up. This undoubtedly explains why the President withdrew his proposal so hastily.

21

THE FIRE STORM

AFTER being advised of his firing. Archibald Cox rightly appraised what was at stake for America in the Saturday-Night Massacre: "Whether we shall be a government of laws and not of men is for Congress and ultimately the American people to decide." The American people did not hesitate to say what they wished their country to be.

When he perpetrated the Saturday-Night Massacre on the nation, President Nixon grossly miscalculated the tolerance of the people of America for plain executive tyranny. In consequence, he provoked them into an angry reaction, which General Haig called a fire storm.

During the next few days untold thousands of them bombarded the White House and congressional and committee offices on Capitol Hill with telephone calls, telegrams, and letters condemning the President's action. The committee alone received approximately 125,000 of these protests during the ensuing ten-day period. In volume and intensity of denunciation this outcry of the people was without the faintest precedent in the annals of the country.

Many of the protesters expressed opinions in accord with those of Chesterfield Smith, the courageous and outspoken president of the American Bar Association. He declared that President Nixon had attempted "to abort the established processes of justice" and had "instituted an intolerable assault upon the courts, our first-line of defense against tyranny and arbitrary power." The American Bar Association itself urged Congress to create by law a Special Prosecutor with authority to investigate Watergate-related crimes, and to make him "absolutely independent of the direction and control of those whom he is investigating."

The more irate of those who protested expressed sentiments in harmony with those of the AFL-CIO Convention, which adopted a resolution calling on President Nixon to resign, and urging Congress to remove him from office by impeachment and conviction if he failed to do so.

Responsible journals and organizations asserted that the President had lost the confidence of the nation and ought to resign in the public interest. His ratings in the polls dropped to a new low of 27 percent.

After Cox had rejected President Nixon's proposal, the White House forwarded a summary of it to Judge Sirica. Wright was expected to appear before Judge Sirica on the afternoon of October 23 and urge him to accept the summaries envisaged by the proposal in lieu of the nine subpoenaed tapes themselves, as a compliance with the judge's order.

Meanwhile the Nixon White House was astounded and alarmed by the vehemence of the public outcry caused by the Saturday-Night Massacre.

When he appeared before Judge Sirica on October 23, Wright surprised the courtroom audience and possibly the court by stating, "This President does not defy the law, and he has authorized me to say he will comply in full with the orders of the court."

After Judge Sirica had informed him that "the court is very happy that the President has reached this decision," Wright informed him, in response to his inquiry, that the subpoenaed tapes would be delivered to the court for examination *in camera* "as expeditiously as possible."

Before this was done, the White House announced that two of the subpoenaed tapes did not exist, and that an eighteen-minute fifteen-second conversation between the President and Haldeman had been erased in some unknown way from a third. This disclosure precipitated an intensive judicial investigation by Judge Sirica.

On October 23 and 24, eighty-four representatives introduced resolutions calling on the House Judiciary Committee to investigate whether President Nixon had committed an impeachable offense, and ninety-eight representatives offered bills providing for the appointment of a

Special Prosecutor to assume charge of the investigation and prosecution of Watergate-related crimes. Shortly thereafter fifty-seven senators introduced bills providing for a Special Prosecutor for Watergate who would be independent of the President.

The enactment by Congress of any of these bills would have manifested to the nation a lack of congressional confidence in the integrity of President Nixon and that of the Department of Justice controlled by him. For this reason, he reluctantly decided to forestall the passage of any of them by arranging to have the Department of Justice designate a new special prosecutor.

On October 26 he held a stormy televised press conference in which he announced his plan for the appointment of a new special prosecutor, and undertook to justify the firing of Cox.

He assured his nationwide television audience that next week Solicitor General Bork, as Acting Attorney General, would appoint a new Special Prosecutor for the Watergate affair, and that the new Special Prosecutor would have independence and "total cooperation from the Executive Branch." After giving these assurances, he made these statements to justify the firing of Cox:

> The matter of the tapes has been one that has concerned me because of my feeling that I have a Constitutional responsibility to defend the Office of the Presidency from any encroachments on confidentiality which might affect future Presidents in their abilities to conduct the kind of conversations and discussions they need to conduct to carry on the responsibilities of this Office. And, of course, the special prosecutor felt that he needed the tapes for the purpose of his prosecution.
>
> That was why, working with the Attorney General, we worked out what we thought was an acceptable compromise, one in which Judge Stennis, now Senator Stennis, would hear the tapes and would provide a complete and full disclosure, not only to Judge Sirica, but also to the Senate Committee.
>
> Attorney General Richardson approved of the proposition. Senator Baker, Senator Ervin approved of the proposition. Mr. Cox was the only one that rejected it.
>
> Under the circumstances, when he rejected it and indicated that despite the approval of the Attorney General, and, of course, of the President and of the two major Senators on the Ervin Committee, when he rejected the proposal, I had no choice but to dismiss him.
>
> Under those circumstances, Mr. Richardson, Mr. Ruckelshaus felt that because of the nature of their confirmation that their commitment to Mr. Cox had to take precedence over any commitment they might have to carry out an order from the President.

> Under those circumstances, I accepted with regret the resignations of two fine public servants.

President Nixon made these statements to the American people notwithstanding Senator Baker and I had never approved any proposition made by him, and notwithstanding he had fired Ruckelshaus without waiting for his resignation to reach the White House.

Candor compels confessions. I was deeply distressed at the time by President Nixon's public assertions that Senator Baker and I had agreed to have the committee accept summaries of tapes without the consent of the other five members of the committee. Usurpation of authority is alien to my nature.

I was likewise deeply distressed by the President's public assertions that Senator Baker and I had approved his proposal to Cox. Prior to his statement of October 20, I had no information he had ever made any proposal to Cox.

As a trial lawyer and judge for many years, I had expended a major portion of my energy and time in studying and applying the law of evidence, and in consequence I would never have approved that proposal. Upon learning from the President's statement of October 20 the nature of his proposal to Cox, I recognized that the rules of evidence would bar the admission of summaries of tapes in any Watergate-related prosecution, and that the proposal was calculated, if not actually intended, to frustrate Cox in his search for the truth concerning Watergate.

I was strongly tempted to call a press conference and denounce the statements and set the record straight. I realized, however, that by accepting the chairmanship of the committee I had given hostages to fortune, and that my paramount duty to the committee, the Senate, and the country was to refrain from making denunciatory statements and perform with fidelity the obligations resting on me as chairman of the committee. Hence, I exercised restraint and did not undertake to set the record straight.

On November 1 President Nixon nominated Senator William B. Saxbe, of Ohio, to replace Richardson as Attorney General, and Bork, as Acting Attorney General, announced that Leon Jaworski, of Houston, Texas, had accepted appointment as Special Prosecutor.

In making his announcement, Bork stated that Jaworski had been promised complete independence of action, the full cooperation of the executive branch, and freedom to seek the presidential documents he needed. He added that President Nixon had stipulated he would not fire Jaworski without the consent of a substantial majority of the Democratic and Republican leaders of the House and the Senate, and the chairmen and ranking minority members of the House and Senate Judiciary committees. Jaworski declared he accepted the post as a duty to our country.

I had met Jaworski at gatherings of members of the American Bar Association. Besides, I knew that he was acclaimed as one of America's ablest lawyers, that he had made an excellent record as president of the American Bar Association, and that he had reputedly declined an offer of President Lyndon B. Johnson to appoint him to the Supreme Court of the United States.

Since I was otherwise unacquainted with him, I asked my colleague Senator Lloyd Bentsen what kind of a Special Prosecutor his fellow Texan would make. Senator Bentsen responded: "Leon Jaworski is ideally qualified for the job. He is fair-minded, and will not unjustly condemn any man. As a minister's son, he reveres personal integrity as the highest virtue; and as a patriot, he abominates any act disclosing a lack of devotion to the basic principles on which America is founded."

During his service as Special Prosecutor, Jaworski measured up to Senator Bentsen's appraisal of him in all respects.

Jaworski adopted as his own the excellent staff his predecessor, Cox, had assembled, and the office of Special Prosecutor resumed in full measure its dedicated and diligent investigation of Watergate-related crimes. Owing to White House delays, Judge Sirica did not complete the delivery to the Special Prosecutor of Watergate-related portions of the seven existing subpoenaed tapes until December 21, 1973.

22

ENSUING
EVENTS AND
INDICTMENTS

THE Senate Select Committee held nine days of public hearings, during the period beginning September 26 and ending November 6, 1973, investigating unethical campaign activities and "dirty tricks" connected with the presidential campaign of 1972.

One of the witnesses was Patrick J. Buchanan, a White House speech writer, noted for his rugged conservatism and forthrightness. Before his appearance some unidentified person or persons on the committee staff shamefully leaked to the press substantial portions of the prepared statement he had filed with the committee. As one who abhorred committee leaks, I approved Buchanan's eloquent castigation of the offending person or persons.

During the early days of the campaign Senator Muskie was the front runner among those seeking the Democratic nomination. Indeed, he was then outrunning President Nixon in some newspaper polls. Buchanan candidly admitted he was the author of various memorandums detailing the White House policy of destroying by strong partisan attacks the candidacy of Muskie and that of any other person who might succeed him as the front-running Democrat, a policy CREEP afterwards adopted and pursued. Buchanan defended as orthodox politics the practice of the Nixon administration in restricting discretionary federal grants and loans to those supporting conservative causes and Nixon's reelection.

Buchanan denied, however, advocating or encouraging any unethical acts or "dirty tricks," and no evidence inconsistent with this assertion was obtained by the committee.

The testimony received by the committee during the nine days it devoted to this phase of Watergate clearly disclosed that CREEP employed unethical practices and "dirty tricks" in profusion to disrupt, hinder, impede, and sabotage the campaigns of those seeking the Democratic presidential nomination and the campaign of the Democratic nominee, Senator George McGovern.

Robert M. Benz, Berl Bernhard, John R. ("Fat Jack") Buckley, Martin D. Kelly, Frank Mankiewicz, Michael W. McMinoway, Donald H. Segretti, and Rich Stearns testified on this phase of the investigation; and I refer to their testimony for specific details. The evidence of Berl Bernhard, who was Senator Muskie's campaign manager, is especially illuminating. He declared that "the term 'dirty tricks' does not do justice to the slimy deceptions that characterized the CREEP campaign."

I state in epitome the testimony on this phase of the investigation. CREEP expended substantially in excess of $100,000 to employ some twenty-two spies and saboteurs. They deceptively infiltrated the campaign organizations of Democratic candidates; secretly copied and furnished to CREEP their plans, schedules, and other vital documents; impeded their day-to-day functioning; disrupted their fund-raising dinners and political meetings; and deliberately distorted their stands on public issues.

The dirtiest of all the "dirty tricks" perpetrated in behalf of President Nixon's reelection was not the act of CREEP. It was the act of Donald H. Segretti, the White House hired saboteur. By forgeries purporting to originate in Senator Muskie's Florida headquarters in connection with the Florida Democratic primary, Segretti undertook to assassinate the characters of Senators Humphrey and Jackson, who were running against Muskie for the Democratic presidential nomination.

This "dirty trick" is detailed elsewhere, and is invoked at this point merely to explain why Haldeman gave the committee testimony in July 1973 that was both a colossal red herring and a masterpiece in verbal obfuscation.

Segretti was hired to perpetrate "dirty tricks" on Democratic candidates for the presidential nomination by Nixon's appointments secretary, Chapin, with the approval of Nixon's chief of staff, Haldeman, and was paid by Nixon's personal attorney and fund-raiser, Kalmbach, out of Nixon's campaign funds.

To absolve the White House from responsibility for Segretti's conduct, Haldeman asserted, in essence, that the motives of the White House in hiring Segretti were innocent; and to divert the attention of the country from the "dirty tricks" of CREEP and Segretti, Haldeman charged Democratic leaders, whom he did not name, with foul, unethical and criminal acts during the 1972 campaign. To these ends, he gave the committee this astounding testimony:

> The activities we had in mind, and for which we drew careful boundaries, specifically excluded anything remotely connected with the Watergate type of activity.
>
> Moreover, the pranksterism that was envisioned would have specifically excluded such acts as the following: violent demonstrations and disruption, heckling or shouting down speakers, burning or bombing campaign headquarters, physical damage or trashing of headquarters and other buildings, harassment of candidates' wives and families, obscenities, disruption of the national convention by splattering dinner guests with eggs and tomatoes, indecent exposure, rock throwing, assaults on delegates, slashing bus tires, smashing windows, setting trash fires under the gas tank of a bus, knocking policemen from their motorcycles.
>
> I know that this committee and most Americans would agree that such activities cannot be tolerated in a political campaign. But unfortunately the activities I have described are all activities which took place in 1972 against the campaign of the President of the United States by his opponents. Some of them took place with the clear knowledge and consent of agents of the opposing candidate in the last election; others were acts of people who were clearly unsympathetic to the President but may not have had direct orders from the opposing camp.
>
> So far there has been no investigation of these activities and very little publicizing of them, either those which were directly attributable to our opponent or those which certainly served our opponent's interest but did not have his sanction.

By this astounding testimony, Haldeman charged on his oath before the committee and a nation-wide television audience that unnamed Democratic "opponents" of President Nixon had committed foul offenses against President Nixon, his family, and his aides in the campaign of 1972; that some of these foul offenses had been committed with the knowledge and consent of unnamed "agents" of Senator George McGovern, the Democratic presidential candidate; and that some of these foul offenses "were directly attributable" to him.

Senator Weicker was an invaluable member of the committee. Instead of accepting as verity the naked assertions of witnesses, he probed the assertions to disclose what foundations, if any, they had. Weicker put to Haldeman questions designed to elicit from him the identities of the persons he charged with foul crimes and what specific crimes he alleged Democratic candidates and leaders committed. Haldeman dodged these questions by the subterfuge of reading extracts from the obfuscating statement Weicker was striving to have him make explicit.

Finally, however, Weicker put this question to Haldeman: "I want you to tell me exactly which of these illegal acts you ascribe to Senator McGovern and/or the Democratic Party?" Having exhausted his subterfuges, Haldeman confessed: "I am not able to do that at this time, Senator."

Haldeman admitted he had not asked the Department of Justice or the FBI to investigate any of the foul crimes he charged Democrats he would not identify had committed during the presidential campaign of 1972.

Although he insinuated that the Nixon reelection campaign had been buffeted by numerous violent and disruptive acts, Haldeman finally attributed responsibility for only one of them to a Democrat he was willing to name. He stated that McGovern was responsible for a violent demonstration that occurred outside the Century Plaza Hotel in Los Angeles on September 27, 1972, while Nixon was addressing a large Republican fund-raising dinner inside the building.

By its subsequent investigation, the committee discovered that this event was one of the numerous antiwar protests occurring during the Nixon administration, and that McGovern had nothing whatever to do with it.

After Haldeman gave his amazing testimony, I inserted in the record a letter from John H. Davit, chief of the Internal Security Section of the Justice Department, which stated categorically that neither the Internal Security Section nor the FBI had any information that any Democratic presidential candidate or party official had been involved in any way in any violent or disruptive act during the presidential campaign of 1972. I then invited Haldeman to submit to the committee for its investigation any reliable information he had which he contended sustained his charges. He never furnished the committee with any such evidence.

While interrogating Haldeman, Senator Weicker elicited a bit of intriguing evidence relating to Billy Graham Day, which was celebrated in Graham's home city of Charlotte, North Carolina, in October 1971, and which was addressed by President Nixon. Haldeman sent an advance man to Charlotte to make preparations for Nixon's visit. He received a memorandum stating the advance man anticipated that between a hundred and fifty and two hundred "violent" demonstrators, who would be carrying "extremely obscene" signs," would demonstrate at the Billy Graham meeting "not only toward the President, but also toward Billy Graham."

On his copy of the memorandum, Haldeman underlined the words "violent" and "obscene," penciled in the word "good" next to the word "obscene," underlined the words "also toward Billy Graham," and penciled in "great" next to them.

I happened to attend the Billy Graham celebration, and can testify the anticipated demonstration never occurred. Although a handful of demonstrators carrying rather benign signs appeared outside the building in which Nixon extolled Billy Graham and Billy Graham praised Nixon, peace prevailed.

Political partisanship has no rightful place in any search for truth. For this reason, I insisted at all times that the staff of the committee should investigate and present with impartiality the truth in respect to Watergate irrespective of whose wrongdoing might be exposed.

Under Senate Resolution 60, one-third of the professional and clerical members of the committee staff were appointees of the Republican members of the committee. I wished to ensure doubly that allegations of wrongdoing by Democrats in the presidential campaign of 1972 were adequately investigated. To this end, I insisted that Senators Baker, Gurney, and Weicker should assign their appointees to the extent they deemed desirable to the investigation of allegations of this nature, and should present their findings on this score to the public as evidence of the committee.

Staff appointees of Republican committee members investigated allegations of Democratic wrongdoing and presented their findings as committee evidence on November 7. According to these findings, unruly mobs gathered at hotels and on streets during the Republican National Convention in Miami in August 1972; a violent group disrupted a rally of Republican women in Fresno, California, on October

30, 1973; a riotous demonstration took place outside the Commonwealth Armory in Boston while the President's wife was inside the Armory on October 31, 1972; and approximately thirty Nixon reelection committees scattered throughout the country were subjected to spasmodic threats of violence, obscenities, or acts of vandalism. There was no evidence that any responsible Democratic official or organization participated in these events.

Although McGovern managers denied responsibility, the findings also disclosed that scurrilous leaflets comparing Nixon with the Nazis were printed on a machine in a McGovern campaign office in West Los Angeles and distributed by persons described as "McGovern workers" among Jews residing in that area.

The amounts collected and expended in the presidential campaigns of 1972 were unprecedented. The combined expenditures made by the Republican and Democratic parties in behalf of their respective nominees, President Nixon and Senator McGovern, totaled more than $100 million—the bulk of it being attributable to the Nixon campaign. Others who unsuccessfully sought nomination by the two major parties spent other millions.

The committee devoted a substantial part of its manpower and resources to its investigation of the financial aspects of the election. This was necessitated by both the magnitude and the difficulty of the task.

The difficulty of the task was aggravated by two factors: human nature, which prompts contributors, especially those who are actuated by quid pro quo motives, to desire to have their identities and contributions hidden from the public; and the woefully inadequate provisions of the Corrupt Practices Act, which governed contributions to persons seeking federal offices before April 7, 1972. Under this act, contributions avowedly made to aid a candidate seeking nomination rather than election to a federal office were not reportable at all.

As the most successful political fund-raiser in our nation's history, Maurice Stans, chairman of the finance arm of CREEP, exploited to the hilt both the inadequacy of the Corrupt Practices Act and the quid pro quo instincts of potential contributors. He was ably assisted by President Nixon's personal attorney, Herbert W. Kalmbach, who was shown to have solicited almost $11 million for the Nixon reelection campaign.

Stans emphasized to the highest degree that contributions ante-dating April 7, 1972, would be kept secret, and gave this assurance by letter to over 150,000 corporate officers: "Our committee's records of the combined contributions from you and your associates will maximize recognition of your group's support of the President."

His zeal was not abated by this letter which he received from the President of a New Jersey company, who happened to be a strong Nixon supporter:

> I think this is a most unfortunate approach to the solicitation of contributions.
>
> I would strongly object to any pressures, no matter how subtle, imposed upon me by our corporate officers, as I would expect the people in my division to object to any pressures exerted by me.
>
> In addition, your reference to the use of committee records on organization contributions to maximize recognition of support appears to substantiate the Democratic charge of recognition of special interest groups. This certainly highlights the opportunities of the oil interests, as an example, to make a substantial contribution in order to buy further administration support for unfair oil depletion allowances, which are eventually paid for by the taxpayer.

Stans's mundane strategy paid off. During the days preceding April 7, contributions in gigantic amounts poured into the offices of CREEP's finance committee. A substantial proportion of them were in cash. Others were routed to the committee in devious ways to conceal their origins. As was subsequently proved, hundreds of thousands of these pre-April 7 contributions had been directly or indirectly extracted from corporate treasuries in violation of a criminal statute which had been embodied in the federal code for a generation.

In its efforts to investigate impartially and thoroughly the financial aspects of the presidential election of 1972, the committee diligently and impartially sought information from all available sources. Members of its staff interviewed hundreds of persons and examined tens of thousands of documents. The committee itself held five days of public hearings on campaign financing during the period beginning November 7 and ending November 15, 1973.

The activities and discoveries of the committee in this phase of its investigation are detailed in its final report, and I confine further comments on them to contributions from corporations and persons holding or seeking ambassadorships.

Because of the chicanery used to make and hide them, the detection of corporate contributions was exceedingly difficult. In consequence, it is reasonable to assume that many of them went undiscovered.

Up to the time of the filing of the committee's final report, the committee and the Special Prosecutor discovered that corporations had made illegal contributions totaling $780,000 in connection with the presidential campaign of 1972. They allocated $749,000 of these contributions to President Nixon's reelection, and divided the remaining $31,000 in varying amounts among those who unsuccessfully sought the Democratic nomination and Senator McGovern.

Among the corporations making illegal corporate contributions to the Nixon reelection campaign were the following, which gave these amounts: American Airlines, $55,000; American Shipbuilding Company, $100,000; Ashland Oil Company, $100,000; Braniff Airways, $40,000; Goodyear Tire and Rubber Company; $40,000; Gulf Oil Corporation, $100,000; Lehigh Valley Cooperative Farmers, $50,000; Minnesota Mining and Manufacturing Company, $36,000; Northrop Corporation, $100,000; and Phillips Petroleum Corporation, $100,000.

Stans testified before the Select Committee that fund-raisers of the finance arm of CREEP did not solicit or knowingly accept contributions of corporate funds, and that such contributions were returned to their donors wherever their corporate origins were discovered. Evidence received by the committee did disclose, however, that the fund-raisers visited chief executive officers of large corporations in person, and solicited from them enormous contributions without specifically indicating their contemplated sources.

Kalmbach asked George A. Spater, the chief executive officer of American Airlines, for a contribution of $100,000 for CREEP. I put this question to Spater: "Did you draw the inference that he was trying to get the $100,000 from you personally?" Spater replied, "It never entered my mind that he was because I simply do not have the capacity, but that is a subjective evaluation."

Spater and I agreed that federal income taxes and the high cost of living left few places where $100,000 contributions could be obtained "without resorting to corporate funds." The methods whereby representatives of CREEP obtained some contributions of corporate funds must be described as high-handed. When he contacted Spater, Kalmbach said that he wanted a contribution of $100,000, and that he hoped it would be received because all those who made a contribution of as much as $100,000 would be put in a select class.

This solicitation was coercive in nature. The airlines were a heavily regulated industry. At the time of Kalmbach's meeting with Spater, American Airlines had numerous matters pending before federal regulatory agencies. Indeed, it had an application for a merger with Western Airlines, which had reached the White House and was awaiting the President's unreviewable decision. Spater said, "Most contributions from the business community are not volunteered to seek a competitive advantage, but are made in response to pressure for fear of the competitive disadvantage that might result if they are not made. It is particularly dangerous when the pressure is implicit in the position of the individual making the solicitation."

Spater's observation found corroboration in the testimony of Orin Atkins, chairman of the board and chief executive officer of Ashland Oil Company. As he did in the case of many corporate executives, Stans contacted Atkins personally. He asked Atkins for a contribution of $100,000 plus a $10,000 advertisement in the Republican Convention brochure. Although Stans did not specifically ask for a contribution of the moneys of Ashland Oil Company, he had no reason, as far as Atkins knew, for believing that Atkins could personally afford to give CREEP $100,000.

Although he deemed that "Mr. Stans had made an assessment," Atkins felt pressured by the request for a contribution from a former Cabinet officer, and had the contribution made from the funds of Ashland Oil Company because he believed it would benefit the corporation and its stockholders. Atkins told the committee that Stans said the contribution would be kept secret if it was made before April 7. He and I had this colloquy:

> ERVIN: Mr. Stans made a great profession when he was before this Committee that he was merely trying to conceal the identity of contributors. But do you not agree with me that . . . when you conceal the identity of a contributor you also conceal . . . the way by which you can find how the recipient of the contribution got the contribution?
> ATKINS: Yes.
> ERVIN: It certainly is a human weakness or desire for anyone engaged in business to have a friendly ear in Government?
> ATKINS: That is right, very much so.
> ERVIN: And so departing from the realm of politics into the spiritual, the method of raising campaign contributions now borders on extortion, does it not?
> ATKINS: Very much so.

Claude C. Wild, Jr., the vice-president for Governmental Affairs of Gulf Oil Corporation, told the committee that his company made a contribution of its corporate funds totaling $100,000 to CREEP. He further stated the contribution was made after Stans and Lee Nunn, another official of the finance arm of CREEP, had asked for a contribution of that amount, and Nunn had implied to him "that this was the kind of a quota that they were expecting from large corporations." Wild asserted, in essence, that Gulf Oil Corporation made the contribution because it did not wish to be on a blacklist or "at the bottom of the totem pole."

One of the favorite methods by which corporations made and concealed illegal political contributions of corporate funds was practiced by American Ship Building Company, which had some of its officers make individual contributions totaling $100,000 to CREEP and which reimbursed them for their outlays by bonuses.

In investigating the financial aspects of the presidential election of 1972, the committee discovered that eight of the ambassadors named by President Nixon since election day, 1972, had contributed sums totaling $706,000 to his reelection campaign, and that altogether $1.8 million of his campaign contributions can be attributed, in whole or in part, to persons holding ambassadorial appointments from him.

On February 25, 1974, President Nixon denied that his administration had engaged in selling ambassadorships.

As appears from the final report of the committee, on that very day his personal attorney and fund-raiser, Herbert W. Kalmbach, "entered a plea of guilty to having promised, in 1971, then Ambassador to Trinidad and Tobago, J. Fife Symington, a more prestigious European Ambassadorship in return for a $100,000 contribution, which was to be split between 1970 Republican Senatorial candidates by the White House and Mr. Nixon's 1972 campaign."

Kalmbach's plea of guilty was based on a plea-bargaining agreement granting him immunity from further prosecutions based on "contributions from persons seeking ambassadorial posts."

The success of the committee's investigation of campaign financing was attributable in large measure to the untiring efforts of assistant chief counsel David M. Dorsen, who had primary responsibility for it.

As 1973 neared its close the committee had three unfinished investigatory tasks: to complete its investigations of Nixon's involvement in

Watergate, the contributions of the dairy industry to Nixon's reelection campaign, and the $100,000 contribution which billionaire Howard Hughes had given Rebozo for Nixon.

The first of these unfinished tasks was of the greatest moment, and was accorded highest priority by the committee.

The establishment of the Special Services in the Internal Revenue Service, the creation and approval of the Huston plan, and the Fielding burglary were motivated by an insatiable and unrestrained hunger for information. So were the burglary and bugging of the Watergate. The coincidence of motivation for these events excited grave suspicion of the involvement of the Nixon White House in the Watergate affair, but it did not constitute proof that Nixon had prior knowledge of the break-in and bugging.

In June 1973 Dean had given the committee testimony which did implicate Nixon in the unlawful cover-up of these unlawful acts. Rationality called on Nixon to refute Dean's charge, and to do so by convincing means if he could.

Despite suggestions to that effect, he emphatically refused to undertake to refute it by his personal testimony on oath before the committee or by giving the committee access to the taped recordings of his conversations with Dean about the Watergate affair. If he had adopted the first of these courses, he would have subjected himself to cross-examination and the perils of perjury if he ignored truth; and if he had followed the second, he would have released an indisputable contemporary record which his subsequent oral assertions could not successfully contradict. As a consequence, he undertook to refute Dean's charge by ways that circumvented these hazards.

From July 15, 1973, until it ceased to exist, the committee sought in vain to obtain access to the taped recordings of Nixon's conversations with Dean because it believed they would answer conclusively the question whether Dean testified truthfully when he charged the President with complicity in the cover-up of Watergate. During these many months Nixon stood before the press and the people in one televised news conference and speech after another and gave them these solemn assurances:

1. He was not involved in any way in Watergate or its cover-up.

2. As President, he had the absolute and unreviewable power to withhold from congressional committees and courts any evidence whose release he deemed inconsistent with the national interest.

3. He withheld the evidence of his taped and untaped conversations

with Dean and his other former aides from the committee and the courts simply to preserve intact the constitutional powers of the presidency as an essential governmental institution.

In the last analysis, the rationale underlying Nixon's assurances was this: if he revealed to the committee or the courts his taped or untaped conversations with his aides about such criminal acts as Watergate and its cover-up, the constitutional power of all future Presidents to keep confidential their conversations with their aides concerning ways for performing in a lawful manner their presidential duties would be irretrievably destroyed.

I did not know at that time what the President knew, namely, that the release of the tapes the committee had been seeking since July would imperil Nixon as a politician rather than the presidency as an institution. So I merely appraised Nixon's excuse for withholding the tapes to be nonsense.

On November 7, 1973, the Senate indicated agreement with my view by passing without opposition Senate Resolution 194, which had been introduced by all the members of the Senate Select Committee two days previously. This Resolution declared it was the sense of the Senate that Senate Resolution 60 had empowered the committee to issue its subpoenas duces tecum calling on the President to produce before it the tapes of his conversation with Dean about Watergate, and that its access to these tapes was vital to the performance of the legislative task committed to it by the Senate.

After the adoption of this resolution, the committee made a conciliatory approach to the President. On November 13, it approved a resolution offered by Senator Weicker in which it asked the President to meet with the members of the committee in the White House at his earliest convenience, and discuss with them the Watergate investigation. By declining this request of the committee and refusing to obey three new subpoenas duces tecum for additional tapes and documents issued by the committee on December 19, 1973, the President convinced me of his unrelenting purpose to hide from the committee the truth respecting Watergate. After this, I believed the committee's hope of obtaining access to the tapes it sought depended solely on its lawsuit against the President. This hope likewise proved futile for reasons stated elsewhere.

When it adjourned its public hearing on November 15, 1973, the committee did so with the sanguine expectation that it would resume public hearings within a few days, and complete with dispatch its investigation of the dairy and Hughes contributions. It believed the groundwork for so doing had been laid by testimony elicited in prior executive sessions.

On November 27, however, the committee was compelled to postpone further public hearings until January 1974 because of unexpected delays in its receipt of documents relating to the dairy contributions, and the recalcitrance of about twelve Howard Hughes employees who refused to testify to circumstances incident to the Hughes contribution in executive sessions, notwithstanding subpoenas requiring them to do so.

When the committee was on the verge of voting to call their disobedience of the subpoenas to the attention of the Senate for appropriate action, these witnesses relented and agreed to testify before the committee in executive meetings. After that the committee took evidence in private sessions preparatory to the public hearings it contemplated holding in late January.

Before that time came, related events of much moment occurred. With the assistance of its newly appointed special counsel, John M. Doar, and minority counsel, Albert Jenner, Jr., the House Judiciary Committee was substantially augmenting its staff, and preparing to begin its study of whether the President had committed impeachable offenses. President Nixon retained James D. St. Clair, an able Boston lawyer, as his chief counsel and advocate in the impeachment inquiry.

Under the guidance of Special Prosecutor Jaworski and his staff, the Watergate grand jury was expediting its hearings with a view to returning indictments at an early date.

The United States District Court for the Southern District of New York scheduled for February 19, 1974, the trial of Mitchell and Stans, who were under indictment in it for conspiracy, perjury, and obstruction of justice in connection with a contribution of $200,000 in cash by Robert L. Vesco to Nixon's reelection campaign and alleged efforts on their part to impede a Security and Exchange Commission investigation of Vesco's financial dealings.

The Senate committee met on January 23, 1974, to schedule the holding of its postponed public hearings. By this time the three Republican members had reached the conclusion that the time had come for the committee to end its investigation and certify its findings to the House Judiciary Committee for use in its impeachment inquiry. Assistant chief counsel David M. Dorsen and those assisting him had amassed much evidence indicating a causal connection between President Nixon's increase in price supports on dairy products and contributions to his reelection campaign, and the other three Democratic members supported my view that the committee ought to hold limited public hearings to present this evidence. Accordingly, the committee voted four to three by a strict party-line division to schedule six days of additional public hearings beginning January 29 on the dairy and Hughes contributions.

This was the only occasion during its entire existence the committee divided along party lines. I am exceedingly proud of this fact. The committee was charged with conducting an investigation fraught with more political overtones than any other congressional investigation in the nation's history. Despite this, the committee acted impartially and without partisan motivation. Its only party-line split was in respect to a matter on which reasonable minds could reasonably differ.

The committee also voted on January 23 to ask President Nixon to meet with it and seek a solution to the impasse on the tapes. As I expected, the President rejected this request.

The public hearings scheduled to begin on January 29 were never held. Three days before that time United States District Attorney Paul J. Curran, of the Southern District of New York, asked the committee to postpone public hearings until the trial jury in the Mitchell-Stans case had been selected and sequestered to avoid the possibility that pre-trial publicity incident to them might prejudice the trial. The committee voted unanimously to honor this request. I digress to note that Mitchell and Stans were afterwards acquitted in that trial.

On January 30, 1974, Nixon delivered his State of the Union Message to Congress. In it he asserted he had furnished to the Special Prosecutor "all the material he needs to conclude his investigation and to proceed to prosecute the guilty and to clear the innocent." At the same time he assured the joint Senate-House session that he would cooperate with the House Judiciary Committee in its impeachment inquiry "in any way I consider consistent with my responsibilities to the office of the Presidency of the United States."

Having said this, Nixon specified that the only limitation upon his cooperation with the House Judiciary Committee would be this: "I will follow the precedent that has been followed by and defended by every President from George Washington through Lyndon B. Johnson of never doing anything that weakens the office of the President of the United States or impairs the ability of the Presidents of the future to make the great decisions that are so essential to this nation and the world."

This limitation, it is to be noted, was the same specious pretext Nixon had used in efforts to frustrate the Senate committee and the Special Prosecutor from the beginning. In emphasizing a major theme of his State of the Union Message, Nixon said the time has come to bring Watergate investigations to an end, and "for all of us to join together in devoting our full energies to these great issues that I have discussed tonight." By way of emphasis, Nixon declared, "One year of Watergate is enough."

In responding to Nixon's memorable phrase, Senate Majority Leader Mike Mansfield asserted, in essence, that Congress and the courts should continue Watergate investigations for as long as might be necessary to discover the truth, be it months or years. My comment was succinct. I said, "One minute of Watergate was too much." I added that the Senate committee would have completed its task "months ago" if the President had not spent so much time withholding information from it.

On February 1, Special Prosecutor Jaworski met privately with the Senate committee, informed it he was expecting the Watergate grand jury to return indictments against some of the principal former CREEP officials and presidential aides about the first of March, and requested the committee to postpone making its final report on its scheduled date, February 28, to avoid prejudicing the indictments and the trials to be held under them. The committee unanimously acceded to Jaworski's request.

To enable it to comply with Jaworski's request and complete its investigation of the contributions of the dairy industry and Hughes, the Senate adopted two subsequent amendments to Senate Resolution 60. By them, the life of the Senate Select Committee and the time for making its final report was extended from February 28 until June 30, 1974. By the last of these amendments the committee was allowed three months after its expiration date to complete its clerical affairs and entrust its records to the Senate Rules Committee for eventual transfer to the Congressional Library or Archives.

On February 6 the House of Representatives voted 410 to 4 to authorize its Judiciary Committee to continue its inquiry into whether President Nixon had committed impeachable offenses, and gave it subpoena power to obtain testimony needed for that purpose.

As a consequence of the step-up in the activities of the Special Prosecutor and the House Judiciary Committee, the Senate committee agreed on February 19 that "it should be careful not to interfere unduly with the ongoing impeachment process of the House Judiciary Committee or the criminal cases which will soon be prosecuted by the Special Prosecutor." For this reason, it voted unanimously on that day to hold no further public hearings, and to complete its unfinished investigatory tasks in private sessions. In commending the decision of the committee, Senate Majority Leader Mansfield asserted that the House Judiciary Committee and the Special Prosecutor enabled the committee "with good grace, to make an exit."

The Special Prosecutor and the House Judiciary Committee received the evidence they collected for restricted purposes, and could not give the advantage of it to the Senate committee. Since it was not subject to any such inhibition, the committee kept the Special Prosecutor informed of all of its discoveries, and transferred to the House Judiciary for its impeachment inquiry all the evidence it had amassed.

On March 1, 1974, the Watergate grand jury returned its long-awaited indictments. They charged Mitchell, Haldeman, and Ehrlichman with conspiracy to obstruct justice, and with obstruction of justice. They also charged Mitchell and Haldeman with committing perjury before the Senate Select Committee, and Mitchell and Ehrlichman with committing perjury before the grand jury. They also charged Colson, Mardian, Parkinson, and Strachan with Watergate-related crimes.

The Watergate grand jury wanted to indict Nixon for conspiracy and obstruction of justice. Inasmuch as the House Judiciary Committee was currently studying whether Nixon ought to be impeached, Jaworski advised them to refrain from doing so at that time because of the constitutional question whether a President can be prosecuted for crime before his impeachment and removal from office. In consequence, the grand jury voted unanimously to name Nixon an unindicted co-conspirator.

This action was undoubtedly wise. It enabled the courts to proceed with comparative dispatch with the trials of the indictments, and to escape being bogged down interminably while they solved the constitutional question.

Before briefly discussing Nixon's efforts to frustrate the continuing efforts of the Special Prosecutor and the House Judiciary Committee, I will complete the story of the Senate committee.

23

SENATE
COMMITTEE
COMPLETES
ITS TASK

THE three major dairy cooperatives, Associated Milk Producers, Dairy-men, and Mid-America Dairymen, contributed $521,425 of their corporate funds to the campaigns of candidates in the presidential election of 1972. They gave $427,500 of this amount to President Nixon's reelection effort, and divided the remaining $93,925 among the Democratic candidates in these proportions: Wilbur D. Mills, $55,600; Hubert H. Humphrey, $17,225; Fred Harris, $10,000; Henry M. Jackson, $4,500; Edmund S. Muskie, $2,750; George C. Wallace, $2,000; and Vance Hartke, $1,850.

The Senate committee recorded its investigation of these contributions in thirty-four executive hearings during the period beginning November 13, 1973, and ending June 13, 1974. No evidence was received disclosing that any of the beneficiaries of these contributions had any knowledge of their corporate origin.

These contributions revealed the callous contempt of the dominating officers of the participating cooperatives for the law making political contributions of corporate moneys illegal. They also generated this distressing question: Did President Nixon raise the price supports of milk as a quid pro quo for contributions that representatives of the dairy industry pledged to his reelection campaign?

The evidence gathered by the Senate committee established these facts:

—As early as September 1970, officers of the dairy cooperatives promised Nixon's personal attorney and fund-raiser, Kalmbach, the dairy industry would contribute $2 million to Nixon's 1972 reelection campaign. Kalmbach communicated this pledge to White House aides Ehrlichman and Colson.

—After consideration of the relevant facts, Secretary of Agriculture Clifford M. Hardin announced on March 12, 1971, that the federal government would support the price of milk for the 1971–1972 marketing year at 80 percent of parity.

—The dairy industry was deeply disappointed by this action, and its representatives so informed President Nixon at a meeting they held with him in the White House on the morning of March 23, 1971. On the afternoon of that day Nixon and his aides met and discussed the matter, and he decided to overrule his Secretary of Agriculture and order him to set the support price of milk for the coming marketing year at 85 percent of parity.

—The President's decision to raise the price support of milk was immediately communicated to the Associated Milk Producers and Mid-American Dairymen, which thereupon initiated efforts to raise $300,000 forthwith for the President's reelection campaign.

—On the night following the President's decision, Murray Chotiner, a longtime Nixon friend, and Harold S. Nelson, a key dairy lobbyist, met with Kalmbach at their request in Kalmbach's room at the Madison Hotel in Washington. After informing Kalmbach he was acting at Ehrlichman's request, Chotiner stated that Nixon's decision in respect to the price support of milk was to be officially announced the next day, and that he was asking Nelson to reaffirm the pledge the dairy industry had made to Kalmbach to furnish $2 million to Nixon's 1972 reelection campaign. Nelson did so.

—On the next day, March 25, the Secretary of Agriculture officially announced he was rescinding his previous ruling and setting the price support of milk for the 1971–1972 marketing year at 85 percent of parity—an action that increased the cost of this essential product to the consumer by substantially more than half a billion dollars.

By a public pronouncement, Nixon denied there was any causal relation between the contributions and the increase in the price support of milk. He attributed his action to the depressed economic state of the dairy industry, and the fear that Congress would enact a law raising the price support and thus rob him of the credit for so doing in the farm belt. Testimony received by the committee challenged the basis for any such fear.

After receiving the increase in the price support of milk, the dairy industry reneged substantially on its pledge to furnish $2 million to the President's campaign fund.

After the House Judiciary Committee initiated its impeachment inquiry, the question of what constitutes an impeachable offense within the purview of the Constitution was much discussed.

During a televised news conference on March 6, 1974, President Nixon entertained questions. In answering an inquiry of a newsman who asserted his attorneys had taken a narrow view on impeachment by saying "impeachment should be limited to very serious crimes committed in one's official capacity," Nixon said, "When you refer to a narrow view of what is an impeachable crime, I would say that might leave in the minds of some of our viewers and listeners a connotation which would be inaccurate. It is the constitutional view. The Constitution is very precise. Even Senator Ervin agrees that that view is the right one, and if Senator Ervin agrees, it must be the right one."

Four nights later I made a speech to students at Case Western Reserve University in Cleveland, Ohio. In conformity with a policy I steadfastly pursued at all times prior to the filing of the Senate committee's report, I expressed no opinion respecting President Nixon's Watergate-related activities.

My speech was followed by a question-and-answer period. A member of the audience called attention to the President's news conference of March 6, and declared he was surprised by Nixon's statement that he and I agreed as to what constitutes an impeachable offense under the Constitution. I explained that, like President Nixon, I believed a President could not be impeached except for a serious indictable crime occurring within the scope of his official duties. I painstakingly refrained from expressing any opinion on the factual question whether the President had committed an impeachable offense.

My appearance at Case Western Reserve University was covered by a number of reporters. All of the news accounts of it I saw clearly stated that I made no comment whatever concerning President Nixon's Watergate-related activities.

Although I had no knowledge of the fact until Senator Clifford Hansen inserted an editorial by William Randolph Hearst, Jr., in the *Congressional Record* on March 26, a solitary reporter had stated in a story dated March 11 that I made this assertion on my appearance at Case Western Reserve University: "Ervin said the Watergate investigation did not indicate to him that President Nixon had committed an impeachable offense."

The Hearst editorial remarked it was a mystery why this story remained lost for so long, and declared my story was a "real break for the President in his desperate battle against political enemies determined to topple him."

In retrospect, I have surmised the solitary reporter based his statement on his misunderstanding of the colloquy between the questioner and me concerning the views of President Nixon and myself on impeachable offenses.

Be this as it may, staunch Nixon defenders seized on the statement I never made as proof positive that President Nixon had not committed an impeachable offense.

When I was a youth, I read Elbert Hubbard's epigram: "Never explain. Your friends don't require it, and your enemies won't believe you anyway." Being impressed by its wisdom, I made it a practice during my public career to ignore errors in the press and refrain from attempting to correct them unless they were of great magnitude. I deemed this error to be of great magnitude, and was convinced that my obligation to myself, the Senate committee, the country, and the truth required me to correct it.

I knew such action on my part would bring down on me the verbal abuse of the staunch defenders of President Nixon. While I did not relish verbal abuse, I had long since learned, in Harry Truman's phrase, how to stand the heat.

On April 11 I undertook to set the record straight by making on the Senate floor a statement of everything I had said about President Nixon and impeachable offenses. At that time the Senate committee had not completed its investigations of the milk contributions, and had not received the most illuminating testimony on that subject. My statement was as follows:

I am compelled to make this statement by events for which I was not responsible.

During recent days, some of the news media have erroneously asserted, in substance, that I stated in remarks made to the students in a meeting at Case Western University in Cleveland, Ohio, on March 10, 1974, that no evidence had been produced in the Senate Watergate hearings to support impeachment of President Nixon. These assertions were undoubtedly made in good faith on the basis of some honest misunderstanding of a reporter who covered the meeting.

To prevent or minimize the repetition of assertions of this nature, I hereby categorically state that I did not make any such statement at Case Western University or any other place. For reasons hereinafter set forth I have steadfastly refrained from forming or expressing any opinion on the question of whether or not President Nixon has committed any impeachable offense.

I did state to the students at Case Western University, in response to a question, that I agreed with an observation made by President Nixon at one of his recent press conferences that under the Constitution an offense to be impeachable must be a Federal crime.

Much of the confusion in discussion of constitutional questions arises out of the fact that too many men interpret a particular constitutional provision to mean what it would have said if they rather than the Founding Fathers had written it.

The Founding Fathers were determined that the President should be independent of the Congress within the sphere they allotted to him. They knew that their purpose would be thwarted if they put in the Constitution any provision which authorized the impeachment of the President for any reasons not specifically stated in that instrument.

To prevent this from happening, the Founding Fathers expressly declared in article II, section 4 that the President cannot be impeached or removed from office for anything except "treason, bribery, or other high crimes and misdemeanors."

The word "crime" has a definite meaning in law. It is an offense punishable by death, imprisonment, or fine. The word "misdemeanor" also has a definite meaning in law. A misdemeanor is any crime less than a felony.

The constitutional intent that the President can be impeached only for Federal crimes is reinforced by the provision of article III, section 2, which declares that "the trial of all crimes except in cases of impeachment shall be by jury."

Article II, section 4 makes it clear that a President cannot be impeached for just any Federal crime. To be an impeachable offense, a Federal crime must meet these qualifications:

First. The crime must be serious in nature.

Second. The crime must be a crime against Government rather than a crime against an individual.

Treason and bribery have always been regarded as serious crimes. The word "high" which modifies the words "crimes and misdemeanors" signifies that the President can be impeached for other crimes and misdemeanors only if they are serious in nature.

Treason and bribery are clearly crimes against the Government. The words "other high crimes and misdemeanors" must be construed to embrace other high crimes and misdemeanors against the Government rather than crimes or misdemeanors against individuals.

Since one of the primary functions of the Federal Government is to administer justice, the willful obstruction of the administration of justice is a crime against the Federal Government, and for that reason is an impeachable offense; and since the Federal Government is dependent upon taxes for its support, the fraudulent evasion of the payment of Federal income taxes by a President is a crime against the Government, and for that reason is an impeachable offense.

For 15 years of my life preceding my coming to the Senate, I occupied judicial offices. My judicial experience taught me that it is unjust as well as unwise to make any decision on the issue of the guilt or innocence of another until all available evidence is received and weighed.

Some persons have alleged that charges of bribery, an impeachable offense, might be made against the President in connection with contributions made to his campaign by the milk industry. Others have alleged that charges of fraudulent evasion of his income taxes, an impeachable offense, might be made against the President in connection with his income tax returns.

Since I am unaware of the facts surrounding the milk contributions and the preparation and filing of the President's income tax returns, I have not formed or expressed any opinion as to the merits or demerits of any of the allegations based upon these matters.

I have likewise not made any appraisal of what the evidence produced in the Senate Watergate hearings shows in respect to the conduct of the President in the coverup operations. I have refrained from so doing because the Watergate Committee has not been able to obtain from the White House tapes of conversations the President allegedly had with John Dean on September 15, 1972, February 28, 1973, and March 13 and 21, 1973.

I deem tape recordings relating to these conversations crucial to the determination of the credibility of John Dean and to any possible inferences which might be drawn from the testimony of other witnesses.

The Senate Watergate Committee has been trying to obtain the taped recordings of these conversations from the White House since July 1973, and the White House has strenuously resisted all efforts of the Senate Watergate Committee to obtain them.

I am still hoping that the Senate Watergate Committee will be able to have access to these tapes before it completes its report, and thus will not be prevented by the White House from having the benefit of all available evidence in respect to the credibility of John Dean, and in respect to what inferences, if any, should be drawn from the testimony of other witnesses.

For these reasons, I have not formed or expressed any opinions at any time in respect to the question whether or not the President has or has not committed an impeachable offense.

I wish to emphasize at this point that I will never adjudge that the President has committed any impeachable offense unless and until evidence convinces me beyond a reasonable doubt that he has done so.

Nevertheless, I am constrained to say that the President's conduct has engendered these two conclusions in my mind:

First. That the President has needlessly prolonged for himself and the Nation the agony of Watergate by withholding from the Senate Select Committee, the grand jury, and the House Judiciary Committee tapes and documents relevant to the matters they are obligated to investigate.

Second. That the President could have spared himself and the Nation the agony of Watergate if he had acted at the beginning with the forthrightness which ought to characterize the occupant of his high office.

In respect to the first of these conclusions, I find wholly unsatisfactory the excuse given by the President for withholding from the congressional committees and the grand jury relevant tapes and documents. In the final analysis, this excuse amounts to an assertion that the President has the arbitrary power to withhold from the courts and authorized congressional committees information which any one of the other 214 million Americans would have to produce unless he pleads the self-incrimination clause of the Fifth Amendment.

I simply do not believe that the President is above the laws which apply to all other Americans.

With respect to the second of these conclusions, I make these observations. During the darkness of June 17, 1972, five burglars were caught in the Watergate. Within a few days thereafter, the news media made it plain that some weeks before $114,000 of the President's campaign funds had been deposited in a bank account in Miami, Fla., controlled by one of the burglars, Bernard L. Barker; that sometime before the burglars were caught in the Watergate, Barker withdrew thousands of dollars of funds from this bank account in $100 bills; and that 45 of these $100 bills were found in the possession of the burglars at the time they were caught in the Watergate.

When these facts became plain, the President ought to have called into the White House the men to whom he had entrusted the management of his campaign for reelection and his campaign funds, and put to them this crucial question: "How did it happen that when the burglars were caught in the Watergate they had some of my campaign funds in their possession?"

There is certainly reason to believe that had the President done this at that time, the truth in respect to the Watergate affair would have been forthwith revealed.

The Senate committee entrusted to assistant chief counsel Terry F. Lenzner, assistant majority counsel Marc E. Lackritz, chief investigator Carmine S. Bellino, and majority investigator R. Scott Armstrong its investigation of the Hughes contribution, the handling by Rebozo of that and other Nixon campaign contributions, and the payment by Rebozo of Nixon's personal obligations, including the costs of additions and repairs to the Nixon home in Key Biscayne, where Rebozo managed the Key Biscayne Bank and Trust Company.

In their efforts to ascertain the truth in respect to these matters, they left no evidential stones unturned. The massive oral and documentary evidence they collected was presented to the committee in thirty-seven executive sessions during the period beginning on June 25, 1973, and ending on June 14, 1974. This evidence is analyzed in Chapter 8 of the final report of the committee.

I was much distressed during this investigation by inexcusable committee leaks as well as obstructive efforts to deny the committee access to information.

As has been stated, some twelve Hughes employees refused to obey subpoenas requiring them to testify before the committee in executive sessions until the Committee threatened them with Senate disciplinary action. Some prospective witnesses sued the committee in the United States District Court for the District of Columbia in futile efforts to enjoin the committee from enforcing subpoenas served on them. As June 30 neared and the committee's powers were about to expire, some of its subpoenas duces tecum for important documents were ignored, and several subpoenaed witnesses disappeared.

The committee did not ask that those ignoring or disobeying its subpoenas during its final days be prosecuted for contempt of Congress. Its members realized that any prosecution of them would have to be entrusted to the Nixon Department of Justice, and wished to divorce themselves from all Watergate-related matters on the filing of their final report.

Much of the testimony received by the committee was confusing and contradictory. Most of it relating to Rebozo's handling of Nixon campaign funds and financial dealings raised baffling questions and furnished few answers.

On June 6, 1974, Senator Baker and I informed James D. St. Clair, the President's attorney, by letter of the evidence assembled by the committee indicating that Rebozo had paid personal obligations of the President and stating that we wished "to afford the President an opportunity to comment on this material prior to the filing of our report." Eighteen days later St. Clair gave us this response by letter: "I believe that the only useful comment that can be made in response to your letter is to convey the President's assurance that he never instructed C. G. Rebozo to raise and maintain funds to be disbursed for the President's personal behalf, nor so far as he knows was this ever done."

The Hughes contribution consisted of $100,000 in cash which Richard G. Danner, a Hughes official, acting in behalf of the billionaire Howard Hughes, delivered to Rebozo in two cash installments of $50,000 each in 1969 and 1970.

According to Rebozo, the contribution was intended for use in Nixon's 1972 reelection campaign. After its receipt by him, Rebozo said, controversy and litigation about various matters arose in the Hughes industrial empire, and he feared the use of the Hughes contribution in the 1972 election might embarrass President Nixon. As a consequence, Rebozo asserted, he kept the $100,000 untouched in a safe deposit box in his Biscayne bank until June 1973, when he returned the identical bills he had received from Danner to an attorney for Hughes.

The committee's inquiry centered upon allegations that during the times the Hughes contribution was in his custody Rebozo had disbursed parts of the funds to President Nixon's secretary, Rose Mary Woods, his brothers, F. Donald Nixon and Edward Nixon, and unnamed others. Rebozo, Rose Mary Woods, F. Donald Nixon, and Edward Nixon denied these allegations. The testimony received by the committee on this aspect of the investigation generated suspicions, but was insufficient to refute Rebozo's assertion that he kept the entire Hughes contribution untouched in the safe deposit box at all times between his receipt and return of it.

As the time for preparing and filing the committee's final report approached, the Special Prosecutor was preparing for trial the indictments of March 1, and the House Judiciary Committee was studying the question whether President Nixon had committed impeachable offenses.

The Senate Committee did not wish to prejudice the forthcoming trials or appear to usurp the House Judiciary Committee's prerogative. Besides, its members were anxious to make a report which would command their unanimous approval.

After much deliberation, the committee rightly decided it could achieve all of these desirable objectives by making a strictly factual report, which would detail objectively the specific facts relating to every person involved in Watergate and refrain from expressing condemnatory conclusions concerning any of them. I stated at the time: "If you state the facts clearly and logically enough, the conclusions will naturally flow from the facts. In fact, the unstated conclusions will even be stronger if they spring out of a factual report that is presented in an objective way."

As a result of its decision, the committee unanimously approved a final report of 1,094 pages which, in my judgment, constitutes a monument to accuracy and fairness. In addition, the report is as complete as it could have been made without access to the originals of the tapes the committee sought without success to obtain from Nixon.

As chairman of the committee, I filed this report and accompanying concurring and supplementary individual views of Senators Baker, Inouye, Gurney, Weicker, and myself with the Clerk of the Senate on June 27, 1974.

The committee met for the last time in the Senate Caucus Room on July 11, 1974, to discuss its final report with the press. A reporter asked me why the committee failed to make in its report condemnatory conclusions concerning the responsibility of the various persons involved in the Watergate affair. I replied, "You can draw the picture of a horse in two ways. You can draw a very good likeness of a horse, and say nothing. Or you can draw a picture of a horse, and write under it: 'This is a horse.' We just drew the picture."

On July 31, 1974, I made a statement on the Senate floor praising Senators Baker, Talmadge, Inouye, Montoya, Gurney, and Weicker for their patriotic services to the Senate and the American people, and assuring them I would "forever treasure in my heart the recollection of their great aid to me in my capacity as chairman of the Select Committee."

I then commended the principal officers of the majority staff,

Samuel Dash, Rufus L. Edmisten, Arthur S. Miller, David M. Dorsen, James Hamilton, and Terry F. Lenzner, and the principal officers of the minority staff, Fred D. Thompson and Donald G. Sanders, for their fine services.

After so doing, I thanked all the other members of the staff for what they had done, and inserted the name of each of them in the *Congressional Record*.

In its activities, the Senate committee exemplified all of the constitutional functions of congressional investigating committees. In addition to revealing that existing laws were not achieving their objectives and informing the American people concerning a most tragic episode in the nation's history, the committee made numerous recommendations that the Congress adopt specific legislative proposals to safeguard the integrity of the process by which the President and other federal officials are nominated and elected. Many of these proposals have been enacted.

24

RENEWED BATTLE
FOR THE TAPES

WHILE the Senate Committee was concluding its assignment Special Prosecutor Jaworski was endeavoring to prepare for trial by petit jurors the accusations against those indicted on March 1, and the House Judiciary Committee was undertaking to determine whether President Nixon had committed impeachable offenses in the Watergate affair.

Notwithstanding his professed willingness to cooperate with them, President Nixon attempted to frustrate their efforts by dilatory and obstructive tactics similar to those he had employed against the Senate Committee and Archibald Cox.

After Jaworski became Special Prosecutor, the White House delivered to him, for the use of the Watergate grand jury, nineteen tape recordings of presidential conversations with aides and seven hundred documents. The material delivered included that sought by Special Prosecutor Cox in his proceeding against the President.

Even before the Watergate grand jury returned the indictments on March 1, 1974, President Nixon made it plain by his State of the Union Message and his new chief attorney, James D. St. Clair, that his co-operation with Special Prosecutor Jaworski had ended.

During the early days of February the Nixon White House assigned two reasons for rejecting a Jaworski request for additional evidential material. The first was that Jaworski had all the testimony he needed to accomplish his task; and the second was that surrender of the requested material to Jaworski "would be inconsistent with the public interest and the constitutional integrity of the office of the Presidency."

Pursuant to an agreement he had made with the Senate Judiciary Committee at the time of his acceptance of the post of Special Prosecutor, Jaworski reported to it that the President was reneging on his promise to cooperate with him. Although the Watergate grand jury had sufficient evidence for returning indictments, Jaworski asserted, the Special Prosecutor required the additional evidence he was seeking for trial on the merits of the cases which would arise under the indictments. As a consequence of the President's intransigence, Jaworski said, the Special Prosecutor would be compelled to seek subpoenas against the President.

After the return of the indictments on March 1, Jaworski subpoenaed additional White House documents. While it surrendered some of them, the White House withheld the remainder on the pretext that they were not relevant to the Special Prosecutor's task.

For more than two months Jaworski engaged in fruitless negotiations with the President's attorneys for evidential material needed for trial of the March 1 indictments, which was scheduled for September 9.

Becoming wearied of their dilatory tactics, Jaworski obtained from United States District Judge Sirica on April 18, 1974, a third-party subpoena duces tecum commanding President Nixon to produce, for use at the criminal trial of the indicted defendants, sixty-four tape recordings and documents of his conversations with his aides about Watergate. Two of the defendants, Colson and Mardian, joined in the request for the subpoena.

The attorneys for the President moved to quash the subpoena on the ground that the President had an absolute and unreviewable executive privilege to withhold the subpoenaed conversations from the court. Judge Sirica denied the motion to quash, and ordered the President to produce the tapes and documents before him for *in camera* inspection. The President appealed his ruling to the Court of Appeals for the District of Columbia Circuit.

Because of the public importance of the case and the need for its quick decision, Special Prosecutor Jaworski undertook to bypass the Court of Appeals by filing a petition for certiorari with the Supreme Court asking it to assume immediate jurisdiction of the case. The Supreme Court granted the petition, and set the case, which was entitled

United States v. *Nixon,* for hearing in a special post-adjournment session on July 8, 1974.

On that day Jaworski and one of his top aides, Philip A. Lacovara, and St. Clair, the President's attorney, ably argued before the nation's highest tribunal this case, which was of highest constitutional dimension.

Sixteen days later, i.e., on July 24, the Supreme Court by the unanimous vote of the eight sitting Justices affirmed Judge Sirica's order. In so doing, they adjudged in an opinion by Chief Justice Burger that the President is subject to the Constitution he has sworn to support, and cannot invoke executive privilege to withhold from courts evidence of crimes of his aides.

Meantime, the House Judiciary Committee was having a hassle of its own with the White House. On February 25 the House Judiciary Committee asked the White House for forty-two tape recordings of presidential conversations and various documents it deemed relevant to its impeachment inquiry.

A few days later the White House delivered to the committee the nineteen tapes and seven hundred documents it had finally surrendered to the Special Prosecutor. Being unwilling to accept these materials in lieu of those requested on February 25, special attorney Doar and minority counsel Jenner spent a substantial part of their energy and time during succeeding weeks in unproductive efforts to obtain the forty-two additional tapes and documents.

During this period, President Nixon undertook to discredit the committee by charging that it was engaged in a fishing expedition and declaring that he did not intend to "be a party to the destruction of the presidency of the United States" by acceding to its unwarranted demands.

The White House ignored warnings of Peter W. Rodino, Jr., the calm and wise chairman of the House Judiciary Committee, that the committee's patience was wearing thin, and of Republican congressional leaders that the White House's obstructive tactics were inviting President Nixon's impeachment.

Finally, on April 11, the House Judiciary Committee by a vote of 33 to 3 issued its own subpoena duces tecum to President Nixon commanding him to deliver to it by April 25 the forty-two tape recordings it had been seeking since February 25. This was the first subpoena issued to an American President in an impeachment inquiry.

Subsequently, the committee, acting at the President's request, extended the deadline for the delivery of the subpoenaed recordings from April 25 to April 30. Meanwhile the House Judiciary Committee asked the White House for additional tapes and documents. As the deadline for complying with the House Judiciary Committee's subpoena neared, President Nixon devised a desperate strategem.

On the evening of April 29, he made a televised address to the nation which was reminiscent of the Checkers speech which had saved him politically in a bygone day.

Instead of surrendering the forty-two subpoenaed tapes to the House Judiciary Committee as directed by its subpoena on the next day, President Nixon told his nationwide audience he would deliver to it and make public at that time more than 1,200 pages of White House–prepared transcripts of private conversations he had had between September 15, 1972, and April 27, 1973, with his principal aides about Watergate. At the outset, he gave this assurance to the American people: "These actions will at once and for all show that what I knew and what I did with regard to the Watergate break-in and cover-up were just as I have described them to you from the very beginning."

In addition to delivering the White House transcripts to the House Judiciary Committee and making them public, the President assured his audience: "I shall invite Chairman Rodino and the Committee's ranking minority member, Congressman Hutchinson of Michigan, to come to the White House and listen to the actual full tapes of these conversations so that they can determine for themselves beyond question that the transcripts are accurate and that everything on the tapes relevant to my knowledge and my actions on Watergate is included."

The President further affirmed that the White House transcripts would tell everything he "personally knew and did with regard to Watergate and the cover-up"; reveal that he had "nothing to hide in this matter"; and that during the period covered by them he tried "to discover what was right and to do what was right." To bolster this last assertion, he lifted out of context a number of his pious assertions. He blamed "the demand for an impeachment inquiry" on "rumor, insinuation, and charges by just one Watergate witness, John Dean," and inferentially asserted the White House transcripts would refute Dean's accusations.

Prior to and during the Senate committee's hearings, President Nixon had manifested an uneasiness in respect to the contents of the tape of March 21, 1973. In his televised speech to the nation, he undertook to dismiss this tape in this way: "Now I recognize that this tape of March 21 is one which different meanings could be read into by different people, but by the end of the meeting, as the tape shows, my decision was to convene a new grand jury and to send everyone before the grand jury with instructions to testify."

In concluding his speech, President Nixon said that the White House transcripts "will provide all the additional evidence needed to get Watergate behind us and to get it behind us now."

On April 30 the White House delivered to the House Judiciary Committee and released to the public more than 1,200 pages of hastily deciphered and heavily edited White House transcripts of private conversations President Nixon had with his principal aides about Watergate between September 15, 1972, and April 27, 1973.

The transcripts omitted some passages appearing on the original tapes, whose revelation was critical to a full understanding of Nixon's connection with Watergate. The transcripts assigned as the reasons for the omissions that the passages were "unrelated to Watergate" or "unrelated to Presidential actions."

The transcripts were replete with notations that words on the tapes were "inaudible" or "unintelligible," and the expression "expletive deleted," which the editors used to camouflage the foul language President Nixon employed in his private conversations with his aides. Some of the conversations on the tapes were twisted awry by the transcripts, and their real meanings were thereby distorted.

The transcripts were also ambiguous in spots. It is not surprising that this was so. They undertook to transcribe the taped recordings of the intimate conversations of a troubled President and his perplexed aides, who believed they were besieged by enemies, and were seeking some way to escape the peril the truth about Watergate posed for them.

Several hours before it delivered the White House transcripts to the House Judiciary Committee and made them public, the White House released to the press what it claimed was a 50-page summary of them. The thesis of the summary was that the White House transcripts would discredit Dean's testimony before the Senate Select Committee and exonerate President Nixon of any criminal behavior in the Watergate affair.

The White House transcripts did not support the White House summary of them. Despite their ambiguities, inaccuracies, and omissions, the White House transcripts convinced multitudes of Americans for the first time that Dean testified truthfully when he charged Nixon with participating in the cover-up of Watergate and thereby aiding in

the obstruction of justice. In addition, multitudes of others were dis-
illusioned by the picture of Nixon which the transcripts presented.

For these reasons, the White House transcripts boomeranged, and
Nixon's remaining support among the people, the press, and the
politicians dwindled rapidly. A few incidents indicate the erosive impact
of the transcripts on former supporters of Nixon. Two of his former
champions among the press, the Chicago *Tribune* and the Omaha
World Herald, forthwith demanded that he resign. In so doing, the
Chicago *Tribune* said:

> We saw the public man in his first administration and we were
> impressed. Now in about 300,000 words we have seen the private
> man, and we are appalled.
>
> He is preoccupied with appearances rather than substance. His aim
> is to find a way to sell the idea that disreputable schemes are actually
> good, are defensible for some trumped-up cause. He is humorless to
> the point of being inhumane. He is devious. He is vacillating. He is
> profane. He is willing to be led. He displays dismaying gaps in
> knowledge. He is suspicious of his staff. His loyalty is minimal. His
> greatest concern is to create a record that will save him and his ad-
> ministration. The high dedication to grand principles that Americans
> have a right to expect from a President is missing from the transcript
> record.

After crediting Nixon with achievements in foreign affairs, the
Omaha *World-Herald* stated:

> Important as these accomplishments are, they are overshadowed
> now by the appallingly low level of political morality in the White
> House, as indicated in a variety of ways in recent months and con-
> firmed now in damning detail by the White House tapes.
>
> The transcripts have diminished the President's image from that of
> a moral man surrounded by underlings who had betrayed him to
> that of an amoral man who compounded his troubles by withholding
> for more than a year the shocking truth about the mess he and his
> administration were in.

In declaring that his impeachment was inevitable, William
Randolph Hearst, Jr., editor of the Hearst newspapers, who had been a
longtime Nixon supporter, declared that the conversations of the
President and his aides as depicted by the transcripts were those of "a
gang of racketeers."

The comments of Republican senators and representatives reflected
the depth of Nixon's descent in public esteem. Senator Hugh Scott, the
Republican Leader in the Senate, asserted that the transcripts disclosed

"a shabby, disgusting, immoral performance" by all those who participated in the conversations. Senator Jacob Javits was shocked by the lack of concern of the President and his aides for "what was right or fair," and declared the transcripts disclosed a group "of people striving to save their own skins in conditions permeated by unethical and perhaps illegal behavior." Senator Marlow W. Cook commented that the President had "irretrievably lost any claim to the confidence of the American people." Representative John Rhodes, the Republican Leader in the House, remarked that some of the events covered by the transcripts "might possibly be brought up as impeachable offenses having to do with obstruction of justice." Representative William Scherle noted that Nixon had "not yet made the whole record available" and Republicans were concerned with what might come up later to add to the embarrassment of the White House and the President's defenders. Representative John B. Anderson, chairman of the House Republican Conference, predicted that Nixon would be impeached, if he did not resign.

On the day following its receipt of the White House transcripts, the House Judiciary Committee met in closed session to determine what response it should make to the President. After hours of sometimes heated debate, it voted 20 to 18 to notify the President that it refused to accept the transcripts as substitutes for the forty-two subpoenaed tapes, and demanded that he deliver the tapes to it forthwith in obedience to its subpoena.

A comparison made by its staff shortly afterwards revealed there were substantial discrepancies between the transcripts and eight tapes which the committee had previously received.

After the committee's rejection of the transcripts, St. Clair announced that "the President feels he has given them everything he thinks they need," and that the President would not furnish the House Judiciary Committee any additional tapes or documents.

The committee was unwilling to accept the notion that it was the function of the President to judge the evidential needs of its inquiry as to whether he ought to be impeached. Hence, it continued to direct subpoenas to him for additional tapes and documents.

The President spurned the subpoenas. To justify so doing, he invoked the threadbare excuse that he would destroy the constitutional power of all future Presidents of the United States to keep confidential their policy-making discussions with their advisers if he disclosed Watergate-related tapes and documents.

25

IMPEACHMENT INQUIRY

THE House Judiciary Committee, which consisted of 21 Democrats and 17 Republicans, was singularly fortunate from a substantive standpoint in its selection of John M. Doar and Albert E. Jenner, Jr., to head its legal staff for its impeachment inquiry. They were lawyers of outstanding capacity and character. The committee was also fortunate in their selection from a public relations standpoint. Both of them were Republicans.

The House Judiciary Committee received from the Senate Select Committee the mass of evidence it had gathered: from the White House the nineteen tapes and seven hundred documents which it had delivered to Special Prosecutor Jaworski for the consideration of the Watergate grand jury, and from the Watergate grand jury through the agency of Judge Sirica's court a bulging briefcase containing some of the same tapes and other data.

For many months, the House Judiciary Committee, which operated in secret, seemed to be traveling on leaden feet. During this time Doar, Jenner, and their aides diligently studied and analyzed all the evidence available to them. After this, the House Judiciary Committee met in a series of closed hearings, which began on May 9 and ended on July 18, and received this evidence from them, and heard the testimony of witnesses. Some of the witnesses were called at the instance of Doar and others at the request of St. Clair. Most of them had testified previously before the Senate Select Committee.

After receiving the evidence and hearing the witnesses, the members of the committee listened to the arguments of counsel in closed meetings. Doar argued the evidence justified impeachment of President Nixon for obstructing justice, abusing his presidential powers, disobeying the committee's subpoenas, and willfully evading his income taxes; and St. Clair contended it did not disclose any wrongdoing on the President's part "sufficient to justify the grave action of impeachment." Since Jenner shared the views expressed by Doar, deputy minority counsel Samuel Garrison was permitted by the committee to speak to it in behalf of its Republican members who opposed impeachment.

After these arguments the House Judiciary Committee concluded its impeachment inquiry in a series of public meetings which began on July 24—the day on which the Supreme Court handed down its momentous decision in the tapes case—and extended over a period of six days.

These public hearings were telecast "gavel-to-gavel" to a vast nationwide audience. By their conduct during these televised meetings, members of the House Judiciary Committee displayed to millions of Americans a magnificent example of government in action.

The televised meetings were remarkable for many things, such as the dignity and fairness with which Peter W. Rodino, Jr., presided; the high quality of the debates; the impassioned eloquence of Barbara C. Jordan, who championed impeachment, and Charles E. Wiggins, who opposed it; the cogent explanation of circumstantial evidence by William S. Cohen; and the illuminating and tension-easing humor of William L. Hungate.

The committee approved as a first article of impeachment the obstruction of justice by President Nixon by a 27-to-11 vote; as a second article of impeachment the abuse of his presidential powers by President Nixon by a 28-to-10 vote; and as a third article of impeachment the contempt of Congress manifested by President Nixon by a 21-to-17 vote. The gravamen of the third article was the President's disobedience of the committee's subpoenas.

The committee rejected two proposed articles of impeachment—the President's actions relating to his income taxes and his order for the secret Cambodia bombing—by identical votes of 12 to 26.

In concluding its public hearings, the House Judiciary Committee made a report to the House recommending that President Nixon be impeached on the grounds set forth in the three articles of impeachment, and the leadership of the House tentatively scheduled August 19 as the day for the House to begin its consideration of the report.

By their votes on the five proposed articles of impeachment, the members of the House Judiciary Committee divided themselves into three categories.

Eight Democrats—Jack Brooks, John Conyers, Don Edwards, Elizabeth Holtzman, Barbara C. Jordan, Robert W. Kastenmeir, Edward Mezvinsky, and Charles B. Rangel—voted for all the proposals, and ten Republicans—David W. Dennis, Edward Hutchinson, Delbert L. Latta, Trent Lott, Joseph J. Maraziti, Wiley Mayne, Carlos J. Moorehead, Charles W. Sandman, Jr., Henry P. Smith, Jr., and Charles E. Wiggins—voted against all of them.

Thirteen Democrats—George E. Danielson, Harold D. Donohue, Robert F. Drinan, Joshua Eilberg, Walter Flowers, William L. Hungate, James R. Mann, Wayne Owens, Peter W. Rodino, Jr., Paul S. Sarbanes, John F. Seiberling, Ray Thornton, and Jerome R. Waldie, and seven Republicans, M. Caldwell Butler, William S. Cohen, Hamilton Fish, Jr., Harold V. Froehlich, Lawrence J. Hogan, Robert McClory, and Tom Railsbach—voted for some of the proposals and against the others.

The televised meetings reflected the dedication of all the members of the House Judiciary Committee to their task. They gave a convincing lie to charges that the committee was a "kangaroo court" or a "partisan lynch mob" bent on "getting" the President. They did this by demonstrating that many of the Democrats and Republicans who voted for impeachment were impelled to do so by their agonizing appraisals of the evidence and their profound soul-searchings.

26

NIXON'S RESIGNATION

SOMETIME shortly before the Supreme Court handed down its decision in the tapes case on July 24, 1974, Fred Buzhardt listened for the first time to the tapes of three meetings President Nixon had with his then chief of staff Haldeman on June 23, 1972, just six days after the burglars were caught in the Watergate. Buzhardt was so dumbfounded by what he heard he could only mutter, "It's all over, it's all over now."

He must have realized instantly that what he heard was totally incompatible with these words that he had written for Nixon's public statement of May 22, 1973: "At no time did I attempt, nor did I authorize others to attempt, to implicate the CIA in the Watergate matter." Indeed, he must have realized instantly that what he heard gave the lie to Nixon's repeated assurances to the American people that he knew nothing about the cover-up of the Watergate before March 21, 1973, and had never participated in it in any way.

This was true because these tapes revealed in his own words that as early as June 23, 1972, Nixon knew the Watergate break-in was a CREEP-financed operation, and engaged in covering it up for political rather than national security reasons.

Inasmuch as some still-unidentified person had deliberately erased from the tape of June 20 the eighteen-minute conversation Nixon and

Haldeman had on that day, these tapes constituted the earliest existing recordings of what Nixon said about Watergate.

The first of the conversations was taped between 10:04 A.M. and 11:39 A.M. on June 23, 1972, and the portions of it relating to Watergate were as follows:

HALDEMAN: Now, on the investigation, you know the Democratic break-in thing, we're back in the problem area because the FBI is not under control, because Gray doesn't exactly know how to control it and they have—their investigation is now leading into some productive areas—because they've been able to trace the money—not through the money itself—but through the bank sources—the banker. And, it goes in some directions we don't want it to go. Ah, also there have been some things—like an informant came in off the street to the FBI in Miami who was a photographer or has a friend who is a photographer who developed some films through this guy Barker and the films had pictures of Democratic National Committee letterhead documents and things. So it's things like that that are filtering in. Mitchell came up with yesterday, and John Dean analyzed very carefully last night and concludes, concurs now with Mitchell's recommendation that the only way to solve this, and we're set up beautifully to do it, oh, in that and that—the only network that paid any attention to it last night was NBC—they did a massive story on the Cuban thing.

PRESIDENT: That's right.

HALDEMAN: That the way to handle this now is for us to have Walters call Pat Gray and just say, "Stay to hell out of this—this is ah, business here we don't want you to go any further on it." That's not an unusual development, and ah, that would take care of it.

PRESIDENT: What about Pat Gray—you mean Pat Gray doesn't want to?

HALDEMAN: Pat does want to. He doesn't know how to, and he doesn't have, he doesn't have any basis for doing it. Given this, he will then have the basis. He'll call Mark Felt in [W. Mark Felt, FBI deputy associate director in 1972], and the two of them—and Mark Felt wants to cooperate because he's ambitious.

PRESIDENT: Yeah.

HALDEMAN: He'll call him in and say, "We've got the signal from across the river to put the hold on this." And that will fit rather well because the FBI agents who are working the case, at this point, feel that's what it is.

PRESIDENT: This is CIA? They've traced the money? Who'd they trace it to?

HALDEMAN: Well they've traced it to a name, but they haven't gotten to the guy yet.

PRESIDENT: Would it be somebody here?

HALDEMAN: Ken Dahlberg.

PRESIDENT: Who the hell is Ken Dahlberg?

HALDEMAN: He gave $25,000 in Minnesota and, ah, the check went directly to this guy Barker.

PRESIDENT: It isn't from the Committee, though, from Stans?

HALDEMAN: Yeah. It is. It's directly traceable and there's some more through some Texas people that went to the Mexican bank which can also be traced to the Mexican bank—they'll get their names today.

HALDEMAN:—And (pause).

PRESIDENT: Well, I mean, there's no way—I'm just thinking if they don't cooperate, what do they say? That they were approached by the Cubans. That's what Dahlberg has to say, the Texans, too, that they—

HALDEMAN: Well, if they will. But then we're relying on more and more people all the time. That's the problem and they'll stop if we could take this other route.

PRESIDENT: All right.

HALDEMAN: And you seem to think the thing to do is get them to stop?

PRESIDENT: Right, fine.

HALDEMAN: They say the only way to do that is from White House instructions. And it's got to be to Helms and to—ah, what's his name—Walters.

PRESIDENT: Walters.

HALDEMAN: And the proposal would be that Ehrlichman and I call them in, and say, ah—

PRESIDENT: All right, fine. How do you call him in—I mean you just—well, we protected Helms from one hell of a lot of things.

HALDEMAN: That's what Ehrlichman says.

PRESIDENT: Of course, this Hunt, that will uncover a lot of things. You open that scab there's a hell of a lot of things and we just feel that it would be very detrimental to have this thing go any further. This involves these Cubans, Hunt, and a lot of hanky-panky that we have nothing to do with ourselves. Well what the hell, did Mitchell know about this?

HALDEMAN: I think so. I don't think he knew the details, but I think he knew.

PRESIDENT: He didn't know how it was going to be handled though—with Dahlberg and the Texans and so forth? Well who was the asshole that did? Is it Liddy? Is that the fellow? He must be a little nuts!

HALDEMAN: He is.

PRESIDENT: I mean he just isn't well screwed on is he? Is that the problem?

HALDEMAN: No, but he was under pressure, apparently, to get more information, and as he got more pressure, he pushed the people harder to move harder—

PRESIDENT: Pressure from Mitchell?

HALDEMAN: Apparently.

286

PRESIDENT: Oh, Mitchell, Mitchell was at the point (unintelligible)

HALDEMAN: Yeah.

PRESIDENT: All right, fine, I understand it all. We won't second-guess Mitchell and the rest. Thank God it wasn't Colson.

HALDEMAN: The FBI interviewed Colson yesterday. They determined that would be a good thing to do. To have him take an interrogation, which he did, and that—the FBI guys working the case concluded that there were one or two possibilities—one, that this was a White House—they don't think that there is anything at the Election Committee—they think it was either a White House operation and they had some obscure reasons for it—non-political, or it was a Cuban and the CIA. And after their interrogation of Colson yesterday, they concluded it was not the White House, but are now convinced it is a CIA thing, so the CIA turnoff would—

PRESIDENT: Well, not sure of their analysis, I'm not going to get that involved. I'm (unintelligible)

HALDEMAN: No sir, we don't want you to.

PRESIDENT: You call them in.

HALDEMAN: Good deal.

PRESIDENT: Play it tough. That's the way they play it and that's the way we are going to play it.

HALDEMAN: O.K.

PRESIDENT: When I saw that news summary, I questioned whether it's a bunch of crap, but I thought, er, well it's good to have them off us awhile, because when they start bugging us, which they have, our little boys will not know how to handle it. I hope they will though.

HALDEMAN: You never know.

PRESIDENT: Good.

PRESIDENT: When you get in—when you get in (unintelligible) people, say, "Look the problem is that this will open the whole, the whole Bay of Pigs thing, and the President just feels that ah, without going into the details—don't, don't lie to them to the extent to say there is no involvement, but just say this is a comedy of errors, without getting into it, the President believes that it is going to open the whole Bay of Pigs thing up again. And, ah, because these people are plugging for (unintelligible) and that they should call the FBI in and (unintelligible) don't go any further into this case period!"

PRESIDENT: (Inaudible) our cause—

HALDEMAN: Get more done for our cause by the opposition than by us.

PRESIDENT: Well, can you get it done?

HALDEMAN: I think so.

The second conversation was taped between 1:04 P.M. and 1:13 P.M. and the part of it relating to Watergate was as follows:

PRESIDENT: O.K., just postpone (scratching noises) (unintelligible) Just say (unintelligible) very bad to have this fellow Hunt, ah, he

287

knows too damned much, if he was involved—you happen to know that? If it gets out that this is all involved, the Cuba thing it would be a fiasco. It would make the CIA look bad, it's going to make Hunt look bad, and it is likely to blow the whole Bay of Pigs thing which we think would be very unfortunate—both for CIA, and for the country, at this time, and for American foreign policy. Just tell him to lay off. Don't you?

HALDEMAN: Yep. That's the basis to do it on. Just leave it at that.

PRESIDENT: I don't know if he'll get any ideas for doing it because our concern political (unintelligible). Helms is not one to (unintelligible)—I would just say, lookit, because of the Hunt involvement, whole cover basically this.

HALDEMAN: Yep. Good move.

After the second conversation, Haldeman and Ehrlichman met with CIA director Richard C. Helms and deputy director Vernon A. Walters, and informed them that the meeting was being held at the instance of the President, who believed a continuance of the FBI investigation of the money would expose CIA activity in Mexico. Haldeman instructed Walters, in substance, to convey this information to L. Patrick Gray, acting director of the FBI.

The third conversation occurred after this meeting. It was taped between 2:20 P.M. and 2:45 P.M., and the part of it relating to Watergate was as follows:

HALDEMAN: No problem.

PRESIDENT: (Unintelligible)

HALDEMAN: Well, it was kind of interest. Walters made the point and I didn't mention Hunt, I just said that the thing was leading into directions that were going to create potential problems because they were exploring leads that led back into areas that would be harmful to the CIA and harmful to the government (unintelligible) didn't have any thing to do (unintelligible).

HALDEMAN: (unintelligible) I think Helms did to (unintelligible) said, I've had no—

PRESIDENT: God (unintelligible).

HALDEMAN: Gray called and said, yesterday, and said that he thought—

PRESIDENT: Who did? Gray?

HALDEMAN: Gray called Helms and said I think we've run right into the middle of a CIA covert operation.

PRESIDENT: Gray said that?

HALDEMAN: Yeah. And (unintelligible) said nothing we've done at this point and ah (unintelligible) says well it sure looks to me like it is (unintelligible) and ah, that was the end of that conversation (unintelligible) the problem is it tracks back to the Bay of Pigs and it tracks back to some other the leads run out to people who had no involvement in this, except by contacts and connection, but it gets to areas that are liable to be raised? The whole problem (unintelligible) Hunt. So at that point he kind of got the picture. He said, we'll be very happy to be helpful (unintelligible) handle anything you want. I would like to know the reason for being helpful, and I made it clear to him he wasn't going to get explicit (unintelligible) generality, and he said fine. And Walters (unintelligible). Walters is going to make a call to Gray. That's the way we put it and that's the way it was left.

PRESIDENT: How does that work though, how, they've got to (unintelligible) somebody from the Miami bank.

HALDEMAN: (unintelligible) The point John makes—the Bureau is going on on this because they don't know what they are uncovering (unintelligible) continue to pursue it. They don't need to because they already have their case as far as the charges against these men (unintelligible) and ah, as they pursue it (unintelligible) exactly, but we didn't in any way say we (unintelligible). One thing Helms did raise. He said, Gray—he asked Gray why they thought they had run into a CIA thing and Gray said because of the characters involved and the amount of money involved, a lot of dough. (unintelligible) and ah, (unintelligible)

PRESIDENT: (unintelligible)

HALDEMAN: Well, I think they will.

PRESIDENT: If it runs (unintelligible) what the hell who knows (unintelligible) contributed CIA.

HALDEMAN: Ya, it's money CIA gets money (unintelligible) I mean their money moves in a lot of different ways, too.

PRESIDENT: Ya. How are (unintelligible)—a lot of good—

HALDEMAN: (unintelligible).

PRESIDENT: Well you remember what the SOB did on my book? When I brought out the fact, you know.

HALDEMAN: Ya.

PRESIDENT: That he knew all about Dulles? (Expletive deleted) Dulles knew. Dulles told me. I know, I mean (unintelligible) had the telephone call. Remember, I had a call put in—Dulles just blandly said and knew why.

HALDEMAN: Ya.

PRESIDENT: Now, what the hell! Who told him to do it? The President? (unintelligible)

HALDEMAN: Dulles was no more Kennedy's man than (unintelligible) was your man (unintelligible)

PRESIDENT: (unintelligible) covert operation—do anything else (unintelligible)

Buzhardt advised Haig and St. Clair immediately of the contents of the tapes of June 23, 1972, which he reputedly called "the smoking pistol." After listening to them, Haig and St. Clair shared Buzhardt's consternation. Haig informed Vice-President Gerald R. Ford that the tapes were devastating to President Nixon's chances of escaping impeachment or remaining in the White House, and suggested that Ford should be prepared to assume the presidency very soon.

The discovery of the tapes of June 23, 1972, made it manifest that Nixon had been hiding the truth about Watergate from his own lawyers as well as from the Senate Select Committee, the Special Prosecutor, the House Judiciary Committee, the press, and the people.

Under the Supreme Court decision, the tapes of June 23, 1972, were delivered to Judge Sirica for inspection *in camera* on August 2, 1974.

These tapes were potentially embarrassing to Buzhardt and St. Clair. They flatly contradicted in an irrefutable fashion the arguments they had been making to the courts in the utmost good faith on the basis of information supplied them by the Nixon White House that President Nixon had no knowledge of the cover-up of Watergate until March 21, 1973, and had not participated in it in any way at any time.

According to a rumor which permeated Washington at the time, St. Clair threatened to resign as his attorney unless President Nixon forthwith stated publicly that St. Clair and his staff had been ignorant of the contents of the tapes of June 23, 1972.

Be this as it may, President Nixon released to the public on August 5, 1974, transcripts of the tapes of June 23, 1972, and this remarkable statement:

> I have today instructed my attorneys to make available to the House Judiciary Committee, and I am making public, the transcripts of three conversations with H. R. Halderman on June 23, 1972. I have also turned over the tapes of these conversations to Judge Sirica, as part of the process of my compliance with the Supreme Court ruling.
>
> On April 29, in announcing my decision to make public the original set of White House transcripts, I stated that "as far as what the President personally knew and did with regard to Watergate and the cover-up is concerned, these materials—together with those already made available—will tell it all."
>
> Shortly after that, in May, I made a preliminary review of some of the 64 taped conversations subpoenaed by the Special Prosecutor.
>
> Among the conversations I listened to at that time were two of those of June 23. Although I recognized that these presented potential problems, I did not inform my staff or my Counsel of it, or those arguing my case, nor did I amend my submission to the Judiciary Committee in order to include and reflect it. At the time, I

did not realize the extent of the implications which these conversations might now appear to have. As a result, those arguing my case, as well as those passing judgment on the case, did so with information that was incomplete and in some respects erroneous. This was a serious act of omission for which I take full responsibility and which I deeply regret.

Since the Supreme Court's decision twelve days ago, I have ordered my Counsel to analyze the 64 tapes, and I have listened to a number of them myself. This process has made it clear that portions of the tapes of these June 23 conversations are at variance with certain of my previous statements. Therefore, I have ordered the transcripts made available immediately to the Judiciary Committee so that they can be reflected in the Committee's report, and included in the record to be considered by the House and Senate.

In a formal written statement on May 22 of last year, I said that shortly after the Watergate break-in I became concerned about the possibility that the FBI investigation might lead to the exposure either of unrelated covert activities of the CIA, or of sensitive national security matters that the so-called "plumbers" unit at the White House had been working on, because of the CIA and plumbers connections of some of those involved. I said that I therefore gave instructions that the FBI should be alerted to coordinate with the CIA, and to ensure that the investigation not expose these sensitive national security matters.

That statement was based on my recollection at the time—some eleven months later—plus documentary materials and relevant public testimony of those involved.

The June 23 tapes clearly show, however, that at the time I gave those instructions I also discussed the political aspects of the situation, and that I was aware of the advantages this course of action would have with respect to limiting possible public exposure of involvement by persons connected with the re-election committee.

My review of the additional tapes has, so far, shown no other major inconsistencies with what I have previously submitted. While I have no way at this stage of being certain that there will not be others, I have no reason to believe that there will be. In any case, the tapes in their entirety are now in the process of being furnished to Judge Sirica. He has begun what may be a rather lengthy process of reviewing the tapes, passing on specific claims of executive privilege on portions of them, and forwarding to the Special Prosecutor those tapes or those portions that are relevant to the Watergate investigation.

It is highly unlikely that this review will be completed in time for the House debate. It appears at this stage, however, that a House vote of impeachment is, as a practical matter, virtually a foregone conclusion, and that the issue will therefore go to trial in the Senate. In order to ensure that no other significant relevant materials are withheld, I shall voluntarily furnish to the Senate everything from these tapes that Judge Sirica rules should go to the Special Prosecutor.

I recognize that this additional material I am now furnishing may further damage my case, especially because attention will be drawn separately to it rather than to the evidence in its entirety. In considering its implications, therefore, I urge that two points be borne in mind.

The first of these points is to remember what actually happened as a result of the instructions I gave on June 23. Acting Director Gray of the FBI did coordinate with Director Helms and Deputy Director Walters of the CIA. The CIA did undertake an extensive check to see whether any of its covert activities would be compromised by a full FBI investigation of Watergate. Deputy Director Walters then reported back to Mr. Gray that they would not be compromised. On July 6, when I called Mr. Gray, and when he expressed concern about improper attempts to limit his investigation, as the record shows, I told him to press ahead vigorously with his investigation—which he did.

The second point I would urge is that the evidence be looked at in its entirety, and the events be looked at in perspective. Whatever mistakes I made in the handling of Watergate, the basic truth remains that when all the facts were brought to my attention I insisted on a full investigation and prosecution of those guilty. I am firmly convinced that the record, in its entirety, does not justify the extreme step of impeachment and removal of a President. I trust that as the Constitutional process goes forward, this perspective will prevail.

Even before the events of August 5, a nationwide poll disclosed that 66 percent of the persons questioned favored President Nixon's impeachment by the House and that 56 percent favored his conviction by the Senate.

The transcripts of the June 23, 1972, tapes and his statement proved disastrous to President Nixon. Support for him among senators and representatives virtually disappeared. The ten Republican members of the House Judiciary Committee who had voted against impeachment to the last in the committee announced that they would vote for impeachment in the House because the tapes of June 23, 1972, established conclusively the truth of the first article of impeachment, which charged the President with obstruction of justice.

On the late afternoon of August 7 President Nixon summoned Senator Hugh Scott, the Republican Leader of the Senate, Representative John J. Rhodes, the Republican Leader of the House, and Senator

Barry Goldwater, a veteran Republican conservative, to the White House, and discussed with them his standing in the Congress. They told him that only ten or fifteen representatives would vote against his impeachment in the House, and only ten or fifteen senators would vote against his conviction in the Senate.

On the evening after this conference, Nixon decided to resign at noon on August 9, and thus become the first President in history to do so.

Nixon was driven from the presidency by his own misdeeds and his desire to receive the emoluments the laws require the taxpayers to give to unimpeached former Presidents.

In a televised speech to the American people on the evening of August 8, he asserted, however, he was resigning simply because he no longer had "a strong enough political base in the Congress" to justify efforts to remain in office. Nixon resigned at noon on Friday, August 9, 1974, and departed by plane for San Clemente. Vice President Ford forthwith qualified as President of the United States.

The House welcomed Nixon's resignation because it spared the nation the ordeal of an impeachment trial. Notwithstanding the resignation, the House Judiciary Committee prepared and filed with its parent body a 528-page report of its impeachment inquiry. All of its thirty-eight members recommended Nixon's impeachment.

The majority of the members declared that Nixon had committed impeachable offenses by obstructing justice, abusing his presidential powers, and willfully disobeying without just cause the committee's subpoenas. A minority, which consisted of the ten Republican representatives who had opposed impeachment before the release of the June 23, 1972, tapes, asserted that Nixon's only impeachable offense was the obstruction of justice.

On August 20, 1974, the House received and accepted the report of its Judiciary Committee without taking any action in respect to it, and thereby put an end to the impeachment proceeding.

The committee's report was accurately described by one of its members, Charles B. Rangel, in his individual views. He said:

> Even on the day of his resignation, President Nixon attempted to convey to the American people the impression that his resignation was caused by erosion of his political base as a result of some poor

judgments he made during his term of office. The record, as set forth in the committee report, makes it abundantly clear that Richard M. Nixon violated his oath of office as President, that he committed impeachable crimes, and that on the available evidence he would have been impeached by the House of Representatives.

The ten Republican representatives who voted against all impeachment proposals in the House Judiciary Committee made this unforgettable assertion in the statement of their so-called minority views:

> Our gratitude for his having by his resignation spared the nation additional agony should not obscure for history our judgment that Richard Nixon, as President, committed certain acts for which he should have been impeached and removed from office.

By way of elaboration, these ten representatives added:

> We know that it has been said, and perhaps some will continue to say, that Richard Nixon was "hounded from office" by his political opponents and media critics. We feel constrained to point out, however, that it was Richard Nixon who impeded the FBI's investigation of the Watergate affair by wrongfully attempting to implicate the Central Intelligence Agency; it was Richard Nixon, who created and preserved the evidence of that transgression and who, knowing that it had been subpoenaed by this Committee and the Special Prosecutor, concealed its terrible import, even from his own counsel, until he could do so no longer. And it was a unanimous Supreme Court of the United States which, in an opinion authored by the Chief Justice, whom he appointed, ordered Richard Nixon to surrender that evidence to the Special Prosecutor, to further the ends of justice.
>
> The tragedy that finally engulfed Richard Nixon has many facets. One was the very self-inflicted nature of the harm. It is striking that such an able, experienced and perceptive man, whose ability to grasp the global implications of events little noticed by others may well have been unsurpassed by any of his predecessors, should fail to comprehend the damage that accrued daily to himself, his Administration, and to the Nation, as day after day, month after month, he imprisoned the truth about his role in the Watergate cover-up so long and so tightly within the solitude of his Oval Office that it could not be unleashed without destroying his Presidency.

27

THE UNPARDONABLE PARDON

T HE resignation removed any doubt as to whether Nixon was indictable for any Watergate-related crimes he may have committed.
It was followed by an intense discussion in the news media and among
politicians and people as to whether or not he should be indicted and
prosecuted for such crimes.

Inasmuch as its members had unanimously named him an unindicted
co-conspirator, it was a foregone conclusion that the grand jury was prepared to indict him for conspiring with his aides to obstruct justice.
Advocates of indictment and prosecution maintained that our legal system is based on the just principle of equal justice under law for all men,
and that it would shatter the confidence of the American people in
government and their respect for law if Nixon went unwhipped by justice
while his subordinates went to jail for implementing his desires.

Opponents of indictment and prosecution advanced various reasons
for their views. They said that Nixon's constitutional right to a fair
trial by unprejudiced jurors had been destroyed by the unprecedented
publicity relating to Watergate; that he had been punished enough for
any possible misdeeds by the agony of Watergate and the loss of the
presidency; that it would denigrate the nation too much at home and

abroad to put its former President in the dock; and that exempting Nixon from the criminal process would enable the nation to put Watergate behind it and heal the divisions it had caused.

After the resignation became effective, the Special Prosecutor released publicly this previously prepared announcement:

> There has been no agreement or understanding of any sort between the President or his representatives and the Special Prosecutor relating in any way to the President's resignation. The Special Prosecutor's Office was not asked for any such agreement or understanding and offered none. Although I was informed of the President's decision this afternoon, my office did not participate in any way in the President's decision to resign.

By this announcement, Jaworski made it clear that the Special Prosecutor retained the power to invoke the criminal law against Nixon in respect to any Watergate-related crimes he may have committed. By his illuminating book, *The Right and the Power,* he has revealed many things previously unknown to the public. For example, his legal assistants believed that a proper respect for the rule of law required the indictment and prosecution of the former President. They agreed, however, that no decision or action in respect to the matter should be made until the petit jury to try the March 1 indictments had been selected and sequestered. After the resignation the trial of those indictments had been postponed from September 9 until October 1.

Nixon's newly retained attorney, Herbert J. (Jack) Miller, Jr., a Washington lawyer of high character and capability, engaged in two-pronged efforts to secure his client exemption from criminal accountablity. He undertook to convince the Watergate Special Prosecution Force that any effort on its part to secure Nixon's conviction would be futile because the unprecedented publicity attending Watergate had destroyed for all time his constitutional right to a fair trial by unprejudiced jurors. In addition, he sought to persuade President Ford to grant Nixon a pardon, which would constitutionally exempt him forever from all legal accountability for any Watergate-related crimes committed by him.

On November 5, 1973, Ford had appeared before the Senate Rules Committee upon his nomination by President Nixon to fill the post of Vice-President, which Spiro T. Agnew had vacated. At that time Senator Howard W. Cannon put this inquiry to him: "If a President resigned before his term expired, would his successor have the power to prevent or to terminate any investigation or criminal prosecution against the former President?"

Ford responded, "I do not think the public would stand for it, . . . and whether he has the technical authority or not, I cannot give you a categorical answer."

Many people, rightly or wrongly, construed this response to be a pledge by Ford that if he succeeded Nixon in the presidency, he would not pardon him for Watergate-related crimes.

In response to a similar inquiry put to him on August 28, 1974, in his first press conference as President, Ford gave this answer: "In this situation I am the final authority. There have been no charges made, there has been no action by the courts, there has been no action taken by any jury, and until any legal process has been undertaken, I think it is unwise and untimely for me to make any commitment."

Many people rightly or wrongly construed this response to be an assurance by Ford that he would not consider whether he ought to pardon Nixon until he had been indicted, tried, and convicted.

On Sunday, September 8, 1974, President Ford called an unusual press conference, and shocked the nation by granting "a full, free, and absolute pardon unto Richard Nixon for all offenses against the United States which he, Richard Nixon, has committed, or may have committed, or taken part in during the period" he occupied the office of President of the United States.

President Ford undertook to justify his action in a highly emotional statement. After declaring his deep belief in equal justice for all Americans irrespective of their station or former station in life, Ford explained he granted Nixon an absolute pardon for all the crimes he might have committed during his years as President for these reasons:

1. Because Nixon could not obtain during the foreseeable future "a fair trial by jury in any jurisdiction of the United States."

2. Because "during this long period of delay and potential litigation, ugly passions would again be aroused, and our people would again be polarized in their opinions, and the credibility of our free institutions of government would again be challenged at home and abroad."

3. Because, as President, he had "the constitutional power" to write "the End" to the Watergate tragedy.

4. Because "Richard Nixon and his loved ones have suffered enough, and will continue to suffer no matter what I do, no matter what we as a great and good nation can do together to make his goal of peace come true."

The country reacted angrily to President Ford's act of granting Nixon total immunity from prosecution. A public opinion poll conducted by *Newsweek* magazine revealed that 58 percent of the American people questioned condemned his action. Evidently they deemed the pardon an affront to "the credibility of our free institutions of government." The intensity of the opposition to the pardon was illustrated by the act of one man, Ford's longtime friend and biographer, Jerald F. terHorst, who resigned the post of White House press secretary in protest.

On the day following the granting of the pardon, I made this statement to the Senate:

> Candor compels me to answer the numerous inquiries I am receiving concerning President Ford's pardon of former President Nixon.
>
> I do not question the constitutional authority of President Ford to grant an absolute pardon to former President Nixon prior to his indictment, trial or conviction.
>
> I am reminded, however, of the statement of St. Paul which appears in Chapter 10, Verse 23 of First Corinthians: "All things are lawful for me, but all things are not expedient; all things are lawful for me, but all things edify not."
>
> President Ford's action was inexpedient, incompatible with good government, and sets a bad precedent for the future. In granting to former President Nixon an absolute pardon exempting him from all the legal consequences of all crimes which he may have committed against the Constitution, the laws, and the people of the United States while serving in the highest office in our land, President Ford did infinite injury to the indispensable principle of good government embodied in the phrase "Equal justice under law."
>
> President Ford's action will not contribute to the restoration of the confidence of the people in the Federal Government for the reasons set forth below.
>
> After the five burglars were caught in the Watergate complex with some of President Nixon's campaign funds in their possession, various governmental and political aides of Mr. Nixon undertook by lying, perjury, promises of executive clemency, the payment of "hush money," the perversion of governmental processes, and other methods to hide from the American people the identities and activities of the persons responsible for the series of tragedies known collectively as the Watergate affair, and especially the nature and extent of Mr. Nixon's personal involvement in those cover-up operations. As a consequence of these things and Mr. Nixon's failure to take forthright action in accordance with the obligation imposed upon him

by his high office, this Nation has been compelled to endure the agony of Watergate for more than 2 years.

By granting an absolute pardon to Mr. Nixon, President Ford has deprived the only impartial and nonpartisan Department of the Federal Government—that is the Judiciary Department—of the power to conduct judicial inquiries which would reveal to the American people the full nature and extent of Mr. Nixon's personal involvement in these unhappy tragedies.

As a consequence, the pardon aids and abets the efforts of those who have sought to hide the truth in respect to Mr. Nixon's personal involvement in the Watergate affair from the American people, and thus continues the coverup operations.

When Mr. Nixon delivered his last State of the Union message to the Congress, he asserted that "1 year of Watergate is enough." I agree. Indeed, I assert that 1 minute of the Watergate was too much.

President Ford obviously issued the pardon in the hope that such action would relegate the Watergate affair to the past. Believe me, this is a false hope.

Instead of relegating the Watergate affair to the past, the pardon makes it certain that the Watergate affair and President Ford's effort to exempt Mr. Nixon from legal responsibility for it will be injected into the next presidential campaign by those who believe that granting of the ill-timed pardon indicates President Ford's lack of capacity to exercise wisely the awesome power vested in the President by the Constitution.

Pardons are for the guilty—not for those who profess their innocence. A good case can be made for the proposition that the pardon power vested in the President by the Constitution exceeds that of the Almighty, who apparently cannot pardon a sinner unless the sinner first repents of his sins. The President, on the contrary, can grant a full pardon to one who protests his innocence and merely admits that he has made some errors in judgment.

Whether the acceptance of a pardon constitutes a confession of guilt is something which constitutional scholars may argue without satisfactory solution for generations.

President Ford's pardon raises some agonizing questions. What does it portend for those Nixon aides who have gone to jail for their part in the Watergate affair? What does it portend for those Nixon aides who are awaiting sentencing upon pleas of guilt for their part in the Watergate affair? What does it portend for those Nixon aides who are awaiting trial on charges growing out of the Watergate affair?

Does President Ford intend to grant general amnesty to all these Nixon aides, or is he accepting the theory that the legal responsibility of the occupant of the Office of President is insignificant when compared to that of his underlings?

Each day I utter this prayer: "God, be merciful to me, a sinner."

As a consequence, my heart contains great compassion for my erring fellow travelers to the tomb, and I have no desire to see Mr. Nixon suffer. I do desire with all my heart, however, to have our legal and governmental system function wisely.

The writer of Ecclesiastes states in Chapter 3, Verse 1, that: "To everything there is a season, and a time to every purpose under the heaven."

This is true in respect to the exercise of the pardon power. Historically, the pardon power came into being to enable the Executive to correct irretrievable mistakes committed by the courts in adjudging guilt or imposing punishment. It was not conceived to confer upon the Executive the arbitrary power to grant individuals exemption from responsibility which the law imposes upon all people.

These things being true, President Ford ought to have allowed the legal processes to take their course, and not issued any pardon to former President Nixon until he had been indicted, tried, and convicted. He ought to have allowed the presiding judge in those events to determine in the first instance whether or not Mr. Nixon has suffered enough, and I for one would not have quarreled with a decision of the presiding judge to that effect. But I do question most seriously the wisdom of President Ford thwarting the due processes of law by granting a pardon before Mr. Nixon was indicted, tried, and convicted.

In accepting the pardon, Nixon admitted that he "was wrong in not acting more decisively and more forthrightly in dealing with Watergate." But he did not confess any sense of guilt.

I believe the quality of mercy should not be strained for the repentant soul who prays, "God, be merciful to me, a sinner." I still adhere, however, to my original reactions to President Ford's pardon of former President Nixon. The pardon was unpardonable.

When he resigned the presidency, Nixon declared: "I regret deeply any injuries that may have been done in the course of the events that led to this decision. I would say only that if some of my judgments were wrong, and some were wrong, they were made in what I believed at the time to be the best interest of the nation."

The David Frost interviews and his own *Memoirs* generate a deep impression. It is that Nixon still clings to the notion that he committed no evil in respect to Watergate, and that his tragic misfortunes were caused by a hostile news media and political enemies rather than by his own misdeeds. He has never applied to himself this truth embodied in Anne Reeve Aldrich's poem, "Little Parable":

I made the cross myself whose weight
　　Was later laid on me.
This thought is torture as I toil
　　Up life's steep Calvary.

To think mine own hands drove the nails!
　　I sang a merry song,
And chose the heaviest wood I had
　　To build it firm and strong.

If I had guessed—if I had dreamed
　　Its weight was meant for me,
I should have made a lighter cross
　　To bear up Calvary.

28

THE INEXCUSABLE AGREEMENT

O<small>N</small> September 7, 1974, General Services Administrator Arthur F. Sampson entered into an agreement with former President Nixon, which covered forty-two million pages of documents and some 880 taped recordings of presidential conversations made at the expense of the taxpayers during Nixon's incumbency of the presidency. The agreement even embraced the sixty-two tapes covered by the Supreme Court decision. The agreement, which purported to bind the United States, was based on the assumption that Nixon had absolute ownership of all the documents and tapes.

The provisions of the agreement were contemptuous of the need for the documents and tapes for use as evidence in judicial proceedings as well as the demands of historic truth for the preservation of the stuff of which history is made.

Under the agreement, the documents were to be removed from Washington to California, and stored for a time at government expense in some depository near San Clemente. Nixon was given the power to deny access to the materials to others by a provision that he would have as their custodian a key essential to access to them. Neither the Department of Justice nor the Special Prosecutor was consulted in respect to the agreement, which was negotiated in secret and not revealed until the pardon was granted.

The agreement contained astounding provisions relating specifically to the taped recordings. They were to "remain on deposit" until September 1, 1979, and until that date the power to control access to them was reserved to Nixon. The agreement stipulated that the tape recordings were donated to the United States "effective September 1, 1979." The agreement virtually nullified the donation, however, by expressly providing that after September 1, 1979, the administrator of General Services "shall destroy such tapes as Nixon may direct," and that in any event the tapes "shall be destroyed at the time of his death, or on September 1, 1984, whichever event shall first occur." The agreement further prescribed that no tape could be reproduced without Nixon's consent.

In commenting on this strange agreement, Anthony Lewis of *The New York Times* said: "By such provisions Mr. Nixon could achieve in disgrace what he could not in office—the frustration of the Special Prosecution Force. For it needs access to the Nixon White House file not only for the forthcoming cover-up prosecution and other cases but for the final report it must make to Congress."

On September 18, 1974, Senators Gaylord Nelson and Jacob Javits and I introduced S. 4016, a Senate bill which became law as the Presidential Recordings and Materials Preservation Act.

When S. 4016 was being debated in the Senate, its opponents charged that it was an unconstitutional bill of attainder. In replying to this argument, I said:

> I have never heard so many constitutional ghosts, which do not exist, conjured up before in my life. We are told that this is a bill of attainder prohibited by the Constitution.
> A bill of attainder is a legislative act which adjudges someone guilty of a violation of law, and not only does that but inflicts upon him legal penalties for his violation of the law.
> This bill does not contain a word to the effect that Mr. Nixon is guilty of any violation of law. It does not inflict any punishment on him. So it has no more relation to a bill of attainder—if it is to be compared to a bill of attainder—than my style of pulchritude is to be compared to that of the Queen of Sheba.

The Senate approved S. 4016 by a roll call vote of 56 to 7.

In addition to annulling the Nixon-Sampson agreement, the Presidential Recordings and Materials Preservation Act directed the General Services administrator to take complete possession and control of the original tapes of conversations which involved former President Nixon or other federal employees and which were recorded in the White House or other presidential offices during Nixon's incumbency of the presidency; to take complete possession and control of documents "which constitute the presidential historical material of Richard M. Nixon"; to make the tapes and materials available for use in any judicial proceedings, giving priority in this respect to requests of the Watergate Special Prosecution Force; to retain for the United States permanently all tapes and materials relating to Watergate or possessing general historical significance; and to give "to Richard M. Nixon, or his heirs, for his sole custody and use" all other tapes and documents.

The act also directed the General Services administrator to store the retained tapes and materials safely within Washington, D.C., or its metropolitan area, to give "Richard M. Nixon or any person he may designate in writing" access to them at all times, and to adopt regulations to govern public access to them.

The act expressly stipulated that in issuing regulations, the General Services administrator should take into account these factors: (1) the need "to provide the public with the full truth, at the earliest reasonable date, of the abuses of governmental power popularly identified under the generic term 'Watergate'"; (2) "the need to protect national security information"; (3) "the need to protect every individual's right to a fair and impartial trial"; (4) "the need to protect any party's opportunity to assert any legally or constitutionally based right or privilege which would prevent or otherwise limit access" to the retained tapes and materials; and (5) "the need to provide public access to those materials which have general historical significance, and which are not likely to be related to the need described in paragraph (1)."

The act gave the United States District Court for the District of Columbia exclusive jurisdiction of all cases arising under it or the regulations implementing it.

A strong case can be made for the proposition that records relating to matters of public interest made at public expense by a public official during his occupancy of a public office belong in equity and good conscience to the public. The act did not attempt to foreclose this question with respect to Richard M. Nixon's claim to the tapes and materials it directed the General Services administrator to retain for the United States.

304

On the contrary, the act expressly provided that if a final decision of the United States District Court for the District of Columbia holds that any of its provisions "has deprived an individual of private property without just compensation, then there shall be paid out of the general fund of the Treasury of the United States such amount as may be adjudged just by that court."

The Presidential Recordings and Materials Preservation Act has been considered by the Supreme Court in *Nixon* v. *Administrator of General Services* (1977) 433 U.S. 425, where the Court adjudged it to be constitutional, and in *Nixon* v. *Warner Communications, Inc.* (1978) 435 U.S. 589, where the Court rejected under relevant provisions of the act the petition of broadcasters for immediate access to the tapes which had been admitted into evidence at the criminal trial of third persons.

29

END OF THE NATION'S TRAUMA

THE Special Prosecution Force played a crucial role in resolving the Watergate tragedy. Its story has been told by Leon Jaworski in his book, *The Right and the Power*, Richard Ben-Veniste and George Frampton, Jr., in their book, *Stonewall*, and James Doyle in his book *Not Above the Law*. My comments on its achievements will be succinct.

Archibald Cox, Leon Jaworski, Henry S. Ruth, Jr., and Charles F. Ruff, who served successively as Special Prosecutor, and their diligent assistants entertained the abiding conviction that the rule of law is indispensable to the well-being of a free society. This conviction characterized all their activities.

By judicious plea bargaining, the Special Prosecution Force obtained pleas of guilty to appropriate charges from President Nixon's personal attorney and fund-raiser, Herbert W. Kalmbach; former CREEP officials, Jeb Stuart Magruder, Frederick C. LaRue, and Herbert L. Porter; and former White House aides, John W. Dean and Charles W. Colson. All of them went to prison.

United States District Judge Gerhard Gesell of the District of Columbia ably lightened the heavy Watergate burdens of Judge Sirica by presiding over the criminal trial of President Nixon's former appointments secretary, Dwight L. Chapin, who was charged with perjury, and the criminal trial of President Nixon's former chief domestic adviser, John Ehrlichman, and three of the original Watergate burglary group, George Gordon Liddy, Bernard L. Barker, and Eugenio Martinez, who were charged with violating the civil rights of Dr. Fielding in connection with the burglarizing of his office in Beverly Hills.

By successfully prosecuting these cases, the Special Prosecution Force secured the convictions of Chapin, Ehrlichman, Liddy, Barker, and Martinez. Barker and Martinez were placed on probation, and Chapin, Ehrlichman, and Liddy were sentenced to prison. Former White House aide Egil Krogh pleaded guilty to violating the civil rights of Dr. Fielding, and was sentenced to prison. The Special Prosecutor dismissed a similar charge against Felipe De Diego, a resident of Miami, who was also implicated in the Fielding burglary.

While it did not actually prosecute them itself, the Special Prosecution Force was responsible for the prosecution of Donald H. Segretti and George A. Hearing, who were sentenced to prison by the United States District Court at Orlando, Florida, on their pleas of guilty to illegal activities in the Florida Democratic primary of 1972.

The Senate Select Committee and the Special Prosecution Force painstakingly investigated the illegal use of corporate funds in the presidential campaign of 1972. As a result of their discoveries, at least seventeen major corporations and thirty individuals were subjected to criminal penalties for violating the act of Congress making political contributions of corporate funds illegal.

The Special Prosecution Force's most spectacular accomplishment was its successful prosecution of the criminal charges made by the indictments of March 1, 1974.

Before the trial began, the indictments were dismissed as to Colson because he had been sentenced on his plea of guilty to an information charging him with obstruction of justice, and the trial of Strachan had been severed from that of the others for reasons of legal strategy.

The other five defendants—Mitchell, Haldeman, Ehrlichman, Mardian, and Parkinson—were placed on trial upon the indictments before Judge Sirica and a petit jury.

The trial, which began October 1, 1974, and ended January 1, 1975, was distinguished by the intellectual clashes between James F. Neal, Richard Ben-Veniste, and Jill Volner, who headed the prosecution, and the able defense attorneys against whom they were pitted, and is destined to rank among the great trials of history.

When it returned its verdict on New Year's Day, the jury acquitted

Parkinson, and found Mitchell, Haldeman, Ehrlichman, and Mardian guilty of conspiracy to obstruct justice; Mitchell, Haldeman, and Ehrlichman guilty of obstruction of justice; Mitchell and Haldeman guilty of committing perjury before the Senate Select Committee; and Mitchell and Ehrlichman guilty of committing perjury before the grand jury.

Judge Sirica sentenced Mitchell, Haldeman, Ehrlichman, and Mardian to prison. They appealed to the United States Court of Appeals of the District of Columbia Circuit, which affirmed Judge Sirica's judgment as to Mitchell, Haldeman, and Ehrlichman, and granted Mardian a new trial. Mardian was granted a new trial on the ground that his motion for a mistrial and severance ought to have been sustained after his chief attorney became incapacitated by illness during the course of the trial.

The Supreme Court declined to review the ruling of the Court of Appeals, and Mitchell, Haldeman, and Ehrlichman went to prison. Afterwards the Special Prosecutor dismissed the charges as to Mardian and Strachan, and they thereby won their freedom.

The tragedy of Nixon's administration was enhanced by the circumstance that three former members of his Cabinet were adjudged or pleaded guilty to criminal charges.

Former Attorney General Mitchell was sentenced on the verdict of the jury to imprisonment for conspiring to obstruct justice, obstructing justice, and perjury.

Former Secretary of Commerce Stans was not charged by the Special Prosecutor with participating in the break-in or the bugging or efforts to cover them up. But he pleaded guilty and was fined $5,000 on three counts charging violations of the reporting requirements of the Federal Election Campaign Act of 1971, and two counts charging nonwillful receipts of illegal corporate contributions.

Former Attorney General Kleindienst pleaded guilty to an information charging him with refusing to answer a question pertinent to an inquiry being conducted by the Senate Judiciary Committee in violation of 2 U.S.C. 192.

Despite its tragic nature and consequences, Watergate has a positive aspect which ought to give Americans confidence. This is so because it proved our Constitution works. That instrument commands the President to "take care that the laws be faithfully executed." When President Nixon was untrue to his constitutional obligation, Congress and the federal judiciary remained true to theirs. As a consequence, the United

States weathered a great national crisis without turmoil and with all its institutions intact. The federal judiciary was able to perform its constitutional obligations effectively because of the fidelity to duty of the ordinary men and women who served on the Watergate grand and petit juries.

Watergate has taught us the truth embodied in these words of Shakespeare:

> Sweet are the uses of adversity,
> Which, like the toad, ugly and venomous,
> Wears yet a precious jewel in its head.

30

MEDITATIONS

WHEN the Select Committee made its final report to the Senate in June 1974, I added to it an individual statement in which I philosophized about the cause of Watergate and the possibility of avoiding future Watergates. What I said then is still valid, and I believe will remain valid. I close my story of Watergate by quoting it:

> Unlike the men who were responsible for Teapot Dome, the presidential aides who perpetrated Watergate were not seduced by the love of money, which is sometimes thought to be the root of all evil. On the contrary, they were instigated by a lust for political power, which is at least as corrupting as political power itself.
>
> They gave their allegiance to the President and his policies. They had stood for a time near to him, and had been entrusted by him with great governmental and political power. They enjoyed exercising such power, and longed for its continuance.
>
> They knew that the power they enjoyed would be lost and the policies to which they adhered would be frustrated if the President should be defeated.
>
> As a consequence of these things, they believed the President's reelection to be a most worthy objective, and succumbed to an age-old temptation. They resorted to evil means to promote what they conceived to be a good end.

Their lust for political power blinded them to ethical considerations and legal requirements; to Aristotle's aphorism that the good of man must be the end of politics; and to Grover Cleveland's conviction that a public office is a public trust.

They had forgotten, if they ever knew, that the Constitution is designed to be a law for rulers and people alike at all times and under all circumstances; and that no doctrine involving more pernicious consequences to the commonweal has ever been invented by the wit of man than the notion that any of its provisions can be suspended by the President for any reason whatsoever.

On the contrary, they apparently believed that the President is above the Constitution, and has the autocratic power to suspend its provisions if he decides in his own unreviewable judgment that his action in so doing promotes his own political interests or the welfare of the nation. As one of them testified before the Senate Select Committee, they believed that the President has the autocratic power to suspend the Fourth Amendment whenever he imagines that some indefinable aspect of national security is involved.

I digress to reject this doctrine of the constitutional omnipotence of the President. As long as I have a mind to think, a tongue to speak, and a heart to love my country, I shall deny that the Constitution confers any autocratic power on the President, or authorizes him to convert George Washington's America into Gaius Caesar's Rome.

The lust for political power of the presidential aides who perpetrated Watergate on America blinded them to the laws of God as well as to the laws and ethics of man.

As a consequence, they violated the spiritual law which forbids men to do evil even when they think good will result from it, and ignored these warnings of the King James version of the Bible:

1. "There is nothing covered, that shall not be revealed; neither hid, that shall not be known."

2. "Be not deceived; God is not mocked: For whatsoever a man soweth, that shall he also reap."

I find corroboration for my conclusion that lust for political power produced Watergate in words uttered by the most eloquent and learned of all the Romans, Marcus Tullius Cicero, about 2100 years ago. He said:

"Most men, however, are inclined to forget justice altogether, when once the craving for military power or political honors and glory has taken possession of them. Remember the saying of Ennius, 'When crowns are at stake, no friendship is sacred, no faith shall be kept.' "

As one after another of the individuals who participated in Watergate goes to prison, we see in action an inexorable spiritual law which Rudyard Kipling phrased in this fashion in his poem about Tomlinson's Ghost: "For the sin ye do by two and two you must pay for one by one."

As we contemplate the motives that inspired their misdeeds, we acquire a new awareness of the significance of Cardinal Wolsey's poignant lament: "Had I but serv'd my God with half the zeal I serv'd my King, He would not in mine age have left me naked to mine enemies."

Is there an antidote which will prevent future Watergates? If so, what is it?

The Senate Select Committee is recommending the enactment of new laws which it believes will minimize the danger of future Watergates and make more adequate and certain the punishment of those who attempt to perpetrate them upon our country.

Candor compels the confession, however, that law alone will not suffice to prevent future Watergates. In saying this, I do not disparage the essential role which law plays in the life of our nation. As one who has labored as a practicing lawyer, a judge, and a legislator all of my adult years, I venerate the law as an instrument of service to society. At the same time, however, I know the weakness of the law as well as its strength.

Law is not self-executing. Unfortunately, at times its execution rests in the hands of those who are faithless to it. And even when its enforcement is committed to those who revere it, law merely deters some human beings from offending, and punishes other human beings for offending. It does not make men good. This task can be performed only by ethics or religion or morality.

Since politics is the art or science of government, no man is fit to participate in politics or to seek or hold public office unless he has two characteristics.

The first of these characteristics is that he must understand and be dedicated to the true purpose of government, which is to promote the good of the people, and entertain the abiding conviction that a public office is a public trust, which must never be abused to secure private advantage.

The second characteristic is that he must possess that intellectual and moral integrity, which is the priceless ingredient in good character.

When all is said, the only sure antidote for future Watergates is understanding of fundamental principles and intellectual and moral integrity in the men and women who achieve or are entrusted with governmental or political power.

Josiah Gilbert Holland, a poet of a bygone generation, recognized this truth in a poem which he called "The Day's Demand" and which I like to call "America's Prayer." I quote his words:

> God give us men! A time like this demands
> Strong minds, great hearts, true faith and ready hands;

Men whom the lust of office does not kill;
Men whom the spoils of office cannot buy;
Men who possess opinions and a will;
Men who have honor—men who will not lie;
Men who can stand before a demagogue
And damn his treacherous flatteries without winking;
Tall men, sun-crowned, who live above the fog
In public duty, and in private thinking.

INDEX